The Making of the Twentieth Century

This new series of specially commissioned titles focuses attention on significant and often controversial events and themes of world history this century. The authors, many of them already outstanding in their field, have tried to close the gap between the intelligent layman, whose interest is aroused by recent history, and the specialist student at university. Each book will therefore provide sufficient narrative and explanation for the newcomer while offering the specialist student detailed source-references and biblio-graphies, together with interpretation and reassessment in the light of recent scholarship.

In the choice of subjects there will be a balance between breadth in some spheres and detail in others; between the essentially political and matters scientific, economic or social. The series cannot be a comprehensive account of everything that has happened in the twentieth century, but it will provide a guide to recent research and explain something of the times of extraordinary change and complexity in which we live.

The Making of the Twentieth Century

Series Editor: CHRISTOPHER THORNE

Other titles in the Series include

Already published

Anthony Harrison, *The Framework of Economic Activity:
The International Economy and the Rise of the State*
David Rees, *The Age of Containment: The Cold War 1945–1965*

In preparation

Mark Abrams, *The Rise of Public Opinion*
Dennis Austin, *Africa: The Transfer of Power*
George Grün, *The Illusion of Peace: International Relations 1918–1933*
Dennis Gunning, *The Origins of the First World War*
Anthony Hartley, *Gaullism: Its Roots and Development*
Anthony Hartley, *Germany: East/West*
C. P. Hill, *Government, Business and People: The U.S.A. in the
Twentieth Century*
C. P. Hill, *Isolation and Involvement: The United States and the World
in the Twentieth Century*
Desmond King-Hele, *The End of the Twentieth Century?*
Hans Kohn, *The Racial Problem in the Twentieth Century*
J. Miller, *1917 in Russian and World History*
Tony Nicholls, *Weimar and the Rise of Hitler*
B. N. Pandey, *The Break-up of British India*
B. N. Pandey, *Problems of Independence in South and South-East Asia*
P. B. Reddaway, *Literature and Politics in the Soviet Union*
E. M. Robertson, *Mussolini, Abyssinia and the League*
E. M. Robertson, *The European Powers and the Spanish Civil War*
Richard Storry, *Japan and the Decline of the West in Asia*
Ann Williams, *Britain and France in the Middle East*
Elizabeth Wiskemann, *Fascism in Europe*
R. C. Wofinden and A. W. Macara, *Population, Resources and
Public Health*
John Wren-Lewis, *Doubt and Belief in the Twentieth Century*

The Approach of War, 1938–1939

Christopher Thorne

Truly, the souls of men are full of fear:
Ye cannot reason almost with a man
That looks not heavily and full of dread.

Richard III, Act II, Scene iii

Macmillan
London · Melbourne · Toronto
St Martin's Press
New York
1 9 6 7

MACMILLAN AND COMPANY LIMITED
Little Essex Street London WC 2
also Bombay Calcutta Madras Melbourne

THE MACMILLAN COMPANY OF CANADA LIMITED
70 Bond Street Toronto 2

ST MARTIN'S PRESS INC
175 Fifth Avenue New York NY 10010

Library of Congress catalog card no. 67–10649

PRINTED IN GREAT BRITAIN

FOR

B. L. T. and P. D. W.

Contents

Plates and Maps

The cover picture shows Hitler delivering his Sudetenland Ultimatum in the *Sportpalast*, Nuremberg.

PLATES

8*a*   German troops enter Prague, 15 March 1939
  b   Beck arrives for Anglo-Polish talks in London, 3 April
       1939

Grateful thanks are due to the following for permission to
reproduce the plates: 1*a*, Erich Kordt; 1*b*, Austrian National
Library; cover picture, 2*a*, *b*, 3*a*, *b*, 4*a*, *b*, 5*a*, 6*a*, 7*a*, *b*, 8*a*, *b*,
The Radio Times Hulton Picture Library; 5*b*, 6*b*, Central Press
Photos.

MAPS

Grateful thanks are due to the following for permission to
reproduce the maps:

Maps 1, 2: Messrs. Edward Arnold (Publishers) Ltd.,
  based on R. R. Sellmann, *A Student's Atlas of Modern
  History*.

Map 2: Messrs. Hamish Hamilton Ltd., based on A. J. P.
  Taylor, *The Origins of the Second World War*.

Map 3: H.M.S.O., based on J. R. M. Butler, *Grand Strategy*,
  vol. ii of *History of the Second World War*, in the 'United
  Kingdom Military History' Series.

Abbreviations

D.G.F.P.	*Documents on German Foreign Policy, 1918–1945*, Series D (H.M.S.O., vols. i–vii).
D.B.F.P.	*Documents on British Foreign Policy, 1919–1939*, 3rd series (H.M.S.O., 9 vols.).
N.C.A.	*Nazi Conspiracy and Aggression* (Washington, 10 vols.).
New Documents	*New Documents on the History of Munich* (Prague, 1958).
Dirksen Papers	*Documents and Materials Relating to the Eve of the Second World War*, vol. ii (Moscow, 1948).
I.M.T. Proceedings	*The Trial of German Major War Criminals: Proceedings of the International Military Tribunal sitting at Nuremberg* (H.M.S.O., 1946–50, 22 parts).
D.D.I.	*I Documenti Diplomatici Italiani*, 8th series, vols. xii and xiii (Rome, 1952–3).
F.R.U.S.	*Foreign Relations of the United States, 1938*, vol. i, and 1939, vol. i (Washington, 1955 and 1956).

Preface

THIS book does not claim to analyse all the causes of the Second World War. It is essentially a study of the diplomatic activity of the last two years of so-called peace, but I have endeavoured to point out the considerable limitations placed upon the influence and significance of this diplomacy during the period, while giving due weight to other elements. These include the press and public opinion, the destructive savagery of National Socialism, and the personalities and roles of such men as Chamberlain and Mussolini, for both of whom regular diplomatic channels became little more than a tiresome formality. Above all, of course, one has to attempt to penetrate as far as one may the dark recesses of that diseased mind which, more than any other single factor, was to bring war to Europe.

Though the ground has been covered several times before, the clash of rival theories makes an attempt at a fresh assessment still seem worthwhile, and the vast amount of source material has enabled little-known facets to be brought out here and there, as in the case of Memel. I have provided detailed references in a way which enables the non-specialist to ignore them if he chooses, while others may examine more fully the grounds for what I have written. Also, in so brief an essay an indication of where further information may be obtained has often been the most I could offer those wishing to pursue the subject at greater length.

Perhaps I should also add a word concerning the standpoint from which I have approached British foreign policy in particular. The simple, 'guilty men' interpretation of these years is presumably — and rightly — now recognised as an inadequate one. Nor does it become subsequent generations lightly to dismiss that idealism which contributed to the country's weakness when faced with Hitler, or for those who feared for the lives of their children during the Cuban crisis to ignore the voices which were uttering a similar cry in September 1938. I include on page 1 the decorations of the Assistant Editor of *The Times* as a reminder that the most fervent advocates of 'appeasement' had often been tried and not found wanting in the most hideous conditions of warfare.

Yet it remains impossible to ignore the considerable shortcomings of many of those in high places during the approach of war. I have tried to be fair, but I have not altogether followed the advice of some older and wiser heads and removed all traces of the dismay which at times, despite earlier works, accompanied my study of the period. Had I done so a better book might well have resulted, but perhaps a slightly less honest one.

I alone, therefore, am responsible for the opinions which appear below, but despite this and the brevity of the essay there are several to whom I must express much gratitude for the help and encouragement they have given me. The staff of that remarkable institution, the Wiener Library, have been unfailingly kind; Erno Nagy has patiently answered and transmitted to friends my questions on the Central European scene, and in particular Hungary, as he and they saw it at the time; and Luisa Gunning has made good my deficiency by translating documents from Italian. With their great first-hand knowledge of so many aspects of the subject, Elizabeth Wiskemann and the Rt. Hon. Harold Macmillan have been kind enough to read and comment upon the work in typescript and answer further questions, while the immense debt I owe my wife and Philip Whitting is all too inadequately repaid by the book's dedication.

October 1965   C. G. T.

1 Opportunity, Appeasement, and Aggression

Our movement must seek to abolish the present disastrous proportion between our population and the area of our national territory. . . . In striving for this it must bear in mind the fact that we are members of the highest species of humanity on this earth.

Mein Kampf[1]

It is hard to escape when we are, as the Prayer Book says, 'tied and bound by the chains of our sins' stretching all the way back to the General Election of 1918.

R. M. BARRINGTON-WARD, D.S.O., M.C. (Assistant Editor of *The Times*), to a member of his staff, March 1936.[2]

DURING the eighteen months before September 1939 the Great Powers of Europe were nominally at peace; never outside war had the continent known so sustained a period of tension and fear. The conflict which followed was Hitler's; seldom has the way of the aggressor been made so inviting. The circumstances within which the outwardly bloodless conquests of these months took place and the ease with which they were accomplished were the work of other men and earlier events. The natural predominance of Germany in Central Europe was Hitler's opportunity, not his handiwork. In Bohemia the conflict between Czechs and Germans was centuries old, and in Berlin no government since 1919 had genuinely accepted the new frontiers of Eastern Europe as final. Hitler was helped in the 1930's by the internal conflicts of the Austrian people and the nervous credulity of Schuschnigg; by the anomalies and weaknesses of Versailles and the climate of bitterness and idealism in which they had been created; by the weary ignorance of Baldwin, the frightened intrigues of Bonnet, and the moods and opinions of a Britain and a France which were generally given the foreign policies they desired and the politicians they deserved.

For those who had perceived the true nature of Nazi Germany and the opportunities surrounding it, 1938-9 was a time less of surprises than of the fulfilment of their worst fears.[3] The hearts which had 'sung hymns at heaven's gate'[4] as they envisaged the states to be born or recreated from the ruins of the Habsburg, Hohenzollern and Romanov Empires were anxious now. Erected that the transcendent virtues of self-determination might remove the seeds of war, the band of successor states which stretched across Europe offered Germany an opportunity for expansion denied it before 1914. Ominously, the Germans nicknamed them *Saisonsstaaten*.* In varying degrees every one of them suffered from the internal strife which sprang from the ethnographic untidiness of the areas they covered, and from the frequent incompatibility of strict self-determination with historic and strategic considerations. Minorities totalled 34·7 per cent in Czechoslovakia, in Poland 30·4 per cent and in Rumania 25 per cent.[5] In some cases they had been increased by opportunism and force. Linguistic affinity could not remove the years of economic and social distinctiveness between Czechs and Slovaks, nor administrative concessions overcome the deep-rooted antipathy between Czechs and Germans in Bohemia. As the Serbs could never be certain of the loyalty of Slovenes and Croats, so the Poles had always to guard against the centrifugal tendencies of Ruthenes and White Russians. Many such situations were doubtless unavoidable. Often, however, they had been created in the name not of expediency but of principle, and the 'fundamental intellectual dishonesty'[6] involved embarrassed potential friends — especially in Britain — and provided an enemy with both a weapon and an excuse.

Internal weakness was supplemented by international disarray. Though Czechoslovakia, Rumania and Yugoslavia

* That is, states born to exist for a season only.

had sought protection from Hungarian revisionist claims in the Little Entente, other dangers found them divided. For Czechoslovakia, geography and three and a quarter million Germans within her frontiers made Germany the greatest menace; to Yugoslavia, however, tensed at the head of the Adriatic, Germany appeared less as a threat than as a useful counterweight to Italy and, as with Rumania, a natural market for agricultural produce.* The Poles, for their part, waited to retrieve from Czechoslovakia the coal mines and railway junction of Teschen, taken in 1919, and regarded the Ruthenes who occupied the eastern tip of Czechoslovakia as potential agents of discontent among their kinsmen in Eastern Galicia. Yet Rumania shared with Poland an anxious neighbourhood with the Soviet Union and a pact which offered a semblance of protection against the spectre of Bolshevism and the claims of an ancient enemy in Bessarabia.

Anti-Semitism strengthened the Polish-Rumanian bond, and certainly the Poles, aloof from the Little Entente, had need of friendship. To move the Curzon Line, proposed by the Allies as her boundary with the U.S.S.R., 150 miles to the east in 1921 had been a rash if heroic triumph in view of the temporarily dormant German claims on Poland's opposite frontier, and the seizure of Vilna from Lithuania in the same year had added another enemy. Political forethought, like international morality, was not a feature of inter-war Europe.

Both Poland and the Little Entente in the 1920's had been provided with an illusion of safety by France, anxiously

* Rumania, Bulgaria, Yugoslavia and Hungary were all becoming increasingly tied to the German economy, doubly so after the *Anschluss* and disappearance of Czechoslovakia. German tactics included the dumping of industrial goods and the buying of primary products at inflated prices, while insisting on an exaggeratedly favourable exchange rate for the mark. The consequences were steep price rises and ensuing unrest in the ancillary state, the restriction of her own industry, and a growing economic isolation from all but German markets.

I Europe, 1933

searching for the security denied her at Versailles. As German and Soviet strength returned, however, that of France relatively declined, and with it the value of those alliances concluded between 1921 and 1925. In the air, particularly, France was weak, and the mentality which sought security in the Maginot Line was incompatible with that required if German attacks eastward were to be checked by those of France in the west.[7] The failure at Locarno in 1925 to attain parity of international recognition for Germany's eastern with her western frontiers foreshadowed the process of decline, and the inability of the French Foreign Minister, Barthou, to create an Eastern Locarno in 1934 confirmed it. Any likelihood of effective French pressure was further reduced when the Rhineland was remilitarized by Germany in 1936; when Belgium shielded the Ruhr by her declaration of neutrality a year later, it almost disappeared.

By then the alliances which sought to preserve the *status quo* were being strained by the minnow-like darts of policy occasioned by the advent of Hitler's Germany.* Polish *amour-propre* was wounded by an abortive pact between Britain, France, Germany and Italy in 1933, and the subsequent *rapprochement* between France and Italy alarmed Yugoslavia. Any security gained by France and Czecho-slovakia from their alliances with the Soviet Union in 1935 (and in the case of France automatic military assistance was not involved, nor did military conversations ensue) had to be offset against the offence caused to Poland, Rumania and Yugoslavia. Diminished Polish faith in French protection had been one factor behind her own pact with Germany in the previous year, and matters were not improved when

* Despite Hitler's early 'peace offensive'. In the Reichstag on 17 May 1933, for instance, he declared: 'No State can possess a greater under-standing for the young, newly created European national States than the new Germany. . . . Germany wants nothing for herself which she is not prepared to give to others.' N. H. Baynes, *The Speeches of Adolf Hitler* (1942), vol. 2, pp. 1041 ff. The decay of Weimar and rise of Hitler will be the subject of a further essay in this series.

France declined an offer of Polish military aid during the Rhineland crisis of 1936.

The life was dribbling out of the Little Entente. Two of its strongest supporters, Alexander of Yugoslavia and Barthou, were murdered in 1934; another, Titulescu, Foreign Minister of Rumania, was dismissed in 1936, and an authoritarian régime in Yugoslavia signed a treaty of friendship with Italy in the following year. *Sauve qui peut*. Before 1934 the French and Polish Ambassadors in Berlin had been in the habit of dining monthly with their Little Entente colleagues at Horcher's restaurant, but Lipski of Poland did not attend after the Polish-German pact was announced; gradually and symbolically the occasion became less frequent and less frequented.[8]

For France, other events were offering a still more direct threat. The economic and monetary crisis of 1929-32 had swept away the financial strength which had enabled Paris to insist on a preservation of the *status quo*; it had hastened the international disintegration of Europe and in the stricken Sudeten German industrial areas of Czechoslovakia, for instance, had exacerbated internal strife. An early end to reparations and to the Allied occupation of the Rhineland had not prevented the failure of economic and disarmament conferences, and any semblance of ease occasioned by the slackening of the economic storm was dispelled as the Nazi revolution, having purged its own malcontents and hailed the return of the Saar by plebiscite, moved out into Europe. In 1935 Hitler contravened Versailles by announcing conscription and a military air force. The firm front offered by Britain, France and Italy at the Stresa Conference disintegrated as Mussolini plunged into Abyssinia, then Spain, and as Britain condoned Hitler's actions by hastening to conclude an Anglo-German naval agreement without consulting France.*

* The Abyssinian and Spanish episodes, like the rôles of Japan and the U.S.A., will be treated at greater length by further essays in this series.

Abyssinia drove Italy closer to Hitler. The weakness of the West in the face of an abortive Nazi *putsch* in Austria in 1934 had helped make the course a tempting one for Mussolini, and the annoyance of limited sanctions did the rest. The League, already shaken by successful Japanese aggression in Manchuria, received its death blow in the process. Despite Mussolini's misgivings over Austria and the Balkans, the Rome–Berlin Axis was announced in 1936; the longer the Spanish imbroglio distracted attention from Central Europe, as Hitler saw,[9] the more servile would Mussolini become. Spain ruled out a Franco-Italian rapprochement, but not an Anglo-German one, and the independence of Austria was only one instalment of what the Duce had to pay for the friendship he needed in a seller's market.

The Spanish question further divided French opinion, already at odds over the Franco-Soviet pact and embroiled in increasing labour disputes. When Germany reoccupied the Rhineland in March 1936 those who found Hitler less odious than the Popular Front were joined by pacifists on the left in the easy task of ensuring that Flandin went no further than mere posturing. The British public and its politicians gave them every support, many feeling, with the Canadian High Commissioner, that 'French vindictiveness against Germany' offered the real danger. During 'the most nerve-racking hours in his life', as Hitler frequently called them,[10] the French army, burdened by the memory of Verdun and the legacy of Pétain, watched from the deceptive safety of the Maginot Line as the security of its country was further undermined.

In November of the following year Italy joined Germany and Japan in the anti-Comintern pact. To some in the West the pact was a welcome bulwark against the evils of Bolshevism. Its essential threat, however, in Europe, the Mediterranean and the freshly-inflamed Far East, was in Ciano's words 'unmistakably anti-British',[11] a factor which made the event a vital stage in the development of Nazi

foreign policy. Hitler's decision to follow the promptings of
Ribbentrop, to face away from London and sign with the
other two, was 'a turning point of the highest significance,
above all in south-east Europe'.[12] 'Three nations', noted
Ciano, 'are embarking together on a path which may
perhaps lead them to war. A war necessary in order to break
through the crust which is stifling the energy and the
aspirations of the younger nations'.[13]

The growing tension in the Far East, far more than that
of Europe, raised the question of American involvement in
the pre-war years. Yet even here the overwhelming weight
of American public opinion made the answer at best an
equivocal one, and the opportunity for joint action which
some thought (wrongly) to have been offered Britain in 1931
never reappeared in more substantial form. It is also
doubtful whether the peace-talks initiative which Roosevelt
produced and Chamberlain squashed in January 1938
would have proved as crucial in Europe as critics of the
latter have been inclined to suggest, and when the Austrian
crisis was in the air only a month later the official American
determination to mind her own business was most marked.[14]
The President might talk of 'quarantine' for aggressors in
October 1937, but nothing came of it; and though in July
1939 he denounced his country's commercial treaty with
Japan 'in order that the dictators should not imagine that
they could get away with it',[15] an official denial of any
Anglo-American understanding on joint action had to be
issued within a few days. The neutrality laws clearly
symbolised the unlikelihood of a commitment by the New
World redressing the unhealthy balance within the Old.
During the Sudeten crisis in September 1938 Roosevelt not
only had publicly to declare that America could in no way
be considered part of an anti-German bloc; he secretly
warned the British Ambassador that, even if America were
to become involved in war, only a substantial invasion of
Britain might allow him to send her troops to Europe.[16] In

1938 and 1939 Britain and France, with or without Russia, would have to work out their own salvation. Until the outbreak of war and indeed for a time afterwards, the policies most relied upon to accomplish this task were those commonly embraced by the term 'appeasement'.*

Appeasement was not a British prerogative. It received for a variety of motives, realistic rather than idealistic, the support of many Frenchmen. At times they included Daladier,† outwardly so strong, 'hero' of Professor Furnia's polemic, *The Diplomacy of Appeasement*. More subtle yet more consistent was the adherence of a François-Poncet (Ambassador in Berlin, then Rome), for 'so long as there remained a chance for a wealthy Frenchman to have a share in the prosperity of the New Order, one might reconcile oneself to the changed balance of forces in European diplomacy'.[17] Only by default, through their 'policy of amoral drift', did appeasement receive the support of the majority of Americans, but Joseph Kennedy, their Ambassador in London, was 'a warm admirer'[18] of the British role during the Munich crisis, and he assured his German colleague that he 'understood Germany's Jewish policy completely';[19] he had very little idea, he told a journalist at the end of 1939, what the war was being fought for.[20] Though his colleague in Paris, William Bullitt, was tougher, he, too, was suggesting in the summer of 1938 that America should 'attempt to find some way which will let the French out of their moral commitment (to Czechoslovakia)'.[21] Even the doctrine of 'phoney war', so reviled in America when practised by the West, had been privately preached by Roosevelt himself in 1938,[22] and the President was later to misjudge Stalin as thoroughly as Chamberlain had Hitler.

* So completely has the word come to be interpreted in a pejorative sense only that one uses it with regret; contemporaries and therefore historians have been unable to do without it, however.

† See below, pp. 59–60 and 83–4.

Yet in its influence and in its complexity appeasement was essentially a British phenomenon, some of its many strands held in common, some the predilections of a few, some varying with circumstances. 'The appeasers' were not merely those relatively few people clustered around Neville Chamberlain near the summit of power. If one is forced to use the term in this sense it is not only because of the influence and eventual isolation of such men, but because the currents of appeasement in the country at large still await their historian.* The clarity with which the majority of the nation demanded a firm stand in September 1939 was a relatively new phenomenon, for no thought of resistance had greeted the occupation of the Rhineland and Chamberlain had been welcomed home from Munich with something like hysteria.† In Lord Vansittart's words: 'Mine is a story of failure, but it throws light on my time which failed too'.[23]

It may indeed be suggested that public opinion in a liberal democracy, having in the twentieth century acquired a great deal of power, is unlikely to acquire the judgement or sense of responsibility to match. During and after the Great War a body such as the Union of Democratic Control could win much support for its campaign to abolish the evils of 'secret diplomacy'; it could not guarantee the enlightenment of those policies which, in the name of the people, the new 'open' diplomacy would carry out. It could not educate the public out of what Walter Lippmann has described as 'the propensity to say "No" to a change of course, [which] sets up a compulsion to make mistakes [since] opinion deals with

* A study of the British Press and Germany will be found in R. Kieser, *Englands Appeasementpolitik und der Aufstieg des Dritten Reiches im Spiegel der britischen Presse, 1933–39* (Verlag P. G. Keller, Winterthur, 1964). But Dr. Kieser's work deals only indirectly and here and there with public opinion; he has studied the national but not the provincial press, and editorials rather than letters. The Mass Observation publications from 1937–9 should also be consulted.

† The intoxication of relief and hope is captured by a recording in the BBC archives of the scenes in Downing Street on that occasion: record no. 1955/6.

a situation which no longer exists'.[24] It could not remove indifference or the easy indulgence in criticism which left one's own comfort undisturbed. The storm of indignation raised by the Hoare–Laval agreement brought a righteous glow to many and revealed the full extent of Baldwin's parody of responsible leadership. It did not bring oil sanctions to the help of Abyssinia, and would be slower to show itself when more dangerous causes offered themselves.

Appeasement did not rest solely upon the political prejudices or wishful thinking of few, though they had their part to play. Its greatest strength was drawn from the deep-seated horror of war which had gripped the country since 1918 and which could point to the subsequent failure of armed Western intervention in Russia, Turkey and the Ruhr. Though the victor of the Fulham by-election in 1933 was not a pacifist, and though the Peace Ballot produced a majority of nearly three to one in favour of military sanctions if necessary, both events, together with such straws as the 'King and Country' debate, were rightly taken as reaffirming widespread opposition to rearmament. For some, indeed, passive rather than pacifist, isolation was a temptation. 'Where is Prague?' asked the *Daily Express*: 'If the "Collective Security" madmen get their way you might find yourself there in a trench one day. If the policy of Isolation triumphs, you will . . . not fight anybody unless they come here looking for trouble.'[25] Among those 'collective security madmen', the Labour Party for their part were second to none in ensuring Britain's weakness when the crisis came.[26]

Revulsion against war was accompanied by a blend of guilt and idealism for those who felt that the principles which had been proclaimed so loudly as the basis of lasting peace in 1919 had been denied to Germany. To 'appease' was to settle just grievances, not to cringe and betray. The statement that Munich 'was a triumph for all that was best and most enlightened in British life',[27] though half ironic and perhaps terse enough to be misleading, is likely to enrage

only those who view their history from a comfortable
standpoint. Harold Nicolson, who with every reason was
appalled when the flight to Munich was announced in the
Commons, had himself helped lay bare the apparent
hypocrisy of Versailles.[28] So had Keynes.[29] So, more subtly
and more recently, had E. H. Carr.[30] Was it unreasonable
that after seventeen years Germany should re-enter her own
'back garden' in the Rhineland? 'Treat entrance to zone as
assertion, demonstration of recovered status of equality and
not as an act of aggression',[31] ran advice to Baldwin from
some of his friends, and according to a German source,
Edward VIII talked to the German Ambassador of abdicat-
ing if Britain moved.[32] Was not the bloodless course of the
Anschluss due to 'the will of the people affected'?[33] Or could
Britain, as her Ambassador in Germany asked, deny to the
Sudeten Germans the principle upon which her own Empire
now rested?[34] Should we fight, demanded the *Observer*, 'in a
vain attempt to preserve a state of things which never ought
to have been created by the purblind and botching state-
craft of Versailles?'[35] 'If we are ever to be in a position to
protect the peace of the world', wrote Lord Allen of
Hurtwood, 'we must first of all be just to Germany'.[36]

Such idealist overtones were a particularly British feature
of appeasement, and are prominent when one examines the
arguments of the smaller circle of 'appeasers' in or near the
seats of power. It was necessary, ran one theme, 'to convince
the world that for peace we are prepared to go to absurd
lengths',[37] while as late as April 1939 Halifax was warning
that safety could be found only if men were offered a cause
which 'appealed to the highest elements in their nature'.[38]
The Foreign Secretary's speech on that occasion is, indeed, a
cardinal document for understanding that even after Hitler's
entry into Prague the 'inner Cabinet' (Chamberlain,
Halifax, Simon and Hoare), among whom Free Church
influences were strong, were seeking not so much to build
the most powerful coalition possible as to reaffirm the 'moral

basis' of British foreign policy — the rights of smaller states, the sanctity of international obligations, the repudiation of threats and force.[39] Hitler was faced by the heirs not of Chatham but of Bright.

The burden of responsibility carried by Chamberlain and those close to him added negative, practical reasons for continuing the search for a settlement. It was generally accepted, for instance, that in war the bomber would always get through — a proposition usually thought of in terms of German bombers over Britain and not vice versa. Baldwin had said as much; Guernica and Madrid offered recent, if facile, confirmation. Those at the time who were ready for 'peace at any cost in humiliation'[40] because of Britain's unpreparedness may well have been wrong, but they included men of bravery and experience. 'Chamberlain is of course right', wrote General Ironside in September 1938. 'We have not the means of defending ourselves and he knows it. . . . We cannot expose ourselves now to a German attack. We simply commit suicide if we do.'[41]* It was not only in Central Europe, after all, that danger threatened. Turmoil in Palestine and tension in the Mediterranean were not lessened at the time by the one being partly of British making and the other being heightened by an acceptance of Mussolini's power at his own false valuation. There seemed good reason for doubting whether the Commonwealth, so independent over the Chanak crisis, would swiftly follow a strong British lead. As the Japanese threat increased, the most that the country's one satisfactory military arm could offer was a 'hope' of sending to the Far East one battleship 'by 1942'.[42]

* Not only professional advisers but also Churchill and his supporters overrated German strength, particularly in the air; and the latter by their grim warnings may have helped postpone the very involvement of Britain which they sought, from September 1938 to a less favourable September 1939. Nor should Chamberlain's radical work as Minister of Health be forgotten, nor the sight from his German-bound plane of miles of apparently defenceless London.

It is evident, however, that for some within the narrower
circle of 'appeasers' the need to win time to rearm was an
ex post facto justification; Sir Nevile Henderson, who later
used it,[43] wrote in August 1938 that 'Hitler would not dare
to make war if we really showed our teeth'.[44] For
Chamberlain it was a subordinate consideration during the
Sudeten crisis, just as his declared belief in Hitler's word was
not conducive to an all-out effort thereafter. The appointment of Hore-Belisha to revivify the Army had not been
followed up with the necessary material support, and it was
Chamberlain who had replaced Swinton by Kingsley Wood
at the Air Ministry in 1938; even after Hitler's entry into
Prague he and Sir Horace Wilson attempted (on political
rather than military grounds) to avoid the awkward issue of
conscription.[45] More influential with such men at the time
was the belief that 'in the face of a rising market, the longer
they delayed the higher would be the terms asked'.[46] There
were those, even, who did not believe Britain to be capable
of catching up German rearmament. 'We have spurned
Hitler's repeated offers', wrote one of them. 'They will not
be kept open indefinitely. His price will mount.' [47]

Such men saw no hope in the League — even Chamberlain's brief support for it over Abyssinia was perhaps cynical
at bottom.[48] Few of them, however, wished to return to what
was sometimes termed the 'old diplomacy' of alliances which
had 'brought us into the Great War'; it was, as Baldwin
confessed to a friend, 'an awful dilemma'.[49] It was partly on
these grounds that Chamberlain refused a Soviet offer of
discussions after the *Anschluss*, even though he privately
declared at the time that 'force and determination are most
effectively mobilised by alliances'.[50] Power blocs meant war;
only direct dealings might preserve a just peace.

For some, this attitude was reinforced by a dislike of
Britain's one obvious ally. French weakness and despair
between the wars owed much to cold and sometimes callous
treatment from London, and Baldwin was not exceptional

when he counted as a major comfort of retirement 'that he should not have to meet French statesmen any more'.[51] Repugnance was increased when a left-wing government like Blum's — 'hazardous associates', Garvin called them[52] — were involved. Those like Lord Lothian and Geoffrey Dawson, editor of *The Times*, who admired Hitler's strength often made no secret of their detestation for a weak and untrustworthy France, and they were even less restrained once France had allied with the Soviet Union.[53]

There was a small minority in Britain* who long regarded the threat posed by Hitler as less than that of Bolshevism. Stalin's machinations in Spain aroused increasing distrust, and his purge trials added moral repugnance at the same time as they diminished belief in Soviet military effectiveness.[54] At Cliveden,† the American Ambassador in Moscow 'made his listeners' flesh creep with his Bolshevik stories',[55] whilst in Berlin both Halifax and Sir Horace Wilson were quick to recognise Hitler's 'great services' to European civilisation in resisting the forces of disintegration from the east.[56] Dawson's biographer writes that he, too, was 'certainly influenced by the thought that Nazi Germany served as a barrier to the spread of Communism'.[57] It was 1 September 1939 when the *Daily Telegraph* published a letter from Lord Alfred Douglas which rejoiced that Hitler had saved Britain from the 'odious predicament' of an alliance with Russia, and declared with relief that 'there would be no war'.‡

* Public opinion is difficult to gauge on this matter, though clearer by the summer of 1939 when one survey reported 86 per cent in favour of military alliance with the U.S.S.R. (*News Chronicle*, 3 May 1939, survey by the British Institute of Public Opinion).

† The popular concept of a 'Cliveden set' needs modifying, for the opinions of Lady Astor's guests were diverse; Eden and Henderson might be found at the same table.

‡ Other opponents of Bolshevism, besides Germany, received encouragement from some quarters. In January 1939 Lord Rothermere wrote to Admiral Horthy to express 'much gratification' at Hungary's having joined the anti-Comintern pact. 'It links once and for all', he

By then admiration for the new Germany was stilled in Britain, but in earlier years this, too, had weighed with some public figures associated with appeasement. In the 1920's, official and semi-official organisations in Germany had endeavoured to increase the feeling of guilt over Versailles; thereafter visits by prominent people from Britain were encouraged by Hitler, as by Mussolini, and a subsequent book like Arnold Wilson's *Walks and Talks Abroad* more than repaid the efforts of the Nazi propaganda machine.[58] Some had come back with reports of Hitler's modesty,[59] others, like Lloyd George, struck by his greatness and more ready than ever to espouse the return of Germany's former colonies. Several in 1935 and 1936 were convinced, with Lord Allen and Arnold Toynbee, of 'Hitler's sincerity in desiring peace in Europe',[60] and for those who stayed at home there was the odd but persuasive Ribbentrop, able to make an impression even on those like Sir Thomas Inskip, who feared for the church under Nazism. ('A new reformation', they were told, 'was proceeding in Germany in the interests of religion'). Lord Lothian, indeed, managed to believe that Nazi brutality was 'largely the reflex of the external persecution to which Germans have been subjected since the war'.[61]

Few of the leading appeasers spoke German or had much knowledge of European history. Few — even Halifax who had at least read History at Oxford — had studied *Mein Kampf*. Many in Britain found it hard to credit that Nazism could be quite as appalling as its enemies declared it to be; it was a movement quite beyond the comprehension of men like Baldwin or Halifax, or those who, like Dawson and Lothian, were experienced in Commonwealth spheres rather

wrote, 'Hungary with the powerful neighbouring countries, Germany and Italy. . . . I am sufficiently presumptuous to tell your Serene Highness that the present policy, rigorously pursued, will enable Hungary to secure accretions of territory more important than that secured during the last few months.' *The Confidential Papers of Admiral Horthy* (1965), p. 121.

than nearer home. In the City, particularly, anxiety to preserve the calm setting which good business required easily led to a wilful misinterpretation of the nature of Nazism; between 30 November and 8 December 1937, for instance, the *Financial Times* published a series of articles praising the new Germany, and refused to print the detailed refutation sent by the Focus group round Churchill and Lady Violet Bonham Carter.* Even when disenchantment set in later there was always the hope that those 'good' Germans who remained would put their own house in order, or that Hitler himself would not fight in the last resort.[62]

The political preferences of some leading appeasers gave rise at the time to Soviet sneers against the social, frightened-bourgeois basis of the policies they advocated.[63] Whilst rejecting the ideological fantasies involved, it is possible to recognise that in the case of a few men an element of truth remains. To suggest, as has been done, that Sir Nevile Henderson in Berlin was 'typical of the helplessness with which members of a declining ruling class faced the social transformation of the 1920's and 1930's'[64] is far too sweeping; even in his case one should allow for the way in which continuous diplomatic service abroad, like the Indian Army, could make a man a stranger in his own country. At Nuremberg in September 1938, however, Henderson, the fortunes of whose family were less satisfactory than they had earlier been, assured his German listeners that 'Great Britain should not be rated as a democracy but as an aristocracy', and that the 'aristocratic ruling class was at present on the defensive against the broad mass of the popular front.' He added that all would be well, nevertheless, since 'the English . . . being a virile Germanic race, preferred to be led

* See Spier, *Focus*, pp. 31, 36 and 130. Eugen Spier, a German Jew, helped finance *Focus* and offered his services to the British Government at the outbreak of war. He was immediately interned for two years. For comments on the City's support for Franco, see Liddell Hart, ii, pp. 133–4.

by hunting and shooting men and not their opposites.'[65]
The dedication of Henderson's *Failure of a Mission* 'in
humble recognition ... to the people of the British Isles'
needs to be read *de haut en bas*.

Chamberlain's critics within the Labour Party were inclined to develop the same theme regarding the Prime Minister. In this case it may be said that for Attlee to assume that
'Neville truckles to the dictators because he likes their principles'[66] was as misguided as it would have been to suggest
that Sidney Webb admired the NKVD. Nor can it be proved
that those Conservatives who distrusted Soviet talk of assistance were led by prejudice into total error. During the
Sudeten crisis one German observer in Moscow saw no
preparations that suggested Russia (who as recently as August
had had to fight the Japanese at Lake Khasan) meant business.[67] Stalin himself later told Churchill that he had not been
ready to fight even defensively in 1939,[68] an obvious excuse
to offer, but one which the Finnish campaign and the extent
of German penetration in 1941 would seem to bear out.

It is interesting to note, moreover, that in 1940 the Labour
Party were ready to serve under Halifax, whose appeasement
had been only slightly less whole-hearted than that of his
leader ('his loyalty to Chamberlain and his belief in his
policy', writes Lord Birkenhead, 'were never in question').[69]
Personalities seem to have counted for more than policies,
especially, perhaps, since the latter had not been neatly
divided on party lines; the most Kingsley Martin of the
New Statesman had hoped for in 1938 was a peaceful process
of letting Hitler have all he wanted, and on 2 September
1939 Shinwell and others on the Parliamentary Executive of
the Labour Party were all for abandoning Poland if France
would not fight.[70] The political health of the nation suffered
from the very unfamiliarity of the rôles of the two major
parties as the Left struggled towards a policy of firmness and
official Conservatism preached humility and understanding
in foreign affairs. As in the Commonwealth/Common

Market debate, neither side found the other's clothes entirely comfortable. Such occasions, rare gifts for the political satirist, tend naturally to confuse rather than sharpen the issues at stake, and from a distance the participants themselves as well as the country at large have a somewhat bewildered air about them.

It must also be observed that Chamberlain's critics within his own party do not, in retrospect, emerge with all their judgements and their chosen tactics entirely distinct from his. Can Eden be said to have faced up to the dictators during the Rhineland crisis or the approach of the Austrian? Over Abyssinia Duff Cooper — at times supporter of the horse against the tank and the ship against the aeroplane — was ready to appease, as was Amery,[71] and though it is legitimate to argue that Mussolini had to be weaned from Hitler and that Abyssinia was by no means to be equated with Central Europe, the threat to the Suez Canal and the encouragement to future aggression cannot be denied. Moreover Amery, like Chamberlain, privately doubted after the *Anschluss* whether Britain could help Czechoslovakia, and 'whether we might not have to resign ourselves to falling back, with Italian support, on holding Yugoslavia and the Balkans, and letting Germany find her elbow room in the rest of the Danubian area and in Eastern Europe'.[72] It was, perhaps, a judgement easier to reverse out of office than in it. Clearly 'appeasement' could not be ruled out in all circumstances, as Churchill's government was to demonstrate when submitting to Japanese demands that the Burma road should be closed in 1940.

Moreover, hardly any Conservatives felt able to go as far as Churchill in working for alternative policies to those of Chamberlain's government. If few in the Labour Party were as ready as Dalton to abandon party distinctions after Munich, the leader of the 'Eden group' would not support Harold Macmillan's desire to work for '1931 in reverse'.[73] 'The majority (of Conservatives) are miserably unhappy and

B

would follow an alternative lead, if given one', so Richard
Law assured him on 24 September 1938. It cannot be said
that a radical response was forthcoming, and if the swift
events of the following days and the general incongruity of a
pact with an anti-rearmament Opposition were partly
responsible, so, perhaps, was an undue avoidance of risk
among the constituencies. 'So far we have done virtually no
propaganda', admitted Eden in August 1939, 'and have
allowed charges to be made against us which we have made
no attempt to refute'.[74] Only then to think of changing this
might be considered as tardy as Churchill's inclusion in the
government a month later. 'In this period', writes Captain
Liddell Hart, 'Eden's firmness of purpose did not match his
intelligence and good intentions.'[75]

And yet the particular shortcomings of Chamberlain and
his closer and more prominent supporters remain. A policy
is heady which has, initially, a large measure of public
support and which rests upon the noble aims of peace and
justice, which is reinforced by one's own unpreparedness and
yet the immediate pain of which is borne by others.
Appeasement became a mission. How many can believe in
their mission whilst leaving unimpaired their judgement,
their acceptance of criticism, their feelings for those im-
patiently trampled along the path to achievement? Woodrow
Wilson for one had not been able to do so. Missions can
corrupt as much as power, and Chamberlain, with his
'inexhaustible vanity', found both to his liking.[76] In this
harsh though gentle man, 'love of appeasement', wrote
Amery, 'was coupled with a strong vein of cynicism'.[77]

It appears to have been this growing sense of mission, as
well as changing circumstances and attempted realism,
which facilitated the overlooking of past judgements and the
inconsistency of current ones. Thomas Jones, for instance,
though influential in the Baldwin rather than the Chamberlain period, illustrated the process when in 1936 he 'preached
the duty of resisting Vansittart's pro-French bias' and in

1937 advocated alliance with Germany, for in 1935 he had recognised that 'the French are pacific in intention while the Germans are not'.[78] So did Lord Lothian when he admired as 'a prophet ... one of the creative figures of this generation', the man whom he had declared in 1934 to be 'nothing but a gunman'.[79] For Chamberlain in 1934 and 1935 Nazi Germany was 'the bully of Europe' and the threat of military action 'the only thing Germans understand', sentiments he repeated to the American Treasury as late as March 1937;[80] and the Prime Minister who from 1937 onwards wooed Italy with yielding ardour had acknowledged two years before that 'by showing weakness' one would 'encourage Mussolini to be more intransigent'.[81] As the urgency of the mission grew, one saw what one wished to see. Thus Hitler, whose government was for Chamberlain in May 1938 'utterly untrustworthy and dishonest', became four months later 'a man who could be relied upon when he had given his word';[82] thus the Fuehrer at Munich appeared eager to sign an Anglo-German declaration of friendship when to the third person present he seemed to agree 'with a certain reluctance, and ... only to please Chamberlain'.[83] The testimony of Lord Swinton[84] as to his Prime Minister's innermost thoughts at the time serves only to underline the hollowness of recent attempts to proclaim Munich an exercise in *Realpolitik*. To a far larger extent it was a study in self-delusion.

The mission would not be reconsidered at the urging of friends who might be better informed, or deterred by 'the mischievous continuous barrage of questions on foreign affairs in the House'.[85] Secure in the claims of its higher morality, Sir Horace Wilson could privately and indirectly threaten Eden if the truth of the latter's disagreements with Chamberlain leaked out;[86] Geoffrey Dawson could falsify without acknowledgement a correspondent's report;[87] Chamberlain could blandly assert that he had not, at Berchtesgaden, answered Hitler's question on the right of the Sudetens to self-determination.[88] In the interests of the mission the Czechs had, in Henderson's words, 'to get a real twist of the screw',[89] just as Bonnet could be assisted to undermine the firmness of his own Prime Minister in the face of Italian demands.[90] As in the latter case of Suez, not only decision but discussion narrowed to within the radius of a 'magic circle', by-passing Allied governments and the House of Commons as much as expert advisers.[91] During the Sudeten crisis the Cabinet frequently found themselves committed in advance, and their decision on 2 September 1939 to deliver an ultimatum to Germany that day was reversed without their knowledge.[92]

It was the Indian summer of the heirs of mid-Victorian England, with their Birmingham social conscience and their Gladstonian international high-mindedness, their dedication and their cant. Even Halifax, with his spiritual detachment and his 'negotiating type of mind, always ready for accommodation', was the descendant of a steam-age aristocrat. At the same time courage and ability were not abundant in public affairs. Popular inertia was matched by that of Baldwin and would not be overcome by governments which found a ready place for the Londonderrys and Inskips; the Simons and the Kingsley Woods were the last men to offer their nation that unpalatable information which would demand attention* and which would enable the hasty propaganda of the Left Book Club, for instance, to be seen in true perspective and as something more than the distortions of mere ideologues.

It was also the day of the amateur, and some of the strengths and weaknesses which accompanied his mission were to be found within a small compass in a letter which appeared in *The Times* on 21 March 1939. Hitler, the letter argued, had had to be given every chance to enter constructive paths, and doubly so since, in contrast to the blame

* Daladier's failure in the same field was great also. See Pertinax, op. cit., chaps. 5 and 6.

Britain had to bear over Versailles, he had been 'morally armoured' in his earlier demands; now, by destroying Czechoslovakia, he had committed an appalling crime, but still Britain must strive for peace between the people of the two nations. The high appeal of the letter has to be weighed against the inappropriate timing of its remarks. The naïve earnestness which it breathes contrasts sharply with the anonymity of its writer, 'M.P., House of Commons'.

The efforts of appeasement were to be in vain. In September 1939 'the angel of peace was murdered'.[93] This is not a fashionable statement in some academic circles nowadays; Mr. Taylor's submissions have received sufficient support for there to be talk of 'the rise of a revisionist school' concerning appeasement and the German behaviour to which it was related.[94] Not all its members would feel able to write on the origins of the war a book which 'really has little to do with Hitler',[95] but some, in correcting earlier, over-simplified and determinist views, have come close to throwing out the baby with the bath-water.

It is true that a 'blueprint for aggression' will not be found in *Mein Kampf*. In it, for instance, the inevitable enmity of France for Germany assumes proportions not to be found in 1938–9, whilst England, the object of Hitler's most bitter tirades as war approached, is depicted as a needless opponent in the past and a desirable friend for the future.[96] On the other hand the expansionist themes of the book were never abandoned by Hitler: the 'moral right, from the need of the people, to acquire foreign territory', and the rejection of the frontiers of 1914 as inadequate; the belief that 'he who would live must fight' and that 'those nations will be victorious who are of more brutal will and . . . have not practised self-denial'.[97] These were not simply early dreams which can conveniently be fitted to later, fortuitous events; within a few weeks of coming to power Hitler was addressing his High Command on the need for 'the conquest of new *Lebensraum* in the East and its ruthless Germanization'.[98]

In a similar way, the realisation that the moves Hitler finally made were not part of a carefully prepared timetable has been allowed to overshadow the planned aggression which began to be given clearer expression in 1937. In June of that year, for instance, a directive by Field-Marshal von Blomberg, though dealing mainly with hypothetical events, acknowledged that there was no danger of an attack on Germany, yet warned her armed forces to be ready to take advantage of a fluid political situation.[99] And though the circumstances envisaged in the celebrated Hossbach Memorandum* five months later were not to be present when Austria and Czechoslovakia fell to Germany (who could have foreseen, remarked Hitler later, 'that Czechoslovakia would be served up to me, so to speak, by her friends'[100]), the intention that they *should* fall remained throughout. Hitler's anxiety in the summer of 1939 not 'to slide into a war with England on account of Poland' was not allowed to override the decision 'to isolate Poland' and 'to attack [her] at the first suitable opportunity', despite the risks involved.[101]

The immediate initiative which precipitated events in the pre-war period did indeed often come from the nervous hands of others — Schuschnigg over Austria, Hácha over the rump of Czechoslovakia, and, less directly, Chamberlain over the Sudetenland. It is often forgotten that Mr. Taylor was not the first to recognise this, though he brought it publicity by vividness and a tendency to overstatement; it was Sir Lewis Namier who earlier wrote that, though Hitler expected war in about five years time, as late as February 1938 he 'still preferred the "evolutionary course",' moving only when Schuschnigg 'seemed about to give him the slip' and when 'the Western appeasers became active, as if intent on proving to Hitler that he had nothing to fear from them'.[102] Yet the tension which caused others to act sprang

* *D.G.F.P.* i, no. 19; see below, pp. 40-1.

from the expansionist aims — however unco-ordinated —
of the Third Reich and from the nature of Nazism, and this
is equally true of those occasions when Germans outside the
Reich, their nationalism 'often more intense than that of the
Germans at home',[103] attempted to provoke a crisis to the
alarm not only of conservative German diplomats but even
of SS leaders as well.[104] 'Hitler speaks' shouted the newspaper
placards at their anxious publics. 'In every gathering of
friends', noted one observer in January 1939, 'in every
conversation of twos and threes, there is but one topic: what
does Hitler intend? The world hangs once more on this
man's lips. With him are the issues of peace and war'.

There have been other reinterpretations, however, concerning the armaments and economy of pre-war Germany,
and it is clear that the extent of the former was deliberately
exaggerated from 1935 onwards; even the vaunted *Luftwaffe*
was not fully prepared in September 1939.[105]* There was
then only three months' supply of aviation petrol, armaments
existed in width rather than in depth, and in the face of a
major, extended conflict, the economy contained serious flaws.
The decision to place that economy on a war footing, postponed by a Hitler confident of cheap success as late as 23
August 1939,[106] was taken only on 3 September.[107] even
then it remained on a short-term, *Blitzkrieg* basis until 1942.

Yet it must be remembered when assessing German
weaknesses that detailed economics bored Hitler: he
dreamed of *Blitzkrieg*, and the means were expected to be
found. Nor should it be forgotten that from March 1933 to
March 1939 Germany spent about half as much again on
armaments as Britain and France together,[108] with her
heavy-industry sector increasingly predominant and her
existing drift towards autarchy hastened for reasons of

* For details of the *Luftwaffe's* shortcomings in the spheres of planning
and operational range see, for instance, the study by Dr. Karl Klee in
H.-A. Jacobsen and J. Rohwer (eds.), *Decisive Battles of World War II:
The German View* (1965).

strategy. And though the grave economic and social difficulties consequent upon these and other factors (the problem of full employment prominent among them) helped limit the pace of rearmament, they made the prospect of foreign plunder all the more inviting. 'The only "solution" open to this regime of the structural tensions and crises produced by dictatorship and rearmament was more dictatorship and more rearmament, then expansion, then war and terror, then plunder and enslavement. The stark, ever-present alternative was collapse and chaos'.[109]*

At times, it is true, pride in an ability to obtain cheap successes seems to have struggled in Hitler's mind with a desire to use force, and there were still occasions, particularly in the face of growing British opposition, when in private he appears to have had moments of uncertainty and nervousness. Shortened by the confident and evil promptings of Ribbentrop[110] they were resolved in outbursts of swift, hysterical and partly spontaneous action; such behaviour justified the later observation of a German official that while 'the general objectives of National Socialism were known from the start ... the execution of these basic objectives seemed to be characterised by improvisation as each new situation arose'.[111]

Domestically, there was often alarm, seldom more. In 1933 many Germans had 'quivered as a horse quivers when it feels the master's hand and spurs',[112] and now, in the face of succeeding triumphs, others who might once have opposed procrastinated, served, and did not lack reasoning for their memoirs. For one Beck or Oster there were many Schachts or Weizsäckers. Others confessed themselves mistaken, or bowed to the man they now recognised as

---

* Ernst Nolte in his outstanding work, *Three Faces of Fascism* (1965; pp. 302 and 325) asks whether 'rearmament with its totally irresponsible expansion of credit volume was anything but the state's commitment to cover its obligations by war booty?' He also emphasises that, however much 'revisionism' one may undertake, 'conquest, bluntly and without reservation, was the focal idea in Hitler's policy'.

'Germany's destiny for good and for evil',[113] 'the fate of Germany [which] could not be escaped'.[114]

One important characteristic was shared by Germany and the other Powers and must be borne in mind when studying the approach of war. The diplomatic services of the time tended in varying degrees to be ignored or overriden, to be reduced, in Weizsäcker's self-exculpatory phrase, to 'a technical apparatus'.

In Nazi Germany this was hardly surprising. For Hitler the Foreign Ministry, with its aristocratic tradition, was 'an intellectual garbage dump'. Rosenberg, Goebbels and Hess all took their share in attacking it, and it had to compete with bodies such as the *Auslandsorganisation* and the *Dienststelle Ribbentrop*.[115] Though Ribbentrop, on becoming Foreign Minister, fought for the supremacy of his department over all others, it was only as a personal apparatus that he used it. Friction between diplomats and his private agents continued[116] and the atmosphere in the Ministry was often poisonous;[117] in May 1939 Ribbentrop threatened personally to shoot any official heard doubting the wisdom and success of the Fuehrer's policy over Poland.[118] As crises approached, ambassadors were generally withdrawn from the capitals of the intended victim and its potential allies, and interest was seldom displayed in any reports they might wish to deliver on their return.[119]

Similar limitations imposed upon Soviet diplomats were obvious, and the embarrassed twists and turns of an ambassador like Maisky when asked for an opinion or caught one step behind the Kremlin need no comment;[120] if Litvinov's description of his own function as Foreign Minister as being to 'hand on diplomatic documents' was a little self-effacing, his position, too, hung by a thread. In Japan the diplomats, like the government, had frequently to bow to the wishes of the army. In Italy the Duce preferred to read newspapers, intercepted letters and stolen documents than ambassador's reports, whilst his own policy and reactions were expressed more frequently on the platform or in anonymous letters than through other international channels. The warnings of Attolico from Berlin failed to prevent his unwary government from announcing the Pact of Steel before its terms had been considered, and Ciano's shock on hearing the news of the impending Molotov–Ribbentrop pact would have been avoided had he paid closer attention to reports sent by his ambassador in Moscow.*

The position in the democracies was only a little better. Bonnet, as French Foreign Minister, was close to the centre of affairs, but was deviously pressing his personal desire for appeasement at whatever cost rather than executing government policy through regular diplomatic channels. A question whose answer might help undermine any firmness within one's own cabinet† need not be transmitted officially,[121] just as awkward signs of a forward policy by Moscow could be suppressed.[122] The advice of ambassadors was seldom sought,[123] particularly when, as in the case of Coulondre in Berlin, it was known in advance to be unpalatable, and there was little harmony between Bonnet and Léger, his Secretary-General at the Quai d'Orsay.

The British Foreign Office, for its part, had for many years been working within the context of a popular distrust of 'secret diplomacy' and of the directives of governments anxious to do no more than follow the lumberings of public opinion. Its independence and the weight of its advice were further reduced when Chamberlain, determined in advance to be 'his own foreign secretary', became Prime Minister, and the diplomatic machinery of transmission, information

* See below, pp. 168–9 and an article by M. Toscano in *Revue d'Histoire de la Deuxième Guerre Mondiale*, No. 6 (April 1952).

† As in Britain, the French Cabinet found itself at times little more than a spectator. 'Les Ministres demeurent dans l'ignorance la plus absolue', wrote Jean Zay on 30 August 1939: *Carnets secrets de Jean Zay* (Paris, 1942), p. 74.

and judgement was soon by-passed in a way which recalled those machinations of Lloyd George which Baldwin and Chamberlain himself had so abhorred. For Sir Robert Vansittart, Chief Diplomatic Adviser, there was a position of impotence; for Sir Horace Wilson, Chief Industrial Adviser, there was power and influence 'unequalled', in the opinion of Lord Woolton, 'by any member of the Cabinet except the Prime Minister'.[124] Unofficial channels helped Chamberlain develop his own policies against those of Eden,[125] and the more acceptable advice of Halifax which followed, scrutinised as it was by two former and unhappy foreign secretaries, Simon and Hoare, did not command the support of many permanent officials.[126] Henderson in Berlin was a Chamberlain rather than a Foreign Office man, and was no more consistently loyal to the instructions given him by Halifax* than he was to his colleagues in Vienna and Paris.[127] Even he was by-passed before the end.[128]

It has been suggested that 'the democratic ambassador in a totalitarian country' encounters a particular difficulty, that 'the person who explains glides easily into the role of the person who justifies and advocates'.[129] This may be one of the factors behind Henderson's disastrous performance in these years; it may be why Ciano was able to think that Lord Perth, Henderson's colleague in Rome, had 'come to understand and even to love Fascism'[130] and why François-Poncet assured the same writer that 'he now detested freedom of the press and was coming closer and closer to totalitarian ideals'.[131] The inadequacy of the explanation is evident, however, if one considers the contrast between Henderson and his predecessors at Berlin, between Perth and Sir Percy Loraine at Rome, between François-Poncet and Coulondre. From Tokyo Sir Robert Craigie frequently warned against making an enemy of Japan over China; unlike Henderson his judgement, though far from infallible, does not seem

---

* See below, pp. 50 and 65. It should be remembered that Henderson's health was far from good in these years.

to have been distorted by hysteria, nor his firmness by prejudice.[132] The mounting stress of events from February 1938 to September 1939 tested individuals as it tested governments and nations.

[1] 1939 edition, p. 526.

[2] Quoted in *The History of the Times*, vol. iv, p. 901.

[3] For examples of warnings in earlier years, see *Ambassador Dodd's Diary*, ed. W. and M. Dodd (1941); entries for 1 Dec. 1933, 17 Nov. 1934, 4 Apr. 1935, and 6 Apr. 1936; also I. Colvin, *Vansittart in Office* (1965), and E. Spier, *Focus* (1963). The courage and insight of Norman Ebbutt, *The Times*'s Berlin correspondent, deserve particular recognition.

[4] Harold Nicolson, *Peacemaking, 1919* (1934), p. 33.

[5] Full details of these and other states will be found in C. A. Macartney, *National States and National Minorities* (1934), app. iii.

[6] Alfred Cobban, *National Self-Determination* (1944), p. 33.

[7] See Pertinax, *The Gravediggers of France* (1944), chap. 2.

[8] A. François-Poncet, *The Fateful Years* (1949), pp. 111-14.

[9] *D.G.F.P.* i, no. 19.

[10] P. Schmidt, *Hitler's Interpreter* (1951), p. 41.

[11] *Ciano's Diary, 1937-1938* (1952); entry for 2 Nov. 1937.

[12] E. M. Robertson, *Hitler's Pre-War Policy* (1963), p. 103.

[13] Ciano, op. cit.; entry for 6 Nov. 1937.

[14] See *F.R.U.S.* (1938), i, p. 396 (Hull to the chargé d'affaires in Vienna, 15 February).

[15] *D.B.F.P.* ix, no. 431.

[16] Ibid,. vii, App. iv.

[17] G. Craig and F. Gilbert (eds.), *The Diplomats* (1953), p. 473.

[18] *D.B.F.P.* ii, no. 1222.

[19] *D.G.F.P.* i, no. 457. Many clubs in his native Boston, Kennedy asserted proudly, had admitted no Jews for the past fifty years.

[20] Craig and Gilbert, p. 669.

[21] *F.R.U.S.* (1938), i, pp. 509-12 (Bullitt to Roosevelt, 22 May).

[22] *D.B.F.P.* vii, app. iv.

[23] Lord Vansittart, *The Mist Procession* (1958), p. 550.

[24] Walter Lippman, *The Public Philosophy* (1955), chap. 11.

[25] *Daily Express*, 9 Nov. 1937.

[26] For the struggles over armaments within the Labour Party, see Hugh Dalton, *The Fateful Years* (1957), chaps. 3, 4 and 8.

[27] A. J. P. Taylor, *The Origins of the Second World War* (1961), p. 189.

[28] H. Nicolson, *Peacemaking, 1919* (1934).

[29] J. M. Keynes, *The Economic Consequences of the Peace* (1920).

[30] E. H. Carr, *International Relations Since the Peace Treaties* (1937).

[31] T. Jones, *A Diary With Letters* (1954), p. 180.

[32] F. Hesse, *Hitler and the English* (1954), p. 22; another German source reported in July 1940 that the Duke of Windsor 'believed that continued severe bombings would make England ready for peace' (*D.G.F.P.* x, no. 152).

[33] *The Times*, 17 Mar. 1938; letter from Sir Thomas Moore, M.P.

[34] *D.B.F.P.* i, no. 458 (Henderson to Halifax).

[35] *Observer*, 6 Mar. 1938; article by J. L. Garvin.

[36] M. Gilbert, *Plough My Own Furrow* (1965), p. 365.

[37] Jones, p. 396; written on 20 Mar. 1938.

[38] Halifax in the House of Lords, 19 Apr. 1939; *Hansard*, 5th series, vol. 112 (House of Lords), cols. 686–98.

[39] See Arnold Toynbee, *The Eve of War* (1958), pp. 39–44, and A. L. Rowse, *All Souls and Appeasement* (1961), chap. ix.

[40] Jones, p. 411. Jones's opinion sprang from talks with Lindbergh, who was far from objective.

[41] *The Ironside Diaries*, ed. R. Macleod and D. Kelly (1962); entry for 22 Sept. 1938.

[42] *D.B.F.P.* viii, App. i; Admiralty memorandum of March 1939.

[43] *Failure of a Mission* (1940), pp. 147–8.

[44] *D.B.F.P.* ii, No. 590 (Henderson to Halifax).

[45] R. J. Minney, *The Private Papers of Hore-Belisha* (1960), p. 196, cited as 'Hore-Belisha' hereafter. Cf. Viscount Templewood, *Nine Troubled Years* (1954), pp. 289 and 381, and, for some light on Chamberlain's earlier attitude, Lord Ismay, *Memoirs* (1960), p. 90, and B. H. Liddell Hart, *Memoirs*, vol. ii (1965), pp. 53, 114, and 227.

[46] Cf. L. S. Amery, *My Political Life* (1953 on), vol. iii, p. 228, and I. Macleod, *Neville Chamberlain* (1961), pp. 187–8.

[47] Jones, p. 370.

[48] Amery, p. 174.

[49] Jones, p. 93.

[50] Keith Feiling, *Life of Neville Chamberlain* (1946), p. 342.

[51] Jones, p. 538.

[52] *Observer*, 27 Mar. 1938.

[53] See *Ambassador Dodd's Diary*, entry for 6 May 1937, and Rowse, pp. 6 and 28.

[54] The reports of military observers could be quoted in support of this opinion; see *D.B.F.P.* i, no. 148. Cf. *F.R.U.S.* (1938), i, pp. 57–9.

[55] Jones, p. 210.

[56] *D.G.F.P.* i, no. 31 (Halifax to Hitler); *D.G.F.P.* ii, no. 634 (Wilson to Hitler).

[57] A. J. E. Wrench, *Geoffrey Dawson and our Times* (1955), p. 376. For the views of the American Ambassador in Moscow on the possible outcome of Western suspicions, see J. E. Davies, *Mission to Moscow*, (1942), pp. 193–4 and 223.

[58] See Z. A. B. Zeman, *Nazi Propaganda* (1964), pp. 146 ff., and the relevant essay in D. C. Watt, *Personalities and Policies* (1965).

[59] Jones, p. 201.

[60] Ibid., p. 181; Gilbert, op. cit., p. 359; J. R. M. Butler, *Lord Lothian* (1960), p. 203.

[61] Jones, p. 215, and Butler, p. 206.

[62] Lord Avon, *The Reckoning* (1965), p. 11; statement by Kingsley Wood to Eden. See also Lord Birkenhead, *Halifax* (1965), p. 422.

[63] See J. Degras (ed.), *Soviet Documents on Foreign Policy*, vol. 3, pp. 291-2; an election speech by Litvinov in June 1938.

[64] Craig and Gilbert, p. 553.

[65] *D.G.F.P.* ii, no. 482.

[66] Amery, pp. 298-9.

[67] *D.G.F.P.* iv, no. 476.

[68] Arthur Bryant, *The Turn of the Tide* (1957), p. 472.

[69] Cf. Dalton, pp. 307-9; Amery, p. 371; Rowse, p. 107; and Birkenhead, p. 364.

[70] Dalton, pp. 162 and 265 respectively.

[71] Duff Cooper, *Old Men Forget* (1954), pp. 190-1; Amery, p. 175.

[72] Amery, p. 239.

[73] See Dalton, chap. xiv. Harold Macmillan has confirmed to the author that his object was to bring down the government.

[74] Avon, *The Reckoning*, p. 58; a letter from Eden to Cranborne and Law.

[75] B. H. Liddell Hart, *Memoirs*, vol. i (1965), p. 145. Cf. ibid., ii, pp. 210-11, Colvin, pp. 16 and 150-5, and Spier, p. 11.

[76] Chamberlain's liking for power may be deduced not only from his behaviour in May 1940 but from his conversation at other times; cf. Hore-Belisha, p. 270.

[77] Amery, p. 249.

[78] Jones, pp. 175, 219 and 144 respectively.

[79] Rowse, p. 31, and Butler, p. 236.

[80] Feiling, pp. 256 and 253; J. M. Blum, *From the Morgenthau Diaries* (1959), pp. 463-6.

[81] Feiling, p. 272.

[82] Ibid., pp. 354 and 367.

[83] Schmidt, p. 112. Cf. *F.R.U.S.* (1938), i, pp. 95-7.

[84] Colvin, p. 276. Mr. Colvin (p. 144) attempts to pin down Chamberlain's swing to hope and credulity with some precision — too much so, I feel.

[85] See the cases of Barrington-Ward: *History of The Times*, vol. iv, p. 906, footnote; of Dawson: ibid., p. 734 and Liddell Hart, ii, chap. 4; and of Jones: Jones, p. 281.

[86] Lord Avon, *Facing the Dictators* (1962), pp. 562-3; Sir John Simon's brand of pressure was rather more sly: ibid., p. 585.

[87] Duff Cooper, p. 250.

[88] Cf. *D.G.F.P.* ii, no. 487 and Dalton, op. cit., pp. 176-83. (See below, p. 73.)

[89] *D.B.F.P.* i, no. 512.

90 Ibid., v, no. 376; and App. i (letter from Phipps to Halifax, 28 April 1939).

91 Cf. Templewood, p. 260.

92 Hore-Belisha, pp. 139–48 and 225–6 respectively.

93 W. Hofer, *War Premeditated* (1955), p. 11.

94 See an article under this title by D. C. Watt in the *Political Quarterly*, vol. 36, no. 2, 1965.

95 Taylor, op. cit., 5th impression (1963), 'Second Thoughts'. Here, for instance, Mr. Taylor stresses the significance of President Hácha's asking to go to Berlin in March 1939 instead of being invited by a scheming Hitler. The threat and terror which *made* him ask are not, apparently, of significance.

96 *Mein Kampf*, 1939 edition, pp. 128–39.

97 Ibid., pp. 17, 529, 242 and 124 respectively.

98 Robertson, op. cit., pp. 6–7.

99 Nuremberg Documents, C–175; see *N.C.A.*, i, pp. 480–1. Boris Celovsky writes: 'Hitler konnte diese Entwicklung auf dem Kontinent zufrieden beobachten. Das französische Sicherheits-system wurde gesprengt. Die Engländer zeigten immer deutlicher ihr Desinteressement in Mitteleuropa. Die Lage war reif für den lang vorbereiteten Vorstoss.' *Das Münchener Abkommen* (1958), p. 53.

100 *D.G.F.P.* v, no. 272; Hitler to Csáky.

101 Ibid., vi, no. 433 (Hitler conference of 23 May 1939).

102 *In The Nazi Era* (1952), p. 125.

103 Zeman, op. cit., p. 64.

104 See *D.G.F.P.* v, no. 366 (Heydrich to Ribbentrop over Memel).

105 See the evidence of Field-Marshal Milch, *I.M.T. Proceedings*, pt. 8, pp. 255 and 261–2.

106 *D.G.F.P.* vii, App. i (Halder's Notebook).

107 Ibid., no. 576.

108 H. C. Hillmann, 'The Comparative Strength of the Great Powers', in *The World in March 1939* (R.I.I.A. 1952). Mr. Taylor praises this study in his bibliography, but ignores its conclusions, and has done so again in his *England, 1914–1945* (1965).

109 T. W. Mason, 'Some Origins of the Second World War', in *Past and Present*, no. 29 (Dec. 1964), p. 86; this article provides an excellent analysis of the shortcomings of Mr. Taylor's celebrated work and of B. Klein's *Germany's Economic Preparations For War*, on which several of Mr. Taylor's conclusions are based. For similar contemporary descriptions of the German economy see *D.B.F.P.* iv, app. ii, and *Livre Jaune Français* (Paris 1939), no. 33. A. S. Milward, *The German Economy at War* (1965) is excellent.

110 Testimonies, general and specific, to Ribbentrop's efforts to be 'more Hitlerian than Hitler' are numerous. They include *D.D.I.* xii, no. 503; Ulrich von Hassell, *The von Hassell Diaries* (1948), pp. 30–31; *Ciano's Diary, 1937–1938* (1952), entry for 28 Oct. 1938; R. Coulondre, *De Staline à Hitler* (1950), pp. 290–1; Schmidt, op. cit., p. 106; Ernst von Weizsäcker, *Memoirs* (1951), pp. 127–8.

[111] *I.M.T. Proceedings*, pt. 10, p. 143 (affidavit of Dr. Paul Schmidt).

[112] François-Poncet, p. 50.

[113] General von Fritsch, in Hassell, p. 28.

[114] *I.M.T. Proceedings*, pt. 21, p. 35 (testimony of Field-Marshal von Brauchitsch).

[115] For Goebbels' struggle over propaganda, for instance, see Zeman, op. cit., pp. 58–59; and in general, E. Kordt, *Nicht aus den Akten* (1950), pp. 53–92, and P. Seabury, *The Wilhelmstrasse* (1954).

[116] For the case of Welczeck, Ambassador in Paris, see *D.G.F.P.* vi, no. 676.

[117] See Hassell, p. 26.

[118] Kordt, op. cit., p. 332.

[119] See *Dirksen Papers*, no. 29, and H. von Dirksen, *Moscow, Tokyo, London*, (1951), pp. 219, 230 and 242, for the treatment received by the Ambassador in London on his return to Germany in Aug. 1938 and Mar. and Aug. 1939.

[120] Cf. *D.B.F.P.* v, nos. 581 and 582.

[121] *D.B.F.P.* ii, no. 843 and 852.

[122] Cf. *New Documents on the History of Munich*, no. 26, and G. Bonnet, *Défense de la paix*, vol. 1, p. 199.

[123] See François-Poncet, p. xii.

[124] Lord Woolton, *Memoirs*, (1959), p. 140.

[125] *Ciano's Diplomatic Papers*, pp. 164–84, gives a somewhat highly coloured account of this. See also, Avon, *Facing The Dictators*, and in slight mitigation of Chamberlain's behaviour, Macleod, pp. 211–17. Also Colvin, pp. 190–1.

[126] See Avon, *The Reckoning*, p. 53; letter from a Foreign Office official to Eden, May 1939.

[127] Cf. *D.G.F.P.* i, no. 228, and Dalton, pp. 503–4.

[128] *D.G.F.P.* iv, no. 251 (Chamberlain's chief press adviser to Dr. Hesse of the German Embassy).

[129] Craig and Gilbert, pp. 503–4.

[130] *Ciano's Diary, 1937–1938*; entries for 25 Oct. 1937 and 16 Dec. 1938.

[131] *Ciano's Diary, 1939–1943*; entry for 10 May 1939.

[132] Cf. *D.B.F.P.* viii, no. 453.

2 Anschluss

As long as any conventions of ordinary behaviour between independent nations prevail, I think it scarcely possible to deny the right to a head of a state to resort to a plebiscite if he so desires.

HALIFAX to RIBBENTROP, 10 March 1938.[1]

'DESTINY', according to Hitler, had appointed the frontier region between Germany and Austria as his birthplace, and certainly the merging of those two states was the most likely of his conquests. It was also the most improvised in its execution, an apparent lesson of the easy triumphs to be obtained by ruthless pressure and swift action in the face of a critical but passive Europe.

The break-up of the Habsburg Empire towards the end of the Great War had briefly seemed to offer an end to the nineteenth-century problem of relations between the Germans in the Empire and those who came to be gathered in Bismarck's Reich; but when in November 1918 the former, six and a half million strong, declared themselves part of the new German Republic, self-determination was denied them. By the treaties of Versailles and Saint-Germain the Allies prohibited the union, and in 1922 Austria, in return for international financial assistance, had to affirm that she would in no way alienate her independence. A projected Austro-German customs union had similarly been quashed in 1931 at French insistence, and in the following year fresh loans were accompanied by an extension of the assurance given in 1922.

It was an unhappy situation for the small Republic. Legal obligations and financial necessity clashed with dissatisfaction over a peace settlement which, in Schuschnigg's later words, 'we considered an injustice which we could and

would not recognise as a lawful treaty'.[2] While friction
between the successor and the disinherited states of the
Danube basin prevented the possibility of some wider
association in that direction, union with Germany remained
attractive, perhaps all the more because forbidden fruit.
Pan-German sentiments were strongly implanted in men
like Karl Renner and Dollfuss on either side of the centre, as
well as in the right-wing of Austrian politics; until January
1933 the great majority of the Austrian people were not
averse to the idea of the *Anschluss*.

The advent of Nazi Germany, though making the project
more practicable, diminished its respectability. Many of the
anti-Semitic and anti-Slav roots of National Socialism were
far from alien to Austrian soil (it is a movement, commented
one Viennese professor, 'which puts the Prussian sword at
the disposal of Austrian lunacy'[3]) and in the confused
struggle for power during the early 1930's Berlin, as well as
Rome, was still used by Austrian politicians as a potential
source of influence. But with Dollfuss as Chancellor strong
measures were adopted against the Nazi party, and the
failure of the *putsch* in which Dollfuss was murdered in 1934
helped drive it further underground for the time being.

Yet the internal weaknesses of Austria remained. No
national identity had developed since 1918 to overcome the
ambivalence of being German as well as Austrian. 'Already
in 1934', wrote Dollfuss' successor, 'I was sure of one thing:
never again a war against Germany as in 1866', and he
assured von Papen that 'he was well aware that the historical
position of Vienna had come to an end and that the focal
point of the German mission now lay in Berlin';[4] there were
many besides the new Chancellor who, neither Nazi nor
unswerving Monarchist, were lured by the dream of an
autonomous Vienna becoming the cultural heart of a wider
fatherland which might also include the South Tyrol. Nor
was there sufficient loyalty to Austria to heal the breach
between the anti-clerical socialism of Vienna and the

'Austro-Fascism' of those who had triumphed in the brief but bitter civil war of 1934. 'Both Government and Socialist leaders knew that the decisive hour for Austria was approaching; both felt that the danger could be met only by uniting forces. But it was too late; the chasm of mutual distrust could no longer be bridged.'[5] Ironically, it was only in the last days before Hitler struck that many Austrians began to see themselves as one people.

By then, their country's external protectors had faded away, and the British, French, Hungarian and Italian agreements of 1934 and 1935 to consult if her integrity were endangered counted for nothing. Even before the Stresa front had disintegrated Mussolini was remarking that he 'could not always be the only one to march to the Brenner',[6] and Schuschnigg himself, reflecting the antipathy of many of his countrymen, had made it clear that Italian troops would never be welcome beyond that point.[7] A political agreement which was signed between Austria and Germany in 1936 was, in reality, a token of Rome's diminishing determination; when Goering sounded Mussolini on the *Anschluss* in January 1937 the latter disliked the ominous and abrupt manner in which it was done, but he declared that he would not be bound by his 'watch on the Brenner',[8] and when Schuschnigg arrived in Italy in the spring he was treated with a certain reserve. In September Mussolini was Hitler's guest, and impressive displays of German strength reminded him where his interest lay. Though still unwilling to witness the complete disappearance of Austria, he made no protest two months later when Ribbentrop, on signing the anti-Comintern pact, remarked that the question must be settled, and Ciano in his diary defined the task of the Italian Minister in Vienna as 'that of a doctor who has to give oxygen to a dying man without the dying man's heir noticing'. 'In case of doubt', he added, 'we are more interested in the heir than in the dying man.'[9]

Only Czechoslovakia of Austria's other neighbours need

be watched carefully if Germany moved, and even she had been prevented by the contrast in régimes from drawing closer to Vienna in the face of a common danger. Stoyadinovitch of Yugoslavia had talked to Ciano of the *Anschluss* as 'inevitable', and assured the Nazi leaders in January 1938 that his country would never fight over 'a purely domestic question . . . [wherein] a people wished to be united'.[10] If Admiral Horthy, Regent of Hungary, feared the disappearance of an independent Austria, he too had advised the Germans that they 'only needed a little patience in this question',[11] while from further afield the Foreign Minister of Poland came to swell the reassuring chorus which gladdened the ear of Berlin.[12] As the French Foreign Minister, Delbos, travelled gloomily round Eastern Europe in December 1937, he found no more evidence of a determination to stand firm than he had in London a week before. Even he had privately indicated a readiness to see 'a further assimilation of certain of Austria's domestic institutions with Germany's',[13] and Chautemps, his Premier, 'could see no way to prevent Hitler from swallowing Austria in the relatively near future'.[14]

It had long been evident that Britain would not fight for Austrian independence. Eden, moving towards his final break with Chamberlain over Italy, apparently told Ribbentrop in December that the question 'was of much greater interest to Italy than to England', whose people 'recognised that a closer connection between Germany and Austria would have to come about sometime', though they wished force to be avoided.[15] Despite Eden's later strictures, this was scarcely different language from that used by Halifax to Hitler during his November visit to Germany. England realised, said Halifax on that occasion, 'that one might have to contemplate an adjustment to new conditions, a correction of former mistakes and the recognition of changed circumstances', and though insisting upon peaceful methods he specifically mentioned Danzig, Austria and Czechoslo-

vakia.[16] Any further encouragement needed was being sup-
plied by Henderson, whose talk of Germany's right to absorb
Austria and dominate the whole Balkan and Danube area
was widely reported among the diplomatic community.[17]

Few doubted that some developments would occur over
Austria before very long. The Austrian Nazi Party had
survived their 1934 setback stronger than ever, despite
internal squabbles and Hitler's order that 'a new method of
political penetration' must take the place of terrorism.[18] The
'Gentleman's Agreement' of 1936 whereby Austria, 'recog-
nising herself to be a German State', had had her sovereignty
acknowledged by Germany, had further diluted the ruling
Fatherland Front by the inclusion of members of the pan-
German opposition in the government, and had not eased
the pressure of Nazi propaganda from within and from
across the border. When all para-military formations,
including the Italian-orientated *Heimwehr*, were dissolved
shortly afterwards, another potential weapon in the struggle
for survival was thrown away. Outwardly and reassuringly
conservative and Catholic, the time-serving Franz von
Papen was in Vienna as German Minister 'to undermine
and weaken the Austrian Government',[19] urging Schuschnigg that 'Austria, with heart and soul . . . support the
struggle of the German world for its existence',[20] reinforcing
the demands being pressed on behalf of the 'moderate'
Nazis by the naïve traitor, Seyss-Inquart (appointed
Councillor of State in July 1937), diverting attention by his
own counter-charges from the 'very incriminating' documents which police had discovered in the Austrian Nazi
headquarters in the spring of that year. 'National Socialism',
wrote von Papen to Hitler, 'must and will overcome the new
Austrian ideology.'[21]

With Schuschnigg ready to compromise and still trusting
Seyss-Inquart as a fellow Catholic and a gentleman, it was a
satisfactory situation for Hitler. Rebuking the eager Goering
in September 1937 he stated that 'Germany should cause no

explosion of the Austrian problem in the forseeable future, but . . . should continue to seek an evolutionary solution',[22] and his existing military plans were contingent only upon an attempt in Vienna to restore the Habsburgs. Yet the temptation to succeed by one swift stroke remained, and his readiness to do so should a suitable occasion arise was made clear to his Foreign Minister, War Minister and service commanders on 5 November.[23] Though the so-called Hossbach conference has attracted its full share of controversy,[24] no satisfactory arguments have been advanced to alter the conclusion that in its explicitness and its anti-Western rather than anti-Bolshevik framework here was a significant moment in the development of Nazi expansionism. Taken in conjunction with the changes of the following February, when Ribbentrop replaced Neurath at the Foreign Ministry, Hitler became his own War Minister in place of Blomberg, and servility rather than ability was rewarded in other military and economic posts,[25] the harangue of 5 November marked 'a real turning point in Hitler's pre-war policy'.[26]

Germany, said Hitler, must seek greater space in Europe, and her problems 'could only be solved by means of force [which] was never without attendant risk'. Two 'hate-inspired antagonists, Britain and France', had to be reckoned with, but he was determined to settle matters 'at the latest by 1943-45'; earlier action might be made possible by French internal strife — 'then the time for action against the Czechs had come' — or a French war against Italy. Should war with the West come first, then Austria and Czechoslovakia must be overthrown simultaneously to protect Germany's flank, but he believed 'that almost certainly Britain, and probably France as well, had already tacitly written off the Czechs'. The annexation of both neighbours which could thus be anticipated would provide increased foodstuffs, improve Germany's frontiers, and free her forces 'for other purposes'.

Though the conditions envisaged by Hitler were not to materialise, the new readiness for action was transmitted to the armed forces by Blomberg in December:

Should the political situation not develop, or only develop slowly in our favour, then the execution of operation 'Green' [an attack against Czechoslovakia whilst adopting a defensive posture in the West] will have to be postponed for years. If, however, a situation arises which, owing to Britain's aversion to a general European War, through her lack of interest in the Central European problem and because of a conflict breaking out between Italy and France in the Mediterranean, creates the probability that Germany will face no other opponent than Russia on Czechoslovakia's side, then operation Green will start *before* the completion of Germany's full preparedness for war. The military objective ... is still the speedy occupation of Bohemia and Moravia with the simultaneous solution of the Austrian question in the sense of incorporating Austria into the German Reich. In order to achieve the latter aim military force will only be required if other means do not lead or have not led to success.[27]

'Today we are faced with new tasks,' declared Hitler to the Nazi Old Guard in November, 'for the *Lebensraum* of our people is too narrow. The world seeks to evade the examination of these problems and the answering of these questions. But that it will not be able to do.'[28]

The use of the army against Austria was still no more than an alternative, but Ribbentrop, urging Hitler in January that 'every day that our political calculations are not actuated by the fundamental idea that England is our most dangerous foe *would be a gain for our enemies*', had proclaimed that 'in case of a quick success [in Central Europe] I am fully convinced that the West would not intervene'.[29] Goering, too, was working for an early solution by putting pressure on Guido Schmidt, Schuschnigg's Foreign Minister. Moreover Nazi extremists in Austria, setting an example later to be followed in Czechoslovakia, Memel and Danzig, were striving to bring on a crisis. In the summer of 1937 Berlin had attempted to bring them under firmer control,[30] but on 25 January Austrian police raids uncovered plans to provoke repression on a scale which would bring in the German Army, with the convenient murder of von Papen providing a further justification. Seyss-Inquart, too, though he deplored the reckless indiscipline of the extremists, had come to despair of obtaining further rapid concessions from Schuschnigg, and had to be ordered by Goering not to resign as Councillor of State at the turn of the year.[31]

Schuschnigg's reaction to the chilling news of the Nazi plot, however, was to seek further compromise. 'The incident', wrote Papen to Hitler, 'made the Federal Chancellor conscious of the impossibility of letting the present state of affairs continue. He is most eager for the personal meeting contemplated, and in Glaise's* opinion would also be prepared to change his attitude fundamentally.'[32] Schuschnigg, in fact, dreaded the thought of meeting Hitler, even though some measure of reassurance was provided by the smooth promises of von Papen that the 1936 agreement would be the basis of the talks 'which would in no case be to the disadvantage of the Austrian Government'. The Chancellor privately observed that a psychiatrist would have been a more suitable visitor than himself, and that he would go to Berchtesgaden 'only in order to forestall a "coup" and to gain time until the international situation should improve in Austria's favour'.[33]

But Hitler had apparently forgotten the proposed meeting, engrossed as he was in the internal crisis concerning Blomberg, Fritsch, and the replacement of Neurath, and it was only when von Papen, shaken by dismissal from his Vienna post, arrived at Berchtesgaden on 5 February that the project was revived.[34] The news which reawakened Hitler's interest and restored von Papen to his former position was of fresh signs of nervous Austrian weakness. Instead of preparing a denunciation of illegal Nazi activities,

* Edmund Glaise-Horstenau, a crypto-Nazi member of Schuschnigg's Cabinet.

Schuschnigg was undermining his own position in advance by conceding to Seyss-Inquart an end to discrimination against 'moderate' Austrian Nazis, and their participation in 'the development of military, economic and political relations with the Reich'.[35] On the eve of the visit now fixed for 12 February he went even further, and through Zernatto, Secretary of the Fatherland Front, put forward suggestions for co-operation over press facilities, the closest collaboration between the Austrian and German armies, the appointment of specific Nazis to the Council of State, and the incorporation of certain tenets of National Socialism 'into the political ideology of the new Austria'.[36] Swiftly the trusted Seyss had these good omens conveyed to Berchtesgaden where they arrived before Schuschnigg on the morning of the 12th. The visitor's own proposals would be used against him.

The interview which followed was the most forceful intimation an outsider had yet received that Hitler was not a statesman but a gangster.[37] Summoning his generals to heighten the tension and moderating his verbal assault only briefly, when the murder of Dollfuss was mentioned, he lashed a deferential Schuschnigg with 'the uninterrupted high treason of Austrian history', boasted of his 'mission' as 'perhaps the greatest German of all history', threatened that possibly one day his visitor 'would wake up in Vienna to find the Germans there — just like a spring storm', and issued a deadline of that afternoon by which a prepared agreement on Austro-German relations must be signed. When Schuschnigg pointed out that he could not commit his President in advance he was eventually given three days in which to confirm the protocol he now signed; its provisions included the alignment of foreign policies, the inclusion of Seyss-Inquart in the government as Minister of the Interior with control over security, complete freedom for National Socialists, and their incorporation in the ruling Fatherland Front.[38] While the barest of communiqués was issued to the world, Hitler ordered that the impression be given that serious military preparations were in hand against Austria,[39] and on the 15th the required ratification was to be forthcoming. As the visitors drove away, however, they were assured by von Papen that next time would be different, for 'the Fuehrer could be absolutely charming'. A month later one of the soldiers who now opened a barrier to let them pass was guarding Schuschnigg in a cell he left only to clean SS latrines with his own towel.

In the terrible position in which Schuschnigg found himself after Berchtesgaden he behaved with a mixture of acquiescence and defiance easy to understand but difficult to commend. He scarcely fostered that 'improvement in the international situation' which apparently had been his aim. The full truth of what had happened reached the British and French governments only gradually and informally (at a dinner on 14 February Schuschnigg told the French Minister that Hitler, 'a madman with a mission', had been most brutal[40]) and Vienna followed up an anodyne Austro-German communiqué issued on the 15th by privately seeking to prevent protests and questions from the democracies which might further enrage Hitler.[41] In Paris the uneasiness that was manifest none the less was accompanied by a sense of helplessness and was sharply rebuffed when François-Poncet sought assurances from Ribbentrop over what the latter declared to be solely a domestic affair;[42] in London Chamberlain's attention was firmly fixed upon the need to begin talks with Mussolini and thereby repair the 'endless chances' missed by Eden, who resigned on 20 February;[43] in Berlin Henderson was still on hand, not only to convey an invitation to Hitler to consider a new colonial division in Africa (partly at Portuguese and Belgian expense), but to hint that his own support for the *Anschluss* was nearer the opinions of his government than were the anxious protests of his colleague in Vienna.[44] Mussolini and Ciano for their part swung with pompous impotence between acceptance of

the *Anschluss* as 'inevitable' and anxiety over the consequences of 'Germany at the Brenner', between renewed
hope aroused by stirrings of Austrian patriotism and
despairing attempts to offset in advance their coming loss of
face by obtaining an agreement from the compliant hands
of Chamberlain.[45] Austria, partly through her own actions,
stood alone.

How long this precarious state of affairs would have lasted
had Schuschnigg not belatedly decided upon defiance is
uncertain. Reassuring reports had reached Berlin on 18
February that 'the collapse is so complete that . . . a number
of decisive positions can be captured within the succeeding
weeks', and Keppler, Hitler's Special Commissioner for
Austrian affairs, repeated early in March that 'more and
more concessions' could be wrung from Schuschnigg.[46]
When disgruntled Austrian Nazi extremists like Tavs and
Leopold were reported as planning fresh provocation and
working against Seyss-Inquart they were told by Hitler that
though 'the need for intervention by force might still arise',
their actions 'had been insane'. 'He wanted the evolutionary
course to be taken', he declared to them in private on 26
February, and 'did not now desire a solution by violent
means if it could at all be avoided, since the danger . . . in
the field of foreign policy became less each year and German
military power greater each year.'[47]

On Wednesday, 9 March, however, with a suddenness
and intensity born of despair, determining not 'to wait with
fettered hands until . . . we should be gagged as well',[48]
Schuschnigg attempted to regain some freedom of action.
Already on 24 February he had made a stirring appeal to
Austrian patriotism. Now, with his new Minister of the
Interior openly identifying himself with an equally open
Nazi revolt in Styria,[49] he called upon his countrymen to
vote on the following Sunday for 'a free and German,
independent and social, Christian and united Austria'.
Mussolini, consulted beforehand, advised against so rash a

move. In Berlin, an astonished Hitler, informed through Austrian Nazi channels a few hours before the news became public, 'bordered on hysteria', for as the enthusiasm which greeted Schuschnigg's announcement suggested, the plebiscite was likely to give the latter an overwhelming vote of confidence; this was all the more certain since an age limit of 24 would exclude young Nazi zealots. It was of no significance when on the 10th Seyss-Inquart allowed himself to be persuaded by Schuschnigg to support the move;[50] his role as puppet was about to be made clearer than ever. Keppler was already in Vienna with instructions to prevent Sunday's event taking place or at the least have a question on the *Anschluss* added,[51] whilst the intention to invade 'should other means fail', avoiding provocation but 'breaking ruthlessly' any resistance encountered, was embodied in a directive prepared on the 10th and issued from Hitler to the armed forces the next day. Any Czech forces encountered were to be regarded as hostile, Italians as friends.[52]

Frantically, the *Wehrmacht* prepared an assault so improvised that it was to leave along its path a trail of stranded vehicles; it was time for the kill, and none revelled more in the moment, then or later, than the Reich's Chief Game Warden, Hermann Goering.[53] Hitler himself was still not committed to use force, as the opening sentence of his first directive showed, but during the night of the 10th-11th the Nazis in Austria learned that the Fuehrer had given them 'freedom of action' and would 'back them in everything they did'.[54] It was the method, not the intention, that was still to be decided.

Austrian independence was not to outlive Friday, 11 March. Schuschnigg was woken at 5.30 a.m. with the news that Germany had closed the frontier and was massing troops, and the threat became clearer when Seyss-Inquart and Glaise-Horstenau, obeying instructions they had received by letter from Hitler that morning, declared that unless the plebiscite were called off they would resign. As the three men faced one another within the Vienna Chancellery, eager preparations for Sunday's plebiscite filled the warm streets outside with bustle and a scattering of leaflets. At about 2.30 p.m. Schuschnigg decided to give way, only to be pursued further by a series of telephone calls which Goering, with Hitler's approval, put through to Seyss, Keppler and others in Vienna from 2.45 p.m. onwards.[55] Seyss, with his colleagues, was ordered to demand Schuschnigg's resignation, to get himself appointed Chancellor, and to despatch to Hitler a telegram requesting assistance in restoring order. By 4 p.m. Schuschnigg had again surrendered, and when President Miklas 'resolutely and at times pathetically' refused to appoint Seyss in his place, deadlines were issued under the threat that '200,000 men standing in readiness at the border' would otherwise march and that resistance would be 'summarily dealt with by our tribunals'. Schuschnigg, still caretaking as Chancellor, further diminished any likelihood of resistance by authorising announcements that the plebiscite had been postponed and that the entire Cabinet, except Seyss-Inquart, had resigned; he followed this by personally broadcasting at 7.50 p.m. that the army was withdrawing in order to avoid 'shedding German blood' and that the country was 'yielding to force'.

As Seyss confirmed to Goering by phone that a vacuum now existed, Hitler hesitated no longer. As late as 6 p.m. he had been wavering, and on premature news that Seyss had been appointed had withdrawn his order to march;[56] now, at 8.45 p.m., he gave the word to invade the following morning.[57] Three minutes later Goering dictated to Keppler the text of the telegram Seyss was to send asking for help, ignoring Keppler's remark that 'everything was quiet and orderly': 'He does not have to send the telegram. He has only to say that he did. You get me?' By now Nazi thugs were swarming insolently through the Chancellery and baying in the streets outside; others were seizing control in the provinces. When in the small hours of the morning

Seyss-Inquart pathetically attempted to limit the consequences of his treachery by suggesting that invasion was
no longer necessary, Hitler decreed that it was too late,[58]
and at dawn the German troops crossed the frontier to be
greeted with flowers. In the afternoon the Fuehrer made his
homecoming in person to so tumultuous a welcome that on
the 13th he decided to settle immediately for more than a
union of states under common leadership. That day, as the
mass arrests and pillaging began, Austria was declared to be
a province of the German Reich. 'Destiny' was on the
march. If brutality had accompanied its progress —
Schuschnigg's broadcast on the evening of the 11th, let
alone the reports of diplomats and correspondents, made
this quite clear — who could argue in the face of the 99 per
cent vote of approval soon bestowed by the Austrians
themselves?

In any event, the other European Powers had by then
openly or tacitly acquiesced. On the 11th an anxious Hitler
had almost begged for the Duce's approval now that he
'could no longer remain passive' in the face of Austro-Czech
collusion and anarchy in his homeland, swearing to prove a
steadfast ally and to respect the Brenner frontier for ever;[59]
when Prince Philip of Hesse telephoned from Rome at
10.25 p.m. to convey Mussolini's friendly response he was
swamped by the jubilant relief at the other end of the line.
Already on that day a request for advice from Schuschnigg
to his former protector had met with evasion and coldness,
and an even blunter rebuff greeted French enquiries as to
the possibility of a joint stand.[60] 'After sanctions, the non-
recognition of the Empire, and all the other miseries inflicted
on us since 1935', wrote Ciano of the West, 'do they expect
to rebuild Stresa in an hour with Hannibal at the gates?'[61]
Italy would keep her distaste and disquiet to herself.

Even this was scarcely needed to decide the democracies
against action. France, without a government between the
10th and the 13th, might issue the strongest warnings and

protests,[62] but she could not move without Britain as well as Italy close beside her, and Britain's response to Hitler's action went no further than apologetic indignation. On the 10th, it is true, Halifax solemnly warned Ribbentrop, who was back in London to pay his farewell calls as Ambassador, that aggression might eventually precipitate a general conflict and that though he himself 'did not believe in plebiscites much' he attached 'the utmost importance' to the Austrian one being carried out 'without interference or intimidation'.[63] Ribbentrop, however, was not merely placing his usual overconfident gloss on matters when he reported to Hitler that Britain would do nothing 'of her own accord' to help Austria (though a 'plausible justification' for German action was needed for public opinion).[64] Sir Horace Wilson on the same day was indicating to Erich Kordt of the German Embassy that while 'he hoped very much that [Germany] would succeed as much as possible vis-à-vis Czechoslovakia and Austria without the use of force, the prerequisite ... was, of course, that the other side also played fair', and he did not dissent when Kordt retorted that Schuschnigg's plebiscite was itself not 'fair'.[65] Similarly, at a Downing Street luncheon in Ribbentrop's honour on the 11th Chamberlain was more interested in future agreement than current difficulties. 'Once we have all got past this unpleasant affair', he remarked privately to his guest, 'and a reasonable solution has been found, it is to be hoped that we can begin working in earnest towards a German–British understanding'.[66] Though the atmosphere of cordiality was shattered by the arrival of telegrams indicating the pressure being put on Schuschnigg at that moment, and though an excited and indignant Halifax in particular warned that a setback in relations must follow the use of such 'intolerable' methods, Chamberlain agreed that the plebiscite had best be postponed, and remarked that 'personally he understood the situation'.[67]

The development of events necessitated further protests,

of course, and one was forthcoming later that day 'against such use of coercion backed by force against an independent State in order to create a situation incompatible with its national independence.'[68] But when Schuschnigg asked for immediate advice he was told that 'His Majesty's Government cannot take responsibility of advising the Chancellor to take any course of action which might expose his country to dangers against which [they] are unable to guarantee protection'.[69] Given the need to sound Mussolini this was doubtless a necessary, though cheerless, reply, and Rome ensured that it would not be improved upon; it was of no consequence anyway, since when the message arrived Schuschnigg had already resigned.

There was little more that could be done. Goering, still anxious on the 11th about British reactions,[70] must have been somewhat reassured by Henderson's agreement 'that Dr. Schuschnigg had acted with precipitate folly',[71] and the ensuing rebuke Halifax delivered to his Ambassador for allowing personal views to 'diminish the force' of official protests[72] no more helped Austria than it prevented Henderson from repeating his behaviour on later occasions. The disbelieving laughter of the Opposition which greeted Mr. R. A. Butler's assurance in the Commons that 'solemn representations' were being made in Berlin to secure the withdrawal of the German Army and moderate treatment for Austrian Jews, socialists and Catholics was entirely justified.[73] Chamberlain himself could write privately that 'it was now perfectly evident that force was the only argument Germany understood',[74] and could announce in the Commons on the 14th that a fresh review would be made of the British defence programme, but as has been suggested this did not mean what Churchill hopefully assumed at the time, that 'the scales of illusion had fallen from many eyes ... in high quarters'.[75] The Czech crisis was about to show as much.

[1] *D.G.F.P.* i, no. 145.

[2] Kurt von Schuschnigg, *Austrian Requiem* (1946), p. 155.

[3] Quoted in Zeman, op. cit., p. 119.

[4] Schuschnigg, p. 46, and *D.G.F.P.* i, no. 191.

[5] Schuschnigg, p. 160.

[6] Quoted in Ivone Kirkpatrick, *Mussolini* (1964), p. 286.

[7] Schuschnigg, pp. 98–99.

[8] Cf. Schmidt, p. 64; *Ciano's Diplomatic Papers*, pp. 80–91; *D.G.F.P.* i, no. 208.

[9] *Ciano's Diary, 1937–1938*; entry for 24 Nov. 1937; cf. *Ciano's Diplomatic Papers*, p. 146.

[10] *Ciano's Diplomatic Papers*, p. 100, and *D.G.F.P.* v, no. 163.

[11] *D.G.F.P.* v, no. 152.

[12] Ibid., no. 28 (Beck to Neurath).

[13] Ibid., i, no. 46 (Welczeck to Neurath).

[14] *F.R.U.S.* (1938), i, pp. 24–7 (Bullitt to Hull, February 21st).

[15] *D.G.F.P.* i, no. 50 (Ribbentrop to Neurath).

[16] Ibid., no. 31.

[17] See *Ambassador Dodd's Diary*, entries for 2 June 1937, 23 June 1937, and 12 July 1937; Henderson's later denials of the accuracy of these reports should be compared with, e.g., *D.G.F.P.* i, nos. 138 and 228.

[18] *N.C.A.* iv, pp. 586–96 (Rainer's subsequent report on Nazi activity in Austria).

[19] Ibid., pp. 305–25 (Messersmith affidavit). It should be added that von Papen, who was acquitted at Nuremberg, piously denied the validity of this affidavit; see his *Memoirs* (1952), chap. xxxi.

[20] *D.G.F.P.* i, no. 273.

[21] *N.C.A.* iv, p. 932.

[22] *D.G.F.P.* i, no. 256.

[23] Ibid., no. 19.

[24] Cf. Mason, op. cit., pp. 74–6; Taylor, op. cit., 'Second Thoughts', and 'War Origins Again' in *Past and Present*, no. 30, Apr. 1965; and the interpretations offered later by Goering, Raeder and Neurath in *I.M.T. Proceedings*, pt. 9, pp. 110–11; pt. 14, pp. 110–11; and pt. 17, pp. 127–8 respectively. Jodl, in his diary at the time, accepted that Hitler had produced 'his ideas of future development, intentions, and conduct of policy....'; see *N.C.A.* iv, pp. 360 ff. Also F. Hossbach, *Zwischen Wehrmacht und Hitler* (1949) and R. O'Neill, *The German Army and the Nazi Party* (1966).

[25] See J. Wheeler-Bennett, *The Nemesis of Power* (1961), pp. 363–82.

[26] Robertson, op. cit., p. 113.

[27] *D.G.F.P.* vii, App. iii (k).

[28] Baynes, vol. 2, p. 1370.

[29] *D.G.F.P.* i, no. 93.

[30] Ibid., nos. 257 and 258. Cf. Papen, p. 403.

[31] *N.C.A.* vi, pp. 115 and 197.

[32] *D.G.F.P.* i, no. 279.

[33] *I.M.T. Proceedings*, pt. 16, p. 202 (testimony of Dr. Guido Schmidt); cf. Schuschnigg, p. 19.

[34] von Papen, pp. 406–9.

[35] *D.G.F.P.* i, nos. 282, 285 and 293.

[36] See G. Brook-Shepherd, *Anschluss* (1963), p. 34, and J. Gehl, *Austria, Germany and the Anschluss* (1963), p. 171.

[37] A full account is given in Schuschnigg, pp. 20–32, with additions by Guido Schmidt in *I.M.T. Proceedings*, pt. 16, pp. 210–12.

[38] *D.G.F.P.* i, no. 295.

[39] *N.C.A.* iv, pp. 357 and 360 ff. (Keitel's orders, and Jodl's diary for 11, 13 and 14 Feb.).

[40] *F.R.U.S.* (1938), i, pp. 393 and 394.

[41] See Avon, *The Reckoning*, p. 6, and *Facing the Dictators*, p. 579; also *D.G.F.P.* i, no. 322.

[42] *D.G.F.P.* i, no. 308.

[43] See Avon, *Facing the Dictators*, p. 582.

[44] *D.G.F.P.* i, no. 138; note Henderson's anxiety to cover his tracks: ibid., no. 139.

[45] Cf. *Ciano's Diary, 1937–1938*, entries for 13, 18, 23 and 25 Feb., and Avon, *Facing the Dictators*, App. C.

[46] *D.G.F.P.* i, nos. 313 and 335.

[47] Ibid., nos. 313, 318, and 328. Goering was still inclined to back the extremists: see *N.C.A.* vi, pp. 195–7; also ibid., v, pp. 961–92 (Seyss-Inquart affidavit).

[48] Schuschnigg, p. 39.

[49] For a vivid eye-witness account of the Nazi revolt and later events see G. E. R. Gedye, *Fallen Bastions* (1939).

[50] Schuschnigg, p. 43, and *I.M.T. Proceedings*, pt. 16, pp. 160–4 (evidence of Seyss-Inquart).

[51] *D.G.F.P.* i, no. 339.

[52] *N.C.A.* vi, pp. 911–13.

[53] See *I.M.T. Proceedings*, pt. 9, pp. 101–6 for Goering's glorification of his role, and *N.C.A.* iv, pp. 360 ff. for Jodl's diary.

[54] *N.C.A.* iii, pp. 586 ff. (Rainer's report).

[55] Ibid., v, pp. 628–54 and *D.G.F.P.* i, no. 371.

[56] Jodl's diary, loc. cit.

[57] *N.C.A.* vi, p. 1017.

[58] *D.G.F.P.* i, no. 364. See also *I.M.T. Proceedings*, pt. 16, p. 179; Glaise-Horstenau's recollection that Seyss naïvely expected Hitler to grant him 'five years' tranquillity' as Chancellor of an independent Austria.

[59] *D.G.F.P.* i, no. 352.

[60] *D.B.F.P.* i, no. 27.

[61] *Ciano's Diary, 1937–1938*; entry for 11 Mar. 1938.

[62] *D.G.F.P.* i, nos. 346 and 356.

[63] Ibid., no. 145 and *D.B.F.P.* i, no. 8.

[64] *D.G.F.P.* i, no. 146.

[65] Ibid., no. 148.

[66] Ibid., no. 151.

[67] Ibid., no. 150, and *D.B.F.P.* i, no. 44.

[68] *D.B.F.P.* i, no. 39.
[69] Ibid., no. 25.
[70] See Henderson, op. cit., pp. 124–6.
[71] *D.B.F.P.* i, no. 46.
[72] Ibid., no. 54.
[73] See *D.G.F.P.* i, no. 392 and *Hansard,* 5th Series, vol. 333 (House of Commons), col. 163.
[74] Feiling, p. 341.
[75] *Evening Standard,* 18 Mar. 1938.

3 Munich

The Sudeten German Party must camouflage its profession of National Socialism as an ideology of life and as a political principle.... At heart it desires nothing more ardently than the incorporation of the Sudeten German territory, nay of the whole Bohemian, Moravian, and Silesian area, within the Reich.

KONRAD HENLEIN to HITLER, November 1937.[1]

If we two, Great Britain and Germany, come to an agreement regarding the settlement of the Czech problem, we shall simply brush aside the resistance that France or Czechoslovakia herself may offer to the decision.

SIR HORACE WILSON to THEO KORDT, August 1938.[2]

AT the height of the Austrian crisis, Goering and Neurath had hastened to assure the Czech Minister in Berlin that the event was no more than 'a family affair' and that the Fuehrer desired good relations with Prague on the basis of their arbitration treaty of 1925.[3] No fair words, however, could smooth away the alarm which the *Anschluss* caused Czechoslovakia and her friends. All saw that her defences, so carefully prepared against Germany, had been outflanked, and that her susceptibility to economic pressure had been increased. 'Don't shoot Czechoslovakia', urged a prominent Englishman to a German acquaintance; 'strangle her.'[4]

Tension was also bound to highlight the internal weaknesses of a state created only in 1919. The fissile properties of modern nationalism made the failure to fulfil early promises of 'a régime very much resembling that of Switzerland' of more consequence than a record of minorities treatment which compared favourably with those of Poland, Rumania and Germany herself. Only the $7\frac{1}{4}$ million Czechs were clear and positive supporters of the existing order. The two million Slovaks, 'backward and unbalanced' in many Czech eyes, contained a People's Party which was demanding autonomy in April 1938, whilst history, language and geography pulled the three-quarter million Magyars towards a Hungary which in March was pressing Berlin to concert war aims against the common enemy.[5] The half-million Ruthenes would welcome greater independence from the centre and their territory was eyed as covetously by Hungary as was that of the 90,000 Poles by Warsaw. Beck and Hitler were not alone when in January they 'heartily agreed' that 'the whole structure of the Czech state was impossible'.[6]

Above all the problem of the three and a quarter million Germans — the majority of them in the vital defensive and industrial region which had become known as the Sudeten-land — remained to be solved. Originally created by the eastward movement of German settlers in the twelfth and thirteenth centuries, it had been exacerbated by the economic and political inferiority of the increasingly self-conscious Czechs of Bohemia during the last phase of the Habsburg Empire. In vain did the Allies argue in 1919 that 'the populations of German speech inhabiting the borders of [Bohemia, Moravia and Southern Silesia] should remain associated with them in the development of the national unity with which history has bound them up', for the ensuing reversal of national dominance resulted in bitter German complaints against economic, political, educational and administrative injustices. The industrial declines of 1922–3 and 1931–3 fell with particular severity on the Sudeten areas, with unemployment in the latter period frequently well over 25 per cent of the able-bodied adults, and Germans tending to be laid off before Czechs. Even without such complications, feelings ran too deep for there to be any likelihood of lasting tranquillity. The Sudeten German regarded the Czech as 'a half-educated . . . creature, to some extent saved by German influence, politically intolerable and unreliable, socially never satisfied and always pushing for his nation', while for the Czech the

Sudeten German was 'the invader . . . the apostle of German world hegemony, the economic tyrant living in the land in order to subject the Czech people socially, politically, and in every other way'.[7]

After 1933 the false trumpetings of Nazi propaganda which accused a 'Jewish-run' state of carrying Bolshevism to the heart of Europe brought a growing sense of danger to the Czechs, and the Nazi party was soon disbanded. Three years later secret German hints at an understanding came to nothing[8] and a Defence Law which put frontier fortifications on a war footing further enraged the German population of the areas involved. An agreement in February 1937 between the government and those German 'Activists' who were willing to cooperate only brought fresh vituperation against the latter from across the border. Eduard Beneš, now President of the Republic, was remembered by many Germans as the Foreign Minister who had forestalled their minority petitions at Geneva, and Konrad Henlein's Sudeten German Party continued to demand autonomy. Though in the autumn of 1937 the Prime Minister, Dr. Milan Hodža, was acknowledged by secret German testimony to be 'making persevering efforts to settle the conflict . . . and find a way back to peaceful development',[9] this was to count for less than the fact that Henlein had been in receipt of Nazi funds since 1935. Moreover Hodža's government was a coalition of six parties, and many of them were at one with the Army in resisting concessions as leading inevitably to the break-up of the state on national lines.

The *Anschluss* inflamed the situation. 'It has set in motion', wrote the British Consul at Liberec, 'an avalanche of national feeling amongst the Sudeten Germans', and the military attaché added: 'Nazism has gone to their heads like wine. . . . Nothing short of incorporation in the German Reich will [now] satisfy the majority of people'.[10] 'If today', reported the German Minister in Prague, 'a Sudeten German Party member attempted to speak of the possibility even of a policy of understanding he would indubitably be cried down',[11] and though Ribbentrop despatched agents 'to counsel reason'[12] the Minister was still warning in May that the majority would 'neither await nor accept any other form of political solution' than incorporation.[13] Even the Soviet chargé d'affaires in Germany confessed to the American Ambassador after a tour of the area that 'disagreeable as the admission was to him, at present undoubtedly 90 per cent of the Sudeten Germans favoured union with the Reich'.[14] As the Activist parties were submerged by the waves of extremism which brought Nazi armbands and salutes flaunting into the open, the pressure upon Hitler not to lose face and to implement his own intentions sooner rather than later began to mount.

For those searching anxiously for a grain of comfort in the situation, Henlein could still, perhaps, be said to have set limits to his demands. As formulated in a speech at Karlsbad on 24 April they spelled autonomy rather than schism, though they included 'complete freedom to profess adherence to the German element and German ideology' and were supplemented by the insistence that Czech foreign policy should be 'completely revised'.[15] When visiting Britain in the first half of May he obeyed instructions from Berlin by denying any orders from that quarter,[16] and Vansittart, with whom he remained in touch, found him 'far more reasonable and amenable that I had dared to hope'.[17] In reality, however, Henlein had had a very different course approved by Hitler on 28 March: 'We must always demand so much that we can never be satisfied'.[18] Even if he were to falter there were many around him — notably Karl Hermann Frank — yet more ruthless in their determination to hasten a showdown.[19]

The fresh negotiations that were opened with the government were thus a mockery. Beneš, however, though privately declaring that 'he had long held that Czechoslovakia could not be a national state',[20] could reassure

himself that if things came to a crisis the West, in their own
interests as well as his, must stand by him.[21] As a supposition
it was entirely reasonable and entirely erroneous.

By her treaty of 1925, France was pledged to aid
Czechoslovakia if the latter were attacked, and her own
safety appeared inextricably bound up with the fate of the
Czech fortifications on Germany's opposite frontier. If these
defences had suddenly seemed vulnerable, new works were
frantically thrown up to protect the areas exposed by the
Anschluss, and by September the British military attaché
would be able to see 'no material reason why [the Czech
Army] should not put up a really protracted resistance
single-handed' — a judgement which later received some
support from Hitler and his generals.[22] The Škoda munition
works, too, were an asset which France could surely not see
endangered.

Following the *Anschluss*, it did seem for a moment as if
France would be the France of Poincaré and Barthou. Léon
Blum and his Foreign Minister, Paul-Boncour, went out of
their way to reassure Prague, warn Berlin, and rally
London;[23] they were acutely aware that if Germany were
asked to state her terms it could create 'a terribly dangerous
precedent', and that if she were allowed to drive further
east, 'one could not see where such a process would stop'.
On 10 April, however, Blum's Ministry fell and the new
Prime Minister, Édouard Daladier, expressly rejected a
policy of firmness when selecting Georges Bonnet to succeed
Paul-Boncour.[24] For Bonnet, Czechoslovakia was already 'a
doomed nation'. In his determination to avoid war at any
cost he was quick to explore loopholes in the 1925 treaty,
and the ambiguous Polish position was as welcome to him
as Gamelin's opinion that no swift offensive to save the
Czechs could be mounted against Germany.[25]

Only outwardly was Daladier himself any stronger,
though he was more aware than Bonnet of the humiliation

and danger of the rôle they were playing. He was not, as
Beneš realised, a firm friend of the existing order in Central
Europe, and if the German Ambassador in Paris is to be
believed lent a friendly ear in private to warnings against
the influence of Bolshevism and Jewry in Prague.[26] Though
at their meetings of 28–29 April he was to appeal in moving
terms to Chamberlain and Halifax to stand by the Czechs,
his real position had been made plain to a confidential
agent of the German Embassy in London on the evening of
the 27th: his hope was 'that Chamberlain and Halifax
would themselves suggest that pressure should be put on
Prague, when [he] could acquiesce without seeming to have
taken the initiative in the matter'.[27]

Daladier need have had no anxiety. The British Government were eager to thrust Beneš towards an accommodation
with the plausible Henlein. Though Chamberlain in the
House of Commons on 24 March had mentioned the
possibility of assisting Czechoslovakia to resist aggression
under the Covenant of the League, the only clear conclusion
that could be drawn from his plethora of conditional clauses
was that no binding commitment could be undertaken 'in
relation to an area where [Britain's] vital interests were not
concerned in the same degree as they were in the case of
France and Belgium'.[28] He had already written privately
that 'nothing France or Britain could do could possibly save
Czechoslovakia from being overrun by the Germans if they
wanted to do it',[29] and the Chiefs of Staff had reinforced his
personal inclination against a Churchillian 'Grand Alliance'. Though Chamberlain had written in 1934 that he
had 'practically taken charge of defence requirements of the
country', the military context within which he now had to
work was not entirely of his own making; it was, however, so
appalling that on reading its details in March General Ironside felt that 'no foreign nation would believe it if they were
told',[30] and the Prime Minister and his closest colleagues
were not the men to encourage the most drastic reform.[31]

To coerce or abandon Czechoslovakia was widely held at
the time to be necessary or inevitable. Hore-Belisha is
reported to have remarked privately that 'Germany would
have her fill in Central Europe before the West opposed
her'[32] and the British Minister in Prague advised that 'it
would be no kindness in the long run' to try to maintain
Czechoslovakia in 'her present political position [which] is
not permanently tenable'.[33] 'Keep out of war', wrote Lord
Rothermere in the *Daily Mail*;[34] 'our only concern should
be to keep Britain safe and to rebuild her old prosperity',
and *The Times* suggested that self-determination should be
granted all the minorities within the Czech state, though
Dawson, in defending the leader, thought Hitler 'would
prefer to keep the Sudeten Germans *as a lever and a nuisance*
outside his borders'.[35] 'Czecho?' asked the *Daily Express*.
'No, whatever happens.'[36]

Throughout all such speculation and anxiety, Russia
loomed like a shadow off stage. At French wishes,
Russia's 1935 Treaty with Czechoslovakia had bound her to
aid the latter against aggression only if France acted first,
however, and to Bonnet's delight Poland and Rumania
made it clear that they would not contemplate the passage
of Soviet troops through their countries which such aid
would necessitate. Beneš himself was anxious for help from
the West rather than the East, as German diplomatic
reports, in contradistinction to their propaganda, recognised.[37] And though Litvinov on 17 March announced his
government's readiness to join before it was too late 'in
collective actions ... to stop the further developments of
aggression and eliminate the increased danger of a new
world slaughter', distrust, repugnance and a disbelief in
Soviet military effectiveness brought a negative response
from London. Chamberlain's hopes lay rather in weaning
the Duce away from Hitler, and the signing of an Anglo-
Italian agreement in April, though not to take effect until
the withdrawal of Italian volunteers from Spain was well-

advanced, gave fresh encouragement. In Paris, too, (whose own approaches to Mussolini met with a sharp rebuff in May) there was strong antipathy to Russia in the highest places, and suggestions for combined military talks with Moscow and Prague met with coolness, procrastination and eventually refusal.[38]

It was thus a foregone conclusion when Anglo-French talks in London on 28–29 April produced a decision to put pressure on Beneš to settle the Sudeten question. Neither Daladier's eloquent plea to resist there and then before Germany, having swallowed Czechoslovakia and Rumania, turned on the West, nor Chamberlain's glib assurance that 'it made his blood boil to see Germany . . . increasing her domination over free peoples', nor his promise that Beneš would not be asked 'to accept terms which in effect meant the destruction of his country', represented any more than diplomatic manœuvring.[39] France wanted to be freed from the dilemma of having to fight or lose her honour; Britain wanted to be done with a tiresome and unjust source of friction and to proceed with business as usual. Even if a war were fought and won, remarked Halifax, one would doubt whether the Czech state could be reconstituted on its existing basis.

Thereafter Britain in particular combined strong advice to Prague with somewhat fulsome encouragement for Berlin. Officially, the Germans were merely asked to indicate for British consideration 'the lines of a settlement which in their view would be satisfactory to the Sudeten Deutsch'.[40] Privately, much stronger language was used. According to a report from the German Embassy in London, the new Parliamentary Under Secretary at the Foreign Office, R. A. Butler, speaking 'for those circles who fully understood that Germany had to pursue her national aims in her own way', recognised that the Reich would attain 'her next goal', though the manner in which it was done would be vital.[41] The First Secretary of the British Embassy in Berlin similarly suggested to a German official that if the latter's government would confidentially make known its wishes over the Sudetenland, his own would compel Prague to accede to them;[42] Henderson, too, assured the fulminating Ribbentrop that he was 'preaching to one already converted', and hinted that British soldiers would not again march into a Germany which, if it only had patience, 'would win all along the line' over this matter.[43] Chamberlain himself did his bit by 'leaking' to American and Canadian journalists his readiness to see the Sudetenland ceded to Germany and harshly informing his subsequent questioners in the Commons that he would 'neither admit nor deny the truth of [these] stories'.

As in the case of Austria, therefore, Hitler was encouraged by Britain to satisfy the growing clamour of Nazis outside the Reich; the intention to destroy Czechoslovakia and the brutality by which this was accomplished were his own throughout. At first after the *Anschluss* he appears to have been concerned not further to unsettle Mussolini by a fresh strike. Though 'lightning action' based on an incident such as the murder of the German Minister in Prague (diplomats were expendable items in the Third Reich) was discussed with Keitel on 21 April, Hitler in the middle of May was still ready to wait for 'a particularly favourable opportunity' to occur.[44] Early that month, however, his reassurances over the restless South Tyrol, when on a visit to Rome, had produced a response which must have settled any doubts he himself may have had concerning the compliance of his Axis colleague. As democrats and as objects of Hungarian revisionism, the Czechs were odious to Mussolini. He might procrastinate over an actual military alliance with Germany, but when he declared that 'henceforth no force would be able to separate them' he meant it, and the Fuehrer's eyes had filled with tears.[45] The prospects for Operation Green — conceived not in order to win self-determination for the Sudeten Germans but to seize the whole of Bohemia and

Moravia — were improving. They were about to be invested with fresh and maniacal determination.

On 20–21 May widespread rumours of threatening German troop movements were answered by partial Czech mobilisation. The ensuing tension in the frontier regions, further heightened when two Sudeten Germans on motor-cycles were shot by a Czech policeman on refusing to stop, was transmitted to the capitals of Europe; possibly this was intended by those of the Czech General Staff who felt that an end must be sought to the debilitating effect of German menace and propaganda.[46] Bonnet at once declared that France would 'provide the utmost help' if Czechoslovakia were attacked, and on the 22nd Halifax in a personal message warned Ribbentrop that if 'from any precipitate action' a general conflict were to ensue, Britain should not be counted on to stand aside.[47] It seemed as if the West had resolved upon firmness, and its press rejoiced that Hitler had been rebuffed at last.

Hitler was enraged, doubly so since, apparently, no aggressive troop movements had taken place.[48] His desire to crush the Czechs now became something of a personal vendetta. In a two-hour address to army, state and party leaders on the 28th he declared that Czechoslovakia must disappear from the map; the reason he gave, as recalled by one of those present, further indicated the wider trend of his thoughts already noted in late 1937: it was 'to clear the rear for advancing against the West'.[49] Two days later a new directive for Operation Green confirmed his 'unalterable intention to smash Czechoslovakia by military action in the near future' and listed among pre-requisites 'a convenient apparent excuse and adequate political justification'; a European crisis would be risked, but could be avoided by achieving rapid success.[50] At the same time work was redoubled on Germany's western defences. If France wished to interfere, she would have to be prepared to pay a high price in blood.

France had no wish to interfere, however. During the weekend crisis Bonnet had urged the Czechs not to mobilise further,[51] and had told the British Ambassador that 'if Czechoslovakia were really unreasonable the French Government might well declare that France considered herself released from her bond'.[52] (Halifax, delighted, spent the next six weeks urging that the remark should be repeated to the Czechs, and made clear his displeasure when Bonnet, after much wriggling, was forced to reveal he had not done so.[53]) Daladier, for his part, told the German Ambassador that he 'was certainly not happy' about the Czech alliance, and was later reported as saying that even had Germany attacked he would not have signed the decree of mobilisation.[54]

The French Government's policy became further subordinated to that of London, and Halifax had already warned them at the height of the 'May scare' that Britain must not be relied upon to help protect the Czechs.[55] The episode, in fact, though interpreted by Chamberlain as proof of how 'utterly untrustworthy and dishonest' Hitler was, made him all the more anxious to see a speedy accommodation reached between Czechs and Germans, and whilst a sympathetic reception was still accorded the unofficial communications of Henlein, 'the greatest possible pressure', in Halifax's words, was put upon Beneš. It is difficult, moreover, to avoid the word servility when describing British dealings with Berlin in this period. According to the German Ambassador, for instance, the words Halifax chose when discussing Spain on 8 June were that 'it would be of great value to the British Government if it were possible to eliminate the bombing of British ships and non-military areas', though 'he knew this was a very delicate matter, and wished *at all events* to avoid creating any ill feeling in Germany'.[56] To Hitler's adjutant in July the Foreign Secretary declared his great ambition to be that of seeing

Hitler enter Buckingham Palace with the King amid cheering crowds.[57]

Moreover though Halifax made it clear to Henderson that Germany must still be led to believe that Britain might well be drawn into a Czech conflict, even this manœuvre was sabotaged. Convinced of Hitler's 'love for peace', that for the moment 'a quiet life for the Sudeten' would satisfy him, and that the Teuton and the Slav were 'irreconcilable — just as are the Briton and the Slav',[58] Henderson did more than feed Chamberlain and Halifax with the arguments they wanted to hear on the necessity and essential justice of applying the principle of self-determination. On 1 June he told the German State Secretary, Weizsäcker, that Britain and France had warned Prague that they would abandon her if she would not listen to reason, and his repeated and emphatic assurances at a party in August that 'Britain would not think of risking even one sailor or airman for Czechoslovakia' were passed on to Hitler by the German Secret Service.[59] If further encouragement were needed, the diplomatic correspondents of the *Daily Mail* and the *Sunday Times* referred to Chamberlain's private briefings when urging the press adviser of the German Embassy in London in June that his country would be unduly modest if it demanded no more than autonomy for the Sudetenland.[60]

But Hitler did not need pushing. Though in June his General Staff drew up for him a directive which included the qualification that action would only be taken when it was clear that the West would not move, the obliteration of Czechoslovakia remained 'in the forefront of his intentions'.[61] Ribbentrop, extolling the Fuehrer's infallibility to Weizsäcker in August, declared that the task would be accomplished by force of arms and without interference by mid-October, with himself — quintessence of this vainglorious and deranged lackey — at Hitler's side at the head of the leading armoured division.[62] Already, on 10 August, his master had curtly crushed the apprehensive queries of some of his generals, and he angrily assured them again at the end of the month that 'France wouldn't risk it'.[63] On the 30th he reaffirmed that Operation Green would be set in motion 'by an incident ... which would provide Germany with a pretext for military intervention', and to the accompaniment of further diatribes against fainthearted soldiers the details of preparation were elaborated at conferences on 3 and 9 September.[64] The target date was now the end of the month. When *Gauleiter* Forster of Danzig, a particularly close and particularly coarse friend of Hitler's, boasted to guests at his tea table that Prague would soon be razed to the ground by 1,000 bombers,[65] he did no more than elaborate the joyful anticipation that was occupying the Fuehrer's own mind at the time.

The fears of several prominent German soldiers and administrators had not been assuaged, but for a good many their nascent opposition rested on the expectation of defeat and not on any grounds of principle, and was a sickly growth to match. Schacht might mutter in restaurant corners about the folly of pathological individuals, but speeches of adulation still came easier to him than the thought of final resignation;[66] Weizsäcker might write memoranda of protest, but he locked them away and months later was still bullying the Lithuanian foreign minister in fine style; as for the generals and admirals, they were well advanced on the road to degradation, 'gifts and field-marshal's batons more important to them than the great historical issues and moral values at stake',[67] the ineligibility of a junior officer's fiancée a more likely cause for resignation than any directives for aggression.[68]

There were, however, men of firmer stuff, notably Colonel-General Ludwig Beck, who resigned — or rather refused to serve any more, for his resignation was not at first accepted — as Chief of the General Staff in the second half of August. He, Carl Goerdeler (former Lord Mayor of Leipzig), and a group of officers in the military intelligence organisation of Admiral Canaris were planning in August and September to arrest Hitler as soon as the order for 'Green' was given. Though later assertions that success was denied them only by Chamberlain's decision to fly to Munich are to be doubted,[69] they did their best to warn London to stand firm. Their messengers, however, and those of more cautious German diplomatic circles, aroused uneasiness but not complete acceptance in Chamberlain's mind, and were compared by the latter to 'Jacobites'.[70] It was, indeed, scarcely to be expected that the policies of the West would be reversed and that the horrors of war in what appeared an unjust cause would be accepted on the slender grounds of a possible *putsch*. It was not warnings that Hitler meant business that were looked for by them; they were plentiful and included an assurance by the German military attaché in Belgrade that the Sudeten issue was no more than a pretext for the seizure of the whole state.[71] What the British and French governments wanted was almost any means of peacefully disposing of the frightening possibilities which had come to surround the deadlocked minorities' question in Czechoslovakia.

As the long summer had dragged on, negotiations between the Czech government and the Sudeten German Party had followed suit. The demands of the latter for a separate German *Volkstag* could scarcely have been forced through by Beneš and Hodža against public opinion even had they wished to do so, whilst government drafts of a new Language Law and Nationalities Statute were rejected by Henlein in July. In Bohemia there was a boycott of each other's goods by Czechs and Germans, and accusations of arms smuggling across the German border were countered by complaints against local officials. Children of both nationalities were encouraged to display their chauvinism, and there were protests against the singing of 'ribald songs about Herr Hitler'. There was no doubt in Henderson's mind that the moment had come 'for Prague to get a real twist of the screw'.[72]

Halifax's language was more restrained, though his musings on the possible need for a plebiscite internally and neutrality internationally had been no less ominous for the Czechs. He and Chamberlain decided that a British mediator might avert a crisis, and the idea of 'an ex-Governor of an Indian Province' having been discouraged by Newton in Prague with what tact he could muster, the choice fell on Lord Runciman, past President of the Board of Trade. As a coldly ruthless hatchet-man, '*glabre, impassible*', Runciman had already tidied up the problem of Jarrow after a fashion; for those in the West like Robert Coulondre who had encountered him and in whom the warmer human sentiments had not long since withered, the news was not reassuring. Beneš himself was greatly taken aback when the proposal was put to him, for it appeared a further step in the undermining of his country's sovereignty,[73] but by 23 July he had been driven by threats[74] to despatch the necessary request, ostensibly on Czech initiative alone. Even more transparent was the assertion by London that Runciman would be acting in an entirely independent capacity. No one believed it, and the German reaction was reserved to the point of indifference.

Runciman was to admit that the Czechs welcomed his suggestions 'without at any time standing on their dignity'; he was, he wrote, 'something less than a Dictator and more than an Adviser'.[75] His party also believed Henlein to be 'simple and honest', and went out of its way — unnecessarily so, some thought — to cultivate the Sudeten Germans; but for all the pleasant weekends spent on the great estates of that region a solution seemed no nearer. Insomnia pursued his Lordship. It was, he declared, 'an accursed country'. In vain might Beneš plead with Sudeten German delegates at the end of August for 'a rebuilding of the state'; on the same day, 30 August, that he handed them a memorandum whose proposals, by their own private testimony, 'could have meant the fulfilment of the Karlsbad demands', Hitler was signing a memorandum of his own on Operation Green.[76] 'I am only afraid of two things', the President had said to his German listeners in the library of the Hradschin Palace on the 25th: 'a war and, after it, a Bolshevik revolution'. In all the thousands of pre-war documents, no line is more tragic in its prescience.

As Britain and France sprawled on their holidays, the threat surrounding Beneš and his country mounted. A savage campaign in the Polish press demanded the return of Teschen, and though Hungary was secretly anxious to postpone military action till the spring, her public demands on behalf of her minority across the border became sharper; a conditional agreement involving the renunciation of force which had been negotiated with the Little Entente at Bled was now declared by Budapest to be effective in regard to Rumania and Yugoslavia alone, and Jodl noted that Horthy and his ministers arrived in Germany in August 'with the idea that in the course of a great war, after a few years, and with the help of German troops, the old state of Hungary can be reestablished'.[77]* Mussolini, though kept in ignorance of Hitler's plans, would be compliant.[78] It was announced that there would be additional German troop movements and partial mobilisation in September, and pilots were known to have been recalled from Spain. 'If war breaks out', observed the Commander-in-Chief of the French Air Force on a visit to the German aircraft industry, 'there won't be a single French plane left within a fortnight'.[79] Yet the same General Vuillemin assured Goering that France would honour her obligations. On the face of things the West still had to be reckoned with, and while Sir John Simon spoke publicly of the likelihood of local wars spreading, Bonnet, on

---

* Since the Gömbös period, in particular, Hungary's economy was considerably dependent on that of Germany. Memories of Béla Kun made the tie all the more acceptable.

2 September, delivered a private warning to the German Ambassador.

Governments, diplomats and peoples, however, awaited Hitler's speech to the Nazi rally at Nuremberg with acute apprehension, none more so than Henderson who wanted the British press to help by 'writing up Hitler as the apostle of peace'.[80] As for Bonnet's warnings, they were for the benefit of future readers of French Yellow Books. When he received a report from his chargé d'affaires in Moscow that Litvinov on 2 September had proposed not only an appeal to the League but immediate joint military talks and an Anglo-French-Soviet declaration of resolve, he suppressed the vital part of the message, and did the same after meeting Litvinov at Geneva on the 11th;[81] Halifax, informed of the Soviet proposal through their Ambassador, Maisky, and Churchill, was no more receptive.[82] Moreover Bonnet was eagerly and where possible unofficially collecting ammunition to use against those in his Cabinet — Mandel, Zay, Champetier de Ribes and Reynaud certainly, Daladier possibly — who might wish to stand firm, appearing to Phipps, the British Ambassador, 'completely to have lost his nerve', and assuring the latter on the 14th that he was ready for 'any solution' to avoid war. He was delighted to receive a series of replies from Halifax which emerged from elegant ambiguity in the required direction: the Foreign Secretary 'did not think that British opinion ... or His Majesty's Government would be prepared to enter upon hostilities with Germany on account of aggression by Germany on Czechoslovakia'.[83]

There were still to be moments when British policy seemed only reluctantly acquiescent, but it continued to develop a remorseless trend in that direction. The idea of a visit to Hitler rather than a warning — indeed of a Four-Power settlement of the problem — was already in the air. Henderson's own influence was not negligible, for his advice as 'the man on the spot' reinforced the inclinations of those around Chamberlain, and he had flown home for Cabinet discussion at the end of August.[84] On 3 September, Newton warned a shaken Beneš that Britain would support Henlein's Karlsbad demands rather than risk war, and his colleague de Lacroix followed with similar pressure from Paris.[85] *The Times* added its weight by suggesting on the 7th that Czechoslovakia should cede 'that fringe of alien populations who are contiguous to the nation with which they are united by race'; though *La République* had anticipated this by a day and the *New Statesman* by over a week, it went further than anything Hitler or Henlein had yet openly proposed, and was inevitably regarded as having been officially inspired. Moreover a declaration that Britain might have to fight which Henderson was ordered on the 9th to transmit to Hitler 'without delay' was withheld on the former's pleading that it would be fatal to 'repeat the threat of May 21st', and though warning other German leaders at Nuremberg the Ambassador also 'expressed his aversion to the Czechs in very strong terms'.[86]

Hitler did the same. On the 7th Beneš had offered to concede all the Sudeten demands, and a horrified Henlein had had to order an incident to be arranged which would enable negotiations to be broken off. This was done by the following day, and Hitler's speech to the baying Nuremberg crowds on the 12th, assuring the world that his countrymen in Czechoslovakia were 'neither defenceless nor deserted',[87] provoked riots in the Sudetenland. Huge crowds assembled in Eger and Karlsbad, scores of Jewish shop windows were smashed, and tanks and armoured cars were called in under martial law. K. H. Frank had already gone to Nuremberg to get his orders, and Henlein, having fled to Germany on the 15th, appealed against brutal oppression and openly proclaimed the desire of his people 'to return to the Reich'.[88] Few paused to notice that the Sudetenland had never been in the Reich, and few could share the secret German testimony that the frightened exodus of women and children across the border which followed was caused not by oppression but by Goebbels' false and lurid wireless reports.[89] Though in fact Hitler was still not ready to move, with his trains required for final work on the West Wall as well as for 'Green', the Czech Army was unofficially mobilising. They would have to fight in areas where the population were sullen or hostile, but their equipment was good and their morale high.[90]

It was clearly time for Chamberlain to make the dramatic move he had discussed with Henderson and with which he had startled Halifax. He would go and see the man who 'half-mad', controlled 'the fate of hundreds of millions'.[91] France was not consulted before the message indicating the Prime Minister's anxiety to come across was sent to Berlin on the 13th; her press, however, joined that of the rest of Europe in hailing, in the words of *Le Matin*, 'a man of sixty-nine making his first aeroplane flight . . . to see if he can banish the frightful nightmare which hangs over us and save humanity'. The courage and sincerity of the man and the hope and relief of the moment filled all minds. Few would as yet have accepted Mussolini's judgement on hearing the news that Chamberlain would see Hitler on the 15th: 'There will not be war. But this is the liquidation of English prestige.'[92]

Mussolini was to produce his own contribution on the day of the meeting by publishing an open letter to Runciman which insisted that he propose a plebiscite. Neither Italy nor the fresh demands of Poland and Hungary which she championed were in the forefront of Chamberlain's mind as he journeyed to Berchtesgaden, however. During the three-hour train journey from Munich, troops, guns and army transports passed in seemingly endless columns; as a reminder of what was at stake it was as sombre as the black clouds which descended on the mountains as the party drove up to the Berghof.[93]

The small talk did not last long[94] before Hitler and Chamberlain withdrew for their three-hour discussion. Only the interpreter Schmidt accompanied them, a somewhat trusting move on Chamberlain's part as he realised when a jealous Ribbentrop later tried to withhold the record of what had been said. Pouring out a torrent of 'facts' concerning Czech atrocities — 300 dead, 10,000 refugees, gas attacks — Hitler declared that he would risk a world war in his determination to see the Sudeten Germans incorporated in the Reich. Though Chamberlain protested against this apparent determination to use force, he did not demur when it was hinted that Czechoslovakia's alliances would have to go. He added, moreover, that 'personally he recognised the principle of the detachment of the Sudeten areas', though his Cabinet colleagues, Runciman, and the French would of course have to be consulted. The Czechs appear to have been overlooked. Hitler's military deadline of 30 September could remain unchanged when he agreed to stay his hand in the meanwhile; there was merely this much basis for Chamberlain's impression that 'here was a man who could be relied on when he had given his word'.

Others now had to be brought into line. In Runciman's case this was easy, for at the Cabinet meeting on the 17th he 'was unable to suggest any plan or policy'.[95] Conveniently, he would be able to produce a report four days later recommending the solution Chamberlain had in mind: as correctly interpreted by one commentator at the time[96] it implied 'that Czechoslovakia be required to abolish political liberties, suppress free speech ... relinquish her tie with France and Soviet Russia, give up her responsibilities as a "grown up" member of the League ... accept a guarantee by "the principal Powers", and enter the German economic system'. For the almost one million Czechs, Jews and German liberals who would be handed over to Hitler in the process there was not a word. When the leader of the Sudeten German Social-Democrats later came to London

begging vainly for more visas, however, Runciman did
promise that his name would be found on the list of
contributors to a fund being opened for them by the Lord
Mayor of London.[97]

Others were less compliant, however. On the 17th
Chamberlain was visited by a Labour delegation strong in
the virtuous knowledge of their Movement's recent Blackpool
declaration demanding the firmest support for the Czechs,
and thus enabled to forget their party's abysmal record of
negation and discord over rearmament; they were received
with that blend of naïve complacency, evasion and deceit
which the 'mission' increasingly necessitated. Daladier,[98]
too, though he had been angrily declaring to Mandel that
'he did not intend to sacrifice the entire youth of France
merely to whitewash the criminal errors . . . of Versailles',[99]
appeared to make difficulties when he and Bonnet arrived to
be told what to do on the following day.[100] Neither side
wished to be the first to state the unpleasant truth: the buck
was politely passed to and fro and Daladier voiced his fear
that 'Germany's real aim was the disintegration of Czechoslovakia and . . . a march to the East'. Remorselessly, and
again concealing his personal acceptance at Berchtesgaden,
Chamberlain declared that nothing short of self-determination would avert war; when Daladier gave way he was
further and with much euphemism hounded into admitting
that if Beneš were unco-operative he would have to be
coerced.* The one concession made on the British side —
reluctantly and with no firm resolve for the future — was a
promise to join in a guarantee of the rump of the Czechoslovak State. Only in retrospect and in the light of the events
of the following spring does this reversal of Britain's steady

* Daladier at the time and Bonnet later claimed that Beneš had
secretly agreed to cede three frontier districts; the French Minister in
Prague not only denied this but hinted that Bonnet had tampered with
the documents in question. See H. Noguères, *Munich* (1965), pp. 136-7;
Jean Zay, op. cit., p. 4; H. Ripka, *Munich, Before and After* (1939), pp.
85-93.

refusal (at Locarno, for instance) to be committed in Central and Eastern Europe take on considerable significance. It is also somewhat ironic that, having refused aid to a quite formidable friend, Britain should undertake to guarantee her when she was about to be rendered beyond help.

Beneš, 'greatly moved and agitated', received the Anglo-French advice on the 19th: the dangerous precedent of a plebiscite was to be avoided, but those areas containing 50 per cent or more Germans should be ceded. Coupled with new German-Slovak intrigues, Sudeten *Freikorps* raids across the border, and suggestions from London to withhold mobilisation,[101] the outlook from Prague was grim. Point-blank, the French, together with the Soviet Union, were asked if they would honour their pledges.[102] The latter's assurances, the sincerity of which were never to be tested since France did not act, arrived by telephone on the 20th during a Cabinet meeting,[103] and at 7 p.m. the Anglo-French suggestion was rejected; neither Western government was to include this reply when publishing its documents on the crisis.

The British Minister in Prague also reported, however, that 'he had very good reason to believe that the reply should not be treated as final', and that if he could deliver 'a kind of ultimatum' the Czechs would 'feel able to bow to *force majeure*'. The same suggestion was apparently made by Hodža to Newton's colleague, Lacroix.[104] At 2 a.m. on the 21st, therefore, Beneš, who appears to have been unaware of his Premier's manœuvre, was told in the harshest terms that if he persisted in his refusal, the West would leave him to his fate.[105] Despite the private urgings of some French and British politicians that he should not yield[106] and a further pledge by Litvinov at Geneva on the same day, the Czech acceptance was forthcoming at 5 p.m. Fresh Polish and Hungarian *démarches* were demanding equal concessions for their own Czech minorities, and here, too, London and its diplomats, anxious not to drive Rome and Warsaw closer to

Berlin, were far from unfriendly.[107] Hodža's government resigned on the 22nd and was succeeded by a Government of National Concentration under General Syrový. Beneš looked almost unrecognisable to his friends, 'physically worn out and morally crucified'. In the streets of Prague, men and women wept.

Hitler still hoped to isolate Czechoslovakia and enjoy his triumph. On the 20th he had told the Hungarian Ministers that 'he would present [his] demands to Chamberlain with brutal frankness' and that he viewed the possibility of 'the Czechs submitting to every demand' as 'a danger' to the 'only satisfactory solution' which was military action.[108] Ribbentrop urged him on. When Dirksen passed on to his Foreign Minister the assurances of Czech compliance which Wilson had given him as the latter accompanied Chamberlain to Godesberg on the 22nd, Ribbentrop 'put on his hard face, banged the table with his fist, and called out "Three days" '.[109]

Thus when Chamberlain on the afternoon of the 22nd produced his report of a job well done, his solution was rejected as 'no longer any use';[110] Polish and Hungarian claims, said Hitler, as well as the brutal extermination of many Germans, made delay impossible. The Prime Minister appeared stunned — though previous remarks of his make this a little surprising[111] — complaining that he had 'taken his political life into his hands' and that *Freikorps* were reported to have contributed to unrest by invading Eger and Asch; Britain and France could agree only to an orderly take-over free from the threat of force. An exchange of letters across the Rhine the next day[112] only deepened the gloom among the British delegation and anxiety increased among the crowds watching for the slightest sign of developments.

At a final meeting on the evening of the 23rd Hitler thanked his visitor for his efforts to secure peace. The memorandum he now produced, however, demanded occupation of the Sudetenland beginning on the 26th and to be completed on the 28th up to a line drawn by the German General Staff, with a plebiscite to follow in this and additional areas after 'a certain period for the preparation of the voting'.[113] When Chamberlain described this as an ultimatum, Hitler pointed out that the word 'memorandum' stood at the head of the document. News arrived of Czech mobilisation, and the atmosphere worsened. The only concession Chamberlain could secure was the substitution of 1 October (Hitler's secret deadline in any event) for the two previous dates, and the only promise he would make was that he would pass on the German terms. Though the Fuehrer reaffirmed that this was 'his last territorial demand in Europe' and was bid 'a hearty farewell' by the man who still talked of 'the relationship of confidence' now established between them, the visit appeared to end in deadlock.

The world drew the same conclusion. Even before Godesberg British opinion had hardened; crowds in White-hall on the 22nd shouted 'Stand by the Czechs' and on the 23rd even the *Daily Express* was forced to ask disapprovingly: 'Why do so many people in Britain want to fight?' Now, in the words of *L'Époque*, it seemed evident that 'neither Britain nor France, who had gone a long way beyond simple conciliation, could capitulate without disappearing from the ranks of the great nations'. The matter appeared settled, despite a hint of later wavering in Prague,[114] by the stirring and dignified rejection of Hitler's terms — 'a de facto ultimatum of the sort usually presented to a vanquished nation . . . depriving us of every safeguard for our national existence' — issued by the Czechoslovakians themselves.[115] As Roosevelt and others appealed for peace and the French gloomily manned the Maginot Line, fear, resolve and despair mingled throughout Europe.[116]

The mission would not so easily be abandoned, however. On their return Chamberlain and Wilson had, in fact, advised the Cabinet to accept the Godesberg terms. The

Premier 'was quite calmly for total surrender', wrote Sir
Alexander Cadogan in his diary, and while Halifax
'capitulated totally' Simon, too, moved with the tide as was
his wont.* All four Commonwealth High Commissioners in
London were also insisting that 'there might be a dangerous
reaction in the Dominions to a decision to plunge the Empire
into war on the issue of how Hitler was to take possession of
territory already ceded to him in principle'.[117] Chamberlain
secretly asked the German Embassy to assure Hitler that the
rejection the Czechs had impudently published was 'not the
last word'.[118]

When Daladier flew to London on the 25th to proclaim
that 'confronted with a plan to destroy and enslave
Czechoslovakia and dominate Europe', France would have
to do its duty, he found himself being cross-examined by
Chamberlain and Simon as to his country's preparedness for
action. 'What would happen', asked Chamberlain, 'if war
had been declared and a rain of bombs descended upon
Paris?' He regretted to have to observe to the inwardly
furious defendant that all did not appear well with the
French Air Force.[119] Halifax, however, had by now been
persuaded by Cadogan to oppose total surrender, and
eventually it was agreed that Wilson should take one more
message to Hitler appealing for peace.

The interview took place at 5 p.m. on Monday, the 26th.
It was stormy.[120] At one point Hitler, making as if to leave
the room, shouted 'It is no use talking any more', and he
demanded Czech acceptance of his timetable by 2 p.m. on

* Birkenhead, p. 399. Lord Templewood's clear denial in his
memoirs that Chamberlain advocated surrender can now be ignored.
The writer's own firmness of purpose may possibly be gauged from an
incident which, according to a German report, took place in July 1940:
Lord Templewood's procession through all available offices had terminated at the Embassy in Madrid where the Spanish Foreign Minister
offered the services of his country as an intermediary in an Anglo-German
armistice following the Franco-German example. 'It is possible that it
will sometime come to that', the Ambassador is alleged to have replied.
D.G.F.P. x, no. 160. This could, on the other hand, be termed realism.

that Wednesday. To the accompaniment of a frenzied tirade of abuse against Beneš and promises that no Czechs were wanted in the Reich, he repeated the ultimatum that evening in a speech at the *Sportpalast*. Experienced observers were shattered by the demonic primitiveness displayed;[121] it was, simpered *The Times* the next day, 'a rather offensive statement of . . . a perfectly reasonable case'. Sir Horace, nothing daunted, saw Hitler again the next morning,[122] but his congratulations on the ovation the latter had received ('it must be a wonderful experience for any man') did not prevent further outbursts. 'I will smash the Czechs', Hitler screamed several times, and when in consequence a solemn warning was delivered that France and therefore Britain would become involved, it seemed in vain: 'If France and England strike, let them do so. . . . It is Tuesday today, and by next Monday we shall all be at war.' Wilson apparently had the last word, however: 'I will still try to make those Czechos sensible.'

In London slit trenches and sandbags were beginning to appear. Children had their gas masks fitted and men steeled themselves to withstand the unknown horrors of aerial bombardment; in Prague black-out regulations were enforced and machine-gun posts manned in an atmosphere of 'calm fatalism'. Desperately, Flandin and others brought the pressure of the pacifist Left, and conservative and fascist Right* to bear on the Government in Paris, where many of the population were soon to jam the roads out of the city as they rushed to escape the coming inferno. Poland, confident despite a warning from Russia and efforts by Beneš to arrive at an understanding, was about to demand the immediate cession of Teschen and Freistadt. It must be war.

Still Chamberlain and Halifax would not have it so.

---

* French conservatives and fascists who urged appeasement at this time did so less from pro-German motives than from a hatred of Russia and the conviction that defeat would be inevitable.

Though on the 26th a communiqué was issued which declared that Britain and Russia would act with France, it owed its existence to Churchillian and Foreign Office pressure; London hastily forgot it, while Bonnet brazenly denied its authenticity altogether. Similarly when the British Fleet was mobilized on the 27th it was Duff Cooper at the Admiralty who saw to it that publicity accompanied the move. Wilson, on the other hand, had returned to advise immediate Czech evacuation of the areas demanded, and Halifax was busy misquoting Gamelin and the British military attaché in Prague to prove that resistance could only be short.[123] At 5 p.m. on the 27th a personal message from Chamberlain was despatched warning Beneš that nothing the West could do could prevent his country being overrun, followed shortly afterwards by a new plan for the take-over of Egerland and Asch on 1 October.[124] A reminder was included that even if Hitler were defeated Czechoslovakia would still have to be dismembered; it was not worth fighting. Chamberlain again hinted as much at 8.30 that evening when he broadcast a markedly personal account of the situation.[125] Appalled by the 'horrible, fantastic, incredible' situation which had arisen 'because of a quarrel in a far away country between people of whom we know nothing', he added that 'however much we may sympathise with a small nation confronted by a big and powerful neighbour, we cannot in all circumstances undertake to involve the whole British Empire in war simply on her account. If we have to fight it must be on larger issues than that'. The concluding minutes of the speech made it clear that for Chamberlain those larger issues were not to be found in the current crisis.

Immediately afterwards, a new, faint hope appeared in the form of a letter from Hitler. At 1 p.m. that day the Fuehrer had ordered his storm troops to their action stations,[126] but there was still time to isolate the victim. In his letter, therefore, he not only accused the Czechs — as had Henderson — of trying to provoke 'a general warlike conflagration', but warmly praised the Prime Minister for his efforts and hinted that it might still be worth while for him to try to 'bring Prague to reason'.[127] Chamberlain's reply, sent at 11.30 the next morning, declared that Britain and France could see that Hitler got 'all essentials without war and without delay'; it urged, as did a separate message to Mussolini, a fresh meeting to settle the matter.[128]

There was considerable confusion in the German Chancellery on the morning of the 28th. While amid the bustle Hitler strolled from room to room, pausing to harangue whoever happened to be near on the lines of his *Sportpalast* diatribe,[129] his decision to accept a conference was gradually being formed. The Czechs, after all, might still prove obdurate and be left friendless to face the blow. His own Generals, including Goering, were still infuriatingly nervous, and on the 27th an armoured division had passed through Berlin before silent and apprehensive crowds. If Mussolini were to sponsor the conference no personal loss of face would be involved, and Britain, still liable to fight if France did, now offered a new plan, delivered by Henderson late the previous evening.[130] Moreover at 11.15 a.m. François-Poncet, passing the long tables prepared for the lunch the Fuehrer was to have given his departing warriors, arrived with yet another plan, hot from the clammy hand of Bonnet. It proposed the preliminary cession of three large areas of Bohemia, and as the Ambassador had told Weizsäcker earlier, 'if Czechoslovakia refused, conclusions could be drawn which he did not need to define more closely'.[131] When Attolico, too, hurried twice to the scene to suggest on behalf of the militarily unprepared Mussolini a delay in mobilisation and then a Four-Power conference, the matter was as good as settled; Henderson's arrival at 12.30 p.m. with Chamberlain's message was not decisive. By the time the Prime Minister went down to the Commons that afternoon he must have known that salvation was

possible, though for those listening to his long and carefully
edited version of events the interruption which announced
Hitler's acceptance could not have been more dramatic.
Such was the moment of hysterical relief which followed
that according to one account, to remain seated was to
attract the threats of neighbouring Members.*

The meeting which followed on the 29th in the *Führerhaus*
at Munich was not a turning-point. It neither satisfied
Hitler nor enlightened Chamberlain. Though the latter had
telegraphed the Czechs that he would 'have their interests
fully in mind' the dismemberment of their country was
already assured, and neither they nor the Russians would be
present to make difficulties. The proposals which Mussolini
put forward as a basis for discussion had been drafted for
him in advance by the German Foreign Office,[132] and the
two dictators concerted their tactics as they journeyed
together to the conference. It must be complete satisfaction
or war, said Hitler. 'Besides', he added, 'the time will come
when we shall have to fight side by side against France and
England. All the better that it should happen while the
Duce and I are . . . still young and full of vigour.'[133]

'Munich' was a shambles. The second session was conducted without agenda or minutes to a confused coming and
going of officials and hangers-on. Small groups argued over
maps, and when the climactic moment of signing arrived the
ink well was found to be empty. Daladier briefly attempted
to get Czech delegates included and Chamberlain worried
about details concerning property and compensation, but
they were brushed aside. Neither appeared to mind.
Chamberlain was getting on well with Mussolini, while
according to Ciano and the German record, Daladier,
rejecting the Czech idea that evacuation should be delayed

* On the evening of the 29th, Churchill, Sinclair, Lady Violet Bonham
Carter and others of the Focus group met at the Savoy to obtain
signatures to a telegram adjuring Chamberlain not to betray the Czechs.
Attlee insisted he must wait for his party's approval; Eden refused. See
Spier, *Focus*, p. 11.

until they had constructed fresh defences, privately railed against the pigheadedness of Beneš and 'warmongers' in France; in return, Hitler and Goering apparently expressed a desire to come to Paris, the former to visit the Louvre.[134] The Agreement was signed in the small hours of the 30th:[135] the Sudetenland would be occupied in stages between the 1st and the 10th October up to a line determined by an international commission, with additional plebiscite areas as necessary; once the claims of the Polish and Hungarian minorities had been satisfied, Britain and France would be joined by Germany and Italy in guaranteeing the remainder of the Czech state.

The waiting Czech representatives were summoned before Daladier and a yawning Chamberlain and 'sentence was passed'.[136] As Newton was told to make clear to Beneš, there could be no argument; it had to be a plain acceptance or abandonment. On the same morning as the ultimatum arrived in Prague so did another from Beck, injured vanity reinforcing his determination that Teschen should return to Poland as a private triumph and not as a gift from the Powers.[137] In despair, and before one more appeal to Moscow for advice could be answered,[138] Beneš decided to submit to the dictates of the West. On 1 October he bowed in turn to the Poles. Four days later he resigned.

By then he had spared the West its ultimate humiliation, as he had spared Prague. Perhaps Prague would have been safe anyway; had not Hitler in a private talk with Chamberlain on the morning of the 30th promised his visitor that he would try to spare civilians if the Czechs proved obdurate? Had he not insisted that he 'hated the thought of little babies being killed by gas bombs'?[139] At the same time he had agreed to sign the declaration which Chamberlain had produced and which affirmed 'the desire of their two countries never to go to war with one another again'.[140] It was this paper which Chamberlain waved to the jubilant crowds on his return and which prompted him, impulsive

D

with relief and weariness, to declare that he had brought back not only 'peace with honour' but 'peace in our time'. He could not hear his fellow signatory sneering at the 'nonentities' he had to deal with, or moodily cursing that his 'entry into Prague had been spoiled'.[141] And he would have been incapable of sharing Daladier's amazed contempt when the Paris crowds greeted their returning Premier not with eggs but with flowers.

In the weeks which followed the full consequences of what had happened became apparent. Poland obtained 800 square kilometres containing iron and steel works, chemical and textile plants and high-grade coking coal; thanks to Hitler[142] they, and not Germany, also received Oderberg and its important railway junction. The Hungarians, who cast covetous eyes on the whole of Slovakia and Ruthenia, were to some extent disappointed, for on military and political advice Hitler decided that both should remain autonomous units within Czechoslovakia. The common Polish-Hungarian frontier which would otherwise have come about might not have assisted Germany's eastward expansion, as well as offending Rumania and removing a bargaining counter which might be used with Warsaw to offset the return of Danzig in the future.[143] Hitler was prepared to modify his position as circumstances required but for the moment he was adamant, and Mussolini, who had encouraged Hungary over Ruthenia, had to toe the line. Nevertheless, as a result of the Vienna Award drawn up on 2 November by Ribbentrop and Ciano, Hungary regained the predominantly Magyar areas of southern Slovakia and the southern plain of Ruthenia; the latter area included the one vital east–west railway, whilst the whole brought over 436,000 Czechs, Slovaks and Ruthenians under the control of Budapest. 'Hitler' enthused the Hungarian Prime Minister, 'has changed the turbid waters of European politics into a life-giving stream'.

2 Europe, 1938–1939

In Berlin the farce of the International Commission was duly enacted. 'It might as well be dead for all the use it is', wrote the British chargé d'affaires; 'all questions arising out of the Munich Agreement have been and will be decided at German Nazi dictation'.[144] Months later Henderson, one of its members, would flush with embarrassment when the Committee was mentioned.[145] No plebiscites were held, but by insisting on using the 1910 census as a basis Germany obtained virtually all the Czech fortifications and a line only slightly different from that laid down in their Godesberg memorandum.[146] The Czech railway system was disrupted and 35 divisions were removed from the scales of international power. Altogether the country lost 11,000 square miles, 70 per cent of its iron and steel capacity, 80 per cent of its textiles, 90 per cent of its porcelain, 86 per cent of its glass, 86 per cent of its chemicals, and 70 per cent of its electric power. It also lost, in this apparent triumph for self-determination, about 800,000 citizens of Czech origin.

Munich produced the fiercest differences of opinion throughout Europe and America. The press ranged from the adulation of *The Times* and *L'Action française* to the accusations of the *Daily Herald* and *L'Humanité*; from a Norwegian suggestion that the Nobel Peace prize should go to Chamberlain to the bitter despair of the Czechs. In the Commons Duff Cooper's resignation speech and Churchill's crashing condemnation of 'a disaster of the first magnitude' were met by the Prime Minister's efforts to contrast Munich with Godesberg and Sir Thomas Inskip's firm assurance that the British guarantee of Czechoslovakia was now in force. When it was announced that the Government were providing Prague with £10 million to assist them to raise a loan of £30 million, an opponent of appeasement in the Smoking Room of the House remarked on the changing values of betrayal since Judas Iscariot; he was knocked down by a supporter of Chamberlain.[147] As in Paris, the Administration received an overwhelming vote of approval.

The repercussions of Munich were world-wide. In Spain they brought fresh and decisive German intervention[148] whilst in the Kremlin they increased the conviction that the West would always be pusillanimous. From Shanghai, and in contrast to some wishful thinking from his colleague in Tokyo, the British Ambassador was blunt in the extreme:[149]

The effect of Munich accord on foreign opinion as seen from here is that perfidious Albion has been true to form and let her friends down again. . . . The Japanese reaction . . . is that we are prepared to put up with almost any indignity rather than fight. The result is that, all in all, our prestige is at a low ebb in the East. . . .

In October the Japanese seized Canton and isolated Hong Kong. On 3 November, with Hankow, Hanyang and Wuchang also in their hands, and declaring the Kuomintang to be no more than 'a local régime', they announced their plan to found 'a new order which will ensure permanent stability in East Asia'.

For the moment, however, the greatest impact had fallen upon the economically and strategically vital areas of Central and Eastern Europe. Those as yet unharmed scrambled for safety, and King Carol of Rumania, 'increasingly aware that assistance from France is becoming more and more remote', hastened to make known his desire 'to establish closer relations with Germany than hitherto'; as one of his formerly pro-Western politicians remarked, 'The same might happen to Rumania'.[150] In Prague they would not even have used the word 'might' On 30 September, when the British, French and Italian Ministers there had visited the Foreign Minister to offer their condolences, Newton had been cut short in his stumbling intimation that Chamberlain had done his best. A broken man, Krofta had indicated that he wished his visitors to leave at once. He said only: 'Today it is our turn. Tomorrow it will be the turn of others.'[151]

[1] *D.G.F.P.* ii, no. 23.

[2] *Dirksen Papers*, no. 7.

[3] *D.G.F.P.* ii, nos. 72, 74 and 78.

[4] Ibid., no. 244.

[5] Ibid., no. 65. In 1936 Admiral Horthy had drawn up a memorandum for talks with Hitler urging that 'Germany and Hungary (possibly with the aid of Austria and Poland) overrun Czechoslovakia . . . and exterminate this cancerous tumour'. *The Confidential Papers of Admiral Horthy*, pp. 82-90.

[6] *D.G.F.P.* v, no. 29.

[7] Gustav Peters; quoted in Elizabeth Wiskemann, *Czechs and Germans* (1938; 2nd ed. 1966), p. 118. This work is essential background reading.

[8] See Celovsky, op. cit., pp. 83-90.

[9] *D.G.F.P.* ii, no. 7 (Eisenlohr to Neurath).

[10] *D.B.F.P.* i, nos. 97, 120 and 129.

[11] *D.G.F.P.* ii, no. 123.

[12] Ibid., no. 124.

[13] Ibid., no. 158.

[14] *F.R.U.S.* (1938), i, p. 492 (Wilson to Hull, 6 May).

[15] *D.G.F.P.* ii, no. 135.

[16] Ibid., no. 155.

[17] *D.B.F.P.* i, App. ii.

[18] *D.G.F.P.* ii, no. 107.

[19] Cf. ibid., nos. 68, 164 and 350. Note how the Minister in Prague was left in ignorance of Berlin's intentions.

[20] *D.B.F.P.* i, no. 156; (Newton to Halifax).

[21] Eduard Beneš, *Memoirs* (1954), p. 21, and *New Documents*, No. 19.

[22] *D.B.F.P.* ii, no. 794. Cf. *I.M.T. Proceedings*, pt. 11, p. 2, and pt. 21, p. 48 (evidence of Keitel and Manstein respectively), and Pertinax, op. cit., p. 5.

[23] See *D.G.F.P.* ii, no. 117 and *D.B.F.P.* i, no. 112.

[24] J. Paul-Boncour, *Entre deux Guerres* (1945-7), vol. iii, pp. 96-101.

[25] G. Bonnet, *Défense de la paix* (1946-8), vol. i, pp. 125 and 138, and General M. Gamelin, *Servir* (1946-7), vol. 2, pp. 318-61.

[26] Beneš, p. 38, and *D.G.F.P.* ii, no. 194 (Welczeck to Ribbentrop). Cf. *F.R.U.S.* 1938, i, pp. 581-3 (Bullitt to Hull, 8 Sept.) in which Daladier is reported as blaming the Czechs for their 'most brutal' treatment of the Sudeten Germans.

[27] *D.G.F.P.* ii, nos. 143 and 147.

[28] *Hansard*, 5th Series, vol. 333 (House of Commons), cols. 1403-7.

[29] Feiling, pp. 347-8.

[30] *The Ironside Diaries*, entry for 29 Mar. 1939, giving a detailed summary of British Army strength. For further studies see Liddell Hart, op. cit., vols. i and ii, and the chapters by H. C. Hillmann and Viscount Chilston respectively in the *Survey of International Affairs* volumes, *The World in March 1939* (1955), and *The Eve of War, 1939* (1958).

[31] See Duff Cooper, pp. 219-20, for an example of frustration by Simon and the Treasury.

[32] *New Documents*, no. 10; Cf. *F.R.U.S.*, 1938, i, p. 44.

33 *D.B.F.P.* i, no. 86; (Newton to Halifax, 15 Mar. 1938).

34 *Daily Mail*, 17 June 1938.

35 *History of The Times*, vol. iv, p. 922; (Dawson to John Walter); author's italics for the phrase by which Dawson unconsciously undermined the basis of his position during these years.

36 *Daily Express*, 30 Apr. 1938.

37 *D.G.F.P.* ii, no. 47; (Eisenlohr to Neurath). Cf. L. Noël, *L'Aggression allemande contre la Pologne* (1946), p. 200, for Beneš' own remarks on the subject.

38 Coulondre, pp. 142–53 and 197, and Beneš, p. 42.

39 *D.B.F.P.* i, no. 164.

40 Ibid., no. 172 (Halifax to Henderson, 4 May).

41 *D.G.F.P.* i, no. 750.

42 Ibid., ii, no. 151.

43 Ibid., nos. 154 and 184. Henderson's personal antipathy towards the Czechs finds as clear an expression in the German documents as his vain self-pity does in the British; cf. *D.G.F.P.* ii, no. 482 and *D.B.F.P.* vii, no. 49.

44 *D.G.F.P.* ii, nos. 132, 133 and 175.

45 *Ciano's Diary, 1937–1938*; entry for 9 May 1938. Cf. *D.G.F.P.*, i, no. 745.

46 Cf. *D.B.F.P.* i, nos. 244, 245 and 247 and *D.G.F.P.* ii, no. 181.

47 *D.B.F.P.* i, nos. 261 and 264.

48 Cf. *N.C.A.* iv, pp. 360 ff.; (Jodl's diary) and Henderson, p. 135.

49 *D.G.F.P.* vii, App. iii (H).

50 Ibid., ii, no. 221.

51 *New Documents*, no. 13.

52 *D.B.F.P.* i, no. 286.

53 Ibid., no. 472.

54 *D.G.F.P.* ii, no. 194, and *D.B.F.P.* i, no. 408. Cf. *F.R.U.S.* (1938), i, pp. 493 and 495.

55 *D.B.F.P.* i, no. 271.

56 *D.G.F.P.* iii, no. 600.

57 Ibid., vii, App. iii (H).

58 *D.B.F.P.* ii, nos. 776 and 665.

59 *D.G.F.P.* ii, nos. 233 and 337.

60 Ibid., no. 247.

61 Ibid., no. 282.

62 Ibid., no. 374.

63 See *I.M.T. Proceedings*, pt. 21, p. 48, and *D.G.F.P.* vii, App. iii (K).

64 *D.G.F.P.* ii, nos. 424 and 448.

65 Ibid., no. 410.

66 See *I.M.T. Proceedings*, pt. 13, p. 63.

67 Hassell, op. cit., p. 309.

68 See *I.M.T. Proceedings*, pt. 14, p. 171 (testimony of Raeder).

69 Cf. Hans Rothfels, *The German Opposition to Hitler* (1961), pp. 56–63, and Wheeler-Bennett, op. cit., pp. 404–24.

70 See *D.B.F.P.* ii, app. iv; Colvin, pp. 218–21; Kordt, pp. 245–84.

71 *D.B.F.P.* ii, no. 805. Cf. Liddell Hart, ii, p. 158.

[72] *D.B.F.P.* i, no. 512.

[73] Ibid., no. 521.

[74] Ibid., no. 525.

[75] Ibid., ii, no. 644.

[76] *D.G.F.P.* ii, nos. 398 and 407.

[77] *N.C.A.* iv, p. 360 ff.

[78] See *D.G.F.P.* ii, no. 415, and *Ciano's Diary, 1937–1938*, entry or 17 Sept. 1938.

[79] François-Poncet, p. 265.

[80] *D.B.F.P.* ii, no. 793.

[81] Cf. *New Documents*, no. 26, and Bonnet, vol. i, pp. 199–201.

[82] See W. S. Churchill, *The Gathering Storm* (1948), pp. 263–6.

[83] *D.B.F.P.* ii, nos. 814, 822, 843, 852 and 879.

[84] See Duff Cooper, pp. 226–7, and Colvin, pp. 236–48.

[85] *D.B.F.P.* ii, no. 758, and Bonnet, vol. i, p. 186.

[86] *D.G.F.P.* ii, no. 482.

[87] Baynes, vol. 2, pp. 1487 ff.

[88] *D.G.F.P.* ii, no. 490.

[89] Ibid., no. 516. Cf. *D.B.F.P.* ii, no. 916.

[90] *D.B.F.P.* ii, no. 794; see Gedye, op. cit., for the situation in the Sudetenland.

[91] Feiling, p. 357.

[92] *Ciano's Diary, 1937–1938*; entry for 14 Sept. 1938.

[93] Schmidt, p. 91.

[94] The account of the meetings is based on *D.B.F.P.* ii, nos. 895 and 896; *D.G.F.P.* ii, nos. 487; and Feiling, pp. 366–8.

[95] Duff Cooper, p. 229.

[96] H. F. Armstrong, in *Foreign Affairs*, vol. 17, no. 2, Jan. 1939.

[97] Gedye, p. 491.

[98] Dalton, pp. 176–83.

[99] *F.R.U.S.* (1938), i, pp. 600–2 (Bullitt to Hull, 15 Sept.).

[100] *D.B.F.P.* ii, no. 928.

[101] Ibid., no. 927.

[102] Ibid., no. 960, and *New Documents*, no. 36.

[103] *New Documents*, no. 38.

[104] *D.B.F.P.* ii, no. 979, and Bonnet, op. cit., vol. i, p. 248. But see Noguères, op. cit., pp. 147–9, which again suggests that Bonnet tampered with the documents, and Zay, p. 16. The possible motives behind Hodža's action are discussed by Celovsky, op. cit., pp. 361–5.

[105] *New Documents*, no. 42.

[106] See *D.B.F.P.* ii, no. 1001; Bonnet, *Quai D'Orsay* (1965), p. 188, and Noguères, pp. 150–1.

[107] See *Ciano's Diplomatic Papers*, p. 235, and *D.B.F.P.* iii, no. 43.

[108] *D.G.F.P.* ii, no. 554.

[109] Dirksen, *Moscow, Tokyo, London*, p. 222.

[110] *D.B.F.P.* ii, no. 1033, and *D.G.F.P.* ii, no. 562, and Henderson, chap. v.

[111] See Duff Cooper, p. 231.

[112] *D.G.F.P.* ii, nos. 572 and 573.

[113] Ibid., nos. 583 and 584.

[114] See *D.B.F.P.* ii, no. 1095.

[115] Ibid., no. 1092.

[116] J.-P. Sartre, *The Reprieve* (Penguin, 1963) should be read.

[117] Duff Cooper, p. 234; Birkenhead, p. 399; Vincent Massey, *What's Past is Prologue* (1963), pp. 258–62.

[118] *D.G.F.P.* ii, no. 605.

[119] *D.B.F.P.* ii, nos. 1093 and 1096; for Daladier's feelings see Hore-Belisha, p. 148.

[120] *D.B.F.P.* ii, no. 1118.

[121] See William Shirer, *Berlin Diary* (1941), p. 118, and Baynes, vol. 2, p. 1508 ff.

[122] *D.B.F.P.* ii, no. 1129 and *D.G.F.P.* ii, no. 634.

[123] Cf. *D.B.F.P.* ii, nos. 1143, 1148 and 1202; Pertinax, op. cit., p. 3.

[124] *D.B.F.P.* ii, nos. 1136 and 1140.

[125] B.B.C. archives; record no. 1930.

[126] *D.G.F.P.* ii, no. 654.

[127] *D.B.F.P.* ii, no. 1144.

[128] Ibid., no. 1158.

[129] Schmidt, pp. 105–6. Goering thought 'a Great War could hardly be avoided any longer'; see Jodl's diary, loc. cit.

[130] *D.G.F.P.* ii, no. 655.

[131] Ibid., no. 656, and François-Poncet, pp. 265–7.

[132] The conflicting versions of this episode are assessed by Celovsky, p. 462.

[133] Kordt, pp. 274–5; *Ciano's Diary, 1937–1938*, entry for 29–30 Sept. 1938.

[134] Ibid.; *D.G.F.P.* ii, nos. 670 and 674; Zay, pp. 25–6.

[135] *D.G.F.P.* ii, no. 675.

[136] See Ripka, op. cit., pp. 224–7.

[137] For Beck's own explanation of his policy see his *Dernier Rapport*, (1951), p. 182.

[138] *New Documents*, nos. 57 and 58.

[139] *D.B.F.P.* ii, no. 1228.

[140] App. to the above.

[141] *I.M.T. Proceedings*, pt. 13, p. 4 (evidence of Schacht). See Hassell, p. 18, for similar evidence.

[142] *D.G.F.P.* v, nos. 61 and 62.

[143] See ibid., iv, nos. 35, 39 and 46; and v, no. 254.

[144] *D.B.F.P.* iii, no. 397.

[145] Coulondre, p. 172.

[146] For a detailed analysis of the areas involved see an article by Elizabeth Wiskemann in *Foreign Affairs*, vol. 17, no. 2, Jan. 1939.

[147] Cato, *Guilty Men* (1940), pp. 55–6.

[148] See Hugh Thomas, *The Spanish Civil War* (1961), pp. 612–13.

[149] *D.B.F.P.* viii, nos. 148 and 152.

[150] *D.G.F.P.* v, nos. 227, 228 and 239.

[151] Ibid. iv, no. 3.

4 Prague, Memel, Tirana

If all the world lies in ruins,
What the devil do we care?
We still will go marching on,
For today Germany belongs to us
And tomorrow the whole world.

Nazi marching song

What distresses me more than anything else is the handle which it
will give to the critics of Munich.

HENDERSON to HALIFAX on the German invasion of
Bohemia and Moravia, 15 March 1939.[1]

MUNICH gave Hitler added confidence. 'This fellow
Chamberlain shook with fear when I uttered the word *war*',
he boasted to an acquaintance; 'don't tell me *he* is
dangerous.'[2] Few with eyes to see doubted that further
expansion would come, and when Coulondre warned
Bonnet on 15 December: 'c'est maintenant l'heure du
"Lebensraum" qui sonne',[3] he was merely anticipating
by a day Weizsäcker's confidences to Hassell. Hitler and
Ribbentrop's policy, said the State Secretary, 'was obviously
aimed at war, [though] it had not yet been decided whether
to strike out right away against England, whilst keeping
Poland neutral, or to move first against the East'.[4] And
though Ribbentrop himself, on a visit to Rome in October,
talked soothingly to his hosts of a war against the West in
four or five years' time only, the same bullish spirit was
reflected in the message he brought from the Fuehrer:

The Czechoslovak crisis has shown our power. We have the
advantage of the initiative and are masters of the situation.
We cannot be attacked. The military situation is excellent;

as from the month of September (i.e. 1939) we could face a war with the great democracies.[5]

The Italians were not informed of German thinking in an easterly direction. Here too, however, Hitler knew what he wanted, and though an OKW directive of 21 October talked of 'liquidating the remainder of the Czech state' only 'should it pursue an anti-German policy', a fresh order on 17 December made no mention of provocation as a *casus belli*, and admitted that the case could be prepared 'on the assumption that no appreciable resistance is to be expected'.[6] Coulondre and the German opposition both obtained reliable information that the seizure of Bohemia and Moravia was intended, and Dirksen learned the same from a member of the Fuehrer's entourage.[7] In Hitler's words to the Hungarian Foreign Minister in January, 'an ingenious, territorial solution must be sought for'.[8]

Chamberlain, apparently unaware of all this, remained hopeful. Despite the decision to aim for 6 Regular and 26 Territorial divisions, conciliation still loomed larger in his mind than did the desperate need to rearm, and when Halifax suggested that it was time to bring some of the Opposition and dissident Conservatives into the Government, he was rebuffed; whilst Eden found the Foreign Secretary 'unhappy and counting the hours to the time when he should leave the office', Chamberlain strove increasingly to by-pass all but the entirely faithful.[9] This did not mean, of course, that Halifax himself was fully aware of the danger of Hitler. He wrote to Phipps of German expansion in Central Europe as 'a normal and natural thing',[10] and according to the American Ambassador mused in even more alarming fashion over tea on 12 October. There was no point in fighting Hitler, said Halifax, unless he directly interfered with Britain or the Dominions. The country's air strength should be built up so that she could not be threatened; 'then', Kennedy's report continued, after that to let Hitler go ahead and do what he likes in Central Europe. In other words, there is no question in Halifax's mind that reasonably soon Hitler will make a start for Danzig, with Polish concurrence, and then for Memel, with Lithuanian acquiescence, and even if he decides to go into Rumania it is Halifax's idea that England should mind her own business. He contends again that England would never have got into the Czechoslovak situation if it had not been for France.[11]

It is difficult to believe that Kennedy, for all his gloom and instability, was inventing this, and it appears to harmonise with the phrase used to Phipps. If the report was, indeed, accurate, little comment is needed. The road to salvation as pointed by a man in whose mind Britain and India seemed to have been closer than Britain and Europe would have proved perilous indeed.

During the winter of 1938–9 fresh unofficial feelers were put out from Britain involving a colonial settlement (Lords Allen and Lothian were prominent here), large economic credits for Germany, private visits to Hitler, and even the eventual possibility of a defensive alliance against Russia.[12] Though there was little to show for these endeavours beyond an Anglo-German coal agreement and talks between the Reich Federation of Industry and the Federation of British Industries, Chamberlain did not lose heart. When Hitler in a speech of 30 January declared it would be 'a blessing for the whole world if mutual confidence and co-operation could be established between the two peoples', it further encouraged the Prime Minister; the latter remained considerably more eager than Halifax to seize upon the slenderest evidence of goodwill in Berlin.[13]

Bonnet followed suit, despite the opposition of some members of the French Cabinet. With the Right denouncing the pact with Russia, the Left denouncing Munich, a general strike hanging over the country and production crawling, to temporise might be termed realism. The Foreign Minister did at least call openly for rapid rearmament,[14] and it should

also be remembered that French opinion was understandably
sceptical of British resolve. The continued refusal of London
to inaugurate conscription worsened matters, whatever the
technical merits of the case. 'Take care', remarked a
prominent officer in Paris; 'France does not intend to allow
England to fight her battles with French soldiers.'[15]

Bonnet also desired a clear symbol of *détente* with Germany,
however, and on 6 December Ribbentrop arrived in Paris
to sign a declaration of friendship similar to that obtained by
Chamberlain at Munich. With the two Jewish members of
the French Cabinet absent from the official banquet all
seemed sweetness and light at the time; at a reception in his
Embassy Ribbentrop 'held court', and a large section of
Paris society clustered round to pay tribute while Daladier
remained almost alone and unnoticed in another room.[16]
When Bonnet talked to the Chamber in January of fostering
the French '*présence*' in Central and Eastern Europe, however, it brought forth a claim by Ribbentrop that he had
been privately assured during his visit that France would
disinterest herself in the area.[17] It may be, as Schmidt
suggests, that there had been a misunderstanding. Yet the
two Foreign Ministers had been alone for a time,[18] and
Bonnet's later comment to the German Ambassador is not
without interest:

If a French Foreign Minister, against the storm and wave of
opposition, substantiated [German] claims to the Sudeten
German territory . . . *and then drew his own conclusions privately
from the changed situation in central Europe*, he could not . . . be
expected to withdraw all along the line when facing the
Chamber.[19]

Events continued to impede the eager wishes of both
Bonnet and Chamberlain, however. On 10 November, after
the shooting of a minor diplomat in the Paris Embassy had
offered a pretext, an orgy of destruction and victimisation
fell upon Germany's Jews, with sections of the Berlin press
branding Churchill, Attlee, Duff Cooper and others as

'instigators of Jewish murderers'. Moreover in response to enquiries by Halifax concerning the treatment of non-Nazi Sudeten Germans, Hitler had angrily declared in a speech at Saarbruecken on 9 October that his country 'could not tolerate any longer the tutelage of governesses'. He was also known to have assured German journalists that he no longer placed any value on friendship with Britain.[20] A further snub arrived in December when Berlin declared without consultation that it would now exercise its right, under the exceptional circumstances mentioned in the 1935 naval agreement, to build a submarine fleet which would equal the tonnage of Britain's.

More humiliating still was the barren outcome of all those promises of a guarantee for Czechoslovakia. In this case Chamberlain and Halifax, possibly with more realism than before Munich, had already accepted a passive role for they had insisted to Daladier and Bonnet in London on 24 November that no assistance could be rendered unless three out of the four Powers participated.[21] 'It would be too dangerous', observed Chamberlain, 'so to arrange the guarantee that it might happen that France and Britain would have to go to war because of action on the part of the other two guarantors', and Halifax added that whilst nothing they could do would save the Czechs there was a danger of encouraging the latter to take a provocative line against Berlin. Though the Frenchmen were prepared to put up with a great deal — Chamberlain's deprecatory insinuations concerning their Russian alliance, for instance — this virtual abandonment of Prague did move them to a superficial protest. Having thus soothed their consciences, however, they agreed to the 'three out of four' formula in January.[22] It was to be an academic point, anyway. Germany had repeatedly procrastinated over signing; at the end of February she declared that before the guarantee could be given she must 'await a clarification of the internal development of Czechoslovakia and an improvement of that country's relations with surrounding states'.[23]

By then many rumours and fears concerning other areas had gone chasing round the capitals of Europe. 'The tiger will spring, and very soon', the British chargé d'affaires had written from Berlin on 6 December, and on the 12th hints of an impending *coup* in Memel had brought nervous Anglo-French *démarches* to the German Government. Both the French General Staff and the British military attaché in Berlin were agreed that military action was being prepared for 1939, and in January the threat was rumoured to be imminent and westward.[24] While the Belgian King clung all the more desperately to his neutrality, Britain and France agreed that for them an invasion of Holland or Switzerland would constitute a *casus belli*.[25] It was this situation which caused Chamberlain to declare in the Commons on 6 February that 'any threat to the vital interests of France, from whatever quarter it came, would evoke the immediate cooperation of Great Britain'.[26] The way of a peacemaker was not proving an easy one.

The more intransigent Berlin appeared, the more eagerly did the leading appeasers turn their eyes towards Rome. The Munich conference had raised hopes of Mussolini's good intentions, and François-Poncet was not alone in misreading the ensuing situation when he remarked in October that the Duce was now 'the key to Hitler, who was very subject to [his] influence'.[27] Halifax, for instance, thought it possible 'to increase Mussolini's power of manœuvre and so make him less dependent on Hitler, and therefore freer to resume the classic Italian role of balancing between Germany and the Western Powers'.[28]

Despite the absence of the required withdrawals from Spain, therefore, Britain surrendered to Italian demands that their agreement of April 1938 should now be ratified. Halifax cast an uneasy glance at the effect on public opinion of the bombing of British ships off Spain, but from Rome

Perth urged that if he could secretly convey to the Duce in advance the Cabinet's decision to sign, the latter might even call off his planes. He added that Mussolini and Ciano could be 'thoroughly relied on to keep secret (prior) information'. The bone was duly laid at the master's feet on 26 October. Not only did the Italian press and radio immediately give the details of the coming triumph, but Ciano could now repeat that 'Italy could not further abandon General Franco'. Nor could anything be done, of course, about the Italian planes controlled entirely by Spaniards; but did it matter, since the seamen killed had 'nearly always been Greek'?[29] Perhaps only Henderson among British diplomats could have rivalled Perth in inviting and accepting such treatment. 'It does not alter our policy', observed Mussolini in private on 16 November, the day of signing; 'the Axis remains fundamental'.[30]

The situation was worsened, not improved, by the visit of Chamberlain and Halifax to Rome early in January. Whilst the Prime Minister privately considered that he 'had achieved all he expected to get, and more', since Mussolini 'was emphatic in his assurances that he intended to stand by his agreement with us and ... wanted peace',[31] the latter sneered at 'the tired sons of a long line of rich men, [who] will lose their empire'.[32] Ciano wrote of the visitors:

They would be ready for any sacrifice if they could see the future clearly. This sombre preoccupation of theirs has convinced me more and more of the necessity for the Triple Alliance. Having in our hands such an instrument we could get whatever we want. ... I have telephoned von Ribbentrop that the visit was a fiasco. ...[33]

Already Mussolini had decided to accept the German proposals for turning the anti-Comintern pact into a military alliance;[34] the rôle of reluctant partner was being transferred to Japan, where the anxiety of naval and political circles to avoid a final break with the Anglo-Saxons was not to be overcome by the army until the fall of Konoye's government in the autumn of 1941. Only Hitler's own high-handedness or the cold shock of war on braggadocio could damage the Axis now. When Chamberlain sent a letter in March appealing for help to preserve peace, it merely strengthened Mussolini's resolve to strike at Albania. 'In it', wrote Ciano, 'he finds another proof of the inertia of the democracies.'[35]

Approaches to Italy also strained Anglo-French relations. In the face of Italian demands for concessions in French Somaliland, seats on the Suez Canal Board, and a special status for her nationals living in Tunis, Daladier and Léger were reluctant to make any move 'which was only too likely to encourage Italy to set an impossibly high price on an agreement and [to be] interpreted as a sign of weakness'.[36] With deputies shouting 'Tunis, Corsica, Nice' in the Italian Chamber and fiercely anti-French articles appearing in the Rome press, it was not surprising, therefore, that Paris looked uneasily at the eager signings and visits of London and *The Times*'s talk of Italy's 'legitimate grievances'.[37] Daladier did use unofficial channels to investigate the possibility of a settlement, but deliberate revelations by Ribbentrop soon helped destroy the attempt. And though Western recognition of Franco in February together with the shock to Italy of the destruction of Czechoslovakia helped more formal contacts for a while, Mussolini's drift towards the Pact of Steel and 'the brutal friendship' was inexorable. Early in May, following a firm speech by Daladier, the Duce ordered talks with the French to be broken off.

Bonnet, who, like François-Poncet, had been more accommodating than Daladier and Léger throughout,[38] had received every encouragement from the British Government. Whilst London unofficially pressed her good offices on Paris, Phipps took his timing from Bonnet as to 'when he wants me to attack Daladier again'.[39] The pressure was halted only briefly by the rape of Albania, though Sir Percy Loraine's arrival in Rome in place of Perth did help bring

matters out of cloud-cuckoo land.[40] It might be argued that
Italian neutrality in September 1939 was to justify the softer
line, but the 'gangsters' as Daladier so rightly called them,
were then responding to self-interest rather than to kindness.
Certainly the belief that Mussolini could restrain Hitler was
misplaced, as the events of March were to show.

Czechoslovakia (now officially termed Czecho-Slovakia)
had lost her independence at Munich. 'My country',
observed her Minister in Berlin, 'is no more than a province'.
German demands for an extra-territorial road linking
Breslau with Vienna and for an Oder–Danube canal were
accepted, and the new Foreign Minister, Chvalkovský,
assured Ribbentrop and Hitler in October that Prague
'would now make a complete *volte-face* in her foreign policy'.[41]
Since Hungary was about to adhere to the anti-Comintern
pact, and since the Little Entente, as Gafencu of Rumania
cheerfully agreed with the German Minister, 'had ceased to
exist',[42] this was hardly surprising, but it did not satisfy
Berlin. In January the Czechs were told that if they wanted
a guarantee they should adopt a position of complete
neutrality, align their foreign policy with that of Germany,
leave the League of Nations, reduce their army, surrender
part of their gold reserves, obtain permission before
establishing new industries, dismiss officials unacceptable to
the Reich, permit Nazi insignia, and enact anti-Semitic
laws on the lines of the Nuremberg decrees.[43] New measures
against the Jews did, in fact, follow, as did the 'resignation'
of General Krejči, Chief of the General Staff and a remnant
of the Beneš era. Kundt and other Nazis who remained in
the Czech state confidently awaited the day of liberation,
and German troop trains rolled insolently across Moravia.
    At the same time friction between Prague and Bratislava
was increasing. The autonomy promised the Slovaks at
Pittsburgh in 1918 had been granted in considerable
measure after Munich, but for men like Durčansky, their

Deputy Prime Minister, independence alone would suffice. The expansionist aims of Hungary made it doubly urgent to seek the patronage of Germany, and though Hitler was careful to make no promises (bargains with Poland and Hungary might still be necessary) he gave a warm welcome to those Slovak extremists who arrived to address him as 'My Fuehrer' and 'entrust the fate of their people to his care'.[44] Goering, who had long had his eyes on the economic potential of their land as well as that of Bohemia and Moravia, was visited by Durčansky early in March;[45] at the same time negotiations between Czechs and Slovaks on financial and administrative issues were reaching deadlock. The opportunity Hitler had been looking for was about to arrive.

Though the West had become aware of the extent of German demands on Czechoslovakia, the new act of aggression would take London in particular by surprise. The scares of December and January had passed, blamed by Vincent Massey, for instance, on 'the war-mongering types of mind in the F.O., and elsewhere'.[46] Illness had kept Henderson in England until the middle of February ('a minor disaster', in his own words), but on his return he had repeatedly reassured Halifax that 'a period of relative calm' was approaching, that 'if there had been a war party in Berlin ... its shares were now rapidly falling', and that 'if Ribbentrop had belonged to [that party], he no longer did'. Such unstable swinging from extreme gloom to glib optimism was in the nature of the man; no rebukes from Halifax could prevent it.[47] And though at times his analysis of Germany's problems and mentality was shrewd, the Ambassador still believed that Hitler himself was not on the side of the extremists, expecting him to honour his signature 'so long as Britain remained even comparatively friendly disposed to Germany'.[48] Directly inspired by such happy news, a spring tide of hopefulness rolled out from Downing Street, reaching its height on 10 March as Sir Samuel

Hoare speculated on a new 'golden age' for mankind and Chamberlain assured Lobby correspondents that 'Europe was settling down to a period of tranquillity'. Only Halifax was somewhat perturbed; like Eden of old, he had not been consulted.[49]

On 6 March the Ruthenian Government was dismissed by President Hácha of Czechoslovakia in an attempt to prevent the dissolution of his state. On the 9th, the resumed talks between Czechs and Slovaks broke down, and both Monsignor Tiso, the Slovak Premier, and Durčansky were dismissed and joined the extremist leader, Tuka, in brief imprisonment the next day. Prague strove to minimise discontent, however, by announcing that autonomy would remain and that Sidor, a Slovak member of the central government and head of the Hlinka Guard, would take Tiso's place; early protest demonstrations in Bratislava did in fact attract the support only of a few 'evil-looking ruffians of the lowest possible type armed with poles'. Nevertheless, it was reported that arms were being distributed to German extremists from across the border; bomb explosions were soon to occur, whilst on the evening of the 10th the escaped Durčansky broadcast from the sanctuary of Vienna an appeal to all Slovaks to resist the domination of Prague.

On Saturday the 11th, though the British Consul in Bratislava reported that conditions seemed normal, the German press was declaring that Tiso had appealed to Berlin for help. The German interest became clearer still when the new Slovak Cabinet met that evening under Sidor, for Seyss-Inquart arrived with five generals to inform the gathering that they should proclaim their country's independence. Tiso himself was summoned to Berlin, where already the OKW were drawing up the military terms of an ultimatum to Prague and where Ribbentrop and Weizsäcker were 'making themselves inaccessible' to diplomatic enquirers.[50]

Hitler's decision to screw matters to breaking point was

implemented to the point of no return on Monday, 13th. While the chargé d'affaires in Prague was ordered so to arrange matters that 'during the next few days you and your staff are not in a position to receive any communications from the Czechoslovak Government',[51] 'suggestions' were conveyed to Hungary concerning the fate of Ruthenia. In reply, Horthy expressed his 'boundless gratitude'. 'On the 16th', he wrote, 'a frontier incident will take place, to be followed . . . by the big thrust'.[52] To Tiso and Durčansky Hitler stormed about the intolerable persecution of Germans and the return of the Beneš spirit. Did Slovakia want independence or not? He had sent for them 'to clear up this question *in a very short time*', and 'the fate' to which he would abandon their people if the answer were negative was made clear when Ribbentrop conveniently brought in a report of Hungarian troop movements on the Slovak border. Tiso replied that Hitler 'could rely on Slovakia', and later that evening he was helped to draw up the drafts of a declaration of independence and an appeal for the Fuehrer's protection.[53]

In the two days which followed, Czechoslovakia disappeared. A somewhat unenthusiastic Slovak Diet voted for independence on the 14th after Tiso had made plain the unspoken German threat, and Ruthenia, its new status to endure only for a day, followed suit. A twelve-hour Hungarian ultimatum demanding a Czech withdrawal from Ruthenia on the pretext of intolerable frontier incidents arrived in Prague at 3 p.m.; it was passed to President Hácha and Chvalkovský just before they departed by train, on their own initiative, to see what could be preserved by meeting Hitler himself. By the time the two men reached Berlin German troops had already marched into the Mährisch-Ostrau district.

The two Czechs were taken before the Fuehrer, Keitel, Goering, Weizsäcker and others at 1.15 a.m. on the 15th.[54] Pathetically, the frail and ageing Hácha began by declaring his happiness at meeting the man of 'wonderful ideas' who

held 'the destiny of Czechoslovakia . . . in safekeeping', but
the usual harsh tirade cut him short. Soon the visitors 'sat as
if turned to stone. . . . Only their eyes showed they were
alive'.[55] Their country, they were told, would be invaded at
6 a.m. and incorporated within the Reich. If autonomy were
desired there must be no resistance, which would 'be broken
by brute force' in any case, for Hitler 'was almost ashamed'
that 'for every Czech battalion there was a German division'.
The Fuehrer then left, while Ribbentrop and Goering
pursued the protesting Czechs round the table, thrusting at
them a prepared agreement which they must sign; Goering
added persuasive details of how his bombers would raze
Prague if compliance were withheld. Hácha fainted, and
was revived by injection. Finally, between 3 and 4 in the
morning and after a telephone call to his Cabinet, he signed
the document which announced that to preserve 'calm,
order, and peace', he had 'placed the destiny of the Czech
people and country with confidence in the hands of the
Fuehrer of the German Reich'. The latter then graciously
agreed to take the Czechs 'under his protection', guaranteeing them 'autonomous development'.[56]

At 6 a.m. the *Wehrmacht* marched to put an end to the
'intolerable reign of terror' for Germans in Bohemia and
Moravia. Hungarian troops began occupying Ruthenia on
the same day, and on the 16th Tiso requested Germany to
assume a protectorate over the independent Slovakia. Hitler
was already in the Hradschin Castle, rejoicing at the return
of the provinces which 'for a thousand years had formed
part of the *Lebensraum* of the German people'. His revenge
for the 'May scare' was complete.

Despite the promises of September 1938 there was never
any question of the West intervening. A Foreign Office
memorandum on 13 March repeated the painful truth that
Britain could only take effective action through France, and
added with relief: 'In all the circumstances, His Majesty's
Government would have no *locus standi* for taking any

initiative in this matter, and any attempt to check Herr Hitler by public statements or invoking Signor Mussolini's support would only seem calculated to precipitate a solution unfavourable to Czecho-Slovakia'.[57] Bonnet was fervently agreeing on the same day that 'the less we interfere in this crisis the better', whilst Henderson, as usual, was busy shifting the blame onto Hitler's victim. On the 14th the Ambassador concluded that 'no definite line of action had been decided upon', but that force was 'certainly not excluded if the Prague Government proved recalcitrant'.[58]

The disquietude of London was therefore expressed in the gentlest possible manner. As framed by Halifax on the evening of the 14th it deplored violence in Central Europe, but disclaimed 'the desire to interfere unnecessarily in matters with which other Governments may be more directly concerned'.[59] Henderson himself assured Weizsäcker on the same day that he was not making a *démarche*, and that 'German interests were paramount in the Czech area'.[60] Despite his later outbursts against the 'utter cynicism and immorality' of the Nazi action,[61] he was able to ask Weizsäcker on the 17th 'for arguments which he could give Chamberlain for use against the latter's political opposition at home'.[62] In April, Coulondre was to find his colleague still determined above all to avoid annoying Hitler; 'I have the impression', noted the Frenchman, 'that Henderson has reverted to his attitude of last February as if nothing had happened'.[63]

To Chamberlain's dismay, British public opinion was not to prove so indulgent. When the Prime Minister had carefully explained to the Commons on the 15th that the internal disruption of a state so liable to 'possibilities of change' had rendered past guarantees inoperative, he had not been without support in the press. Developments were 'following along a course which had been foreseen', wrote *The Times*; 'The process is natural', repeated the *Daily Mail*, 'and Europe maintains calm'. Such views could not withstand the rage of the country at large, however. Even 'the finest brute votes in Europe' of the Conservative Party had reached their limit, as Halifax made clear to Chamberlain. By the 16th *The Times* and the *Mail* had hardened, and Sir John Simon's grotesque sleight of hand in the Commons on the same day only produced a storm of indignation. At Birmingham on the 17th, therefore, in a speech marked by 'petulance and wounded vanity', the Prime Minister sounded a new, wavering note of indignation. A stern written protest joined those of France, Russia and America on the desks of the Wilhelmstrasse, and Henderson was recalled to report. So, too, was Coulondre, though Bonnet, like Chamberlain, made the gesture with the greatest reluctance.[64] Their departure preceded Hitler's next *coup* by five days.

The Memel operation and its background, though dismissed in a sentence by many historians, is worthy of study as something of a microcosm of its more celebrated predecessors. The Versailles grievance was there — the port and its hinterland had been surrendered by Germany in 1919 — as was the embarrassing precedent set by the victim, Lithuania, in seizing the territory from Allied control in 1923. So, too, was the enmity of another neighbour, and the bitterness of Lithuanian-Polish relations had certainly not been healed by the latter's action in demanding the reopening of diplomatic channels at the point of a gun in March 1938. The conflict which had seemed possible on that occasion would also have touched one of Germany's interests, for in the event of a Polish victory 'Lithuania would cease to be an object of compensation for the restitution of the Corridor to Germany'.[65] Especially as relations between Berlin and Warsaw became more strained, however, the other interest, the return of Memel and its Germans to the Reich, was the one which predominated. The suppression of Nazi organisations by Lithuania in

1935 had not precluded a treaty of friendship and trade with
Germany in the following year. As in Austria, the Sudetenland, North Schleswig, Latvia, Estonia, and Liechtenstein,[66]
however, there remained enough local fanatics to embarrass
even Berlin by their desire for a swift Nazi take-over. In
July 1938 Dr. Neumann, leader of the Germans in Memel,
was told with Ribbentrop's approval 'to impose a stricter . . .
discipline . . . on the young hotheads . . . who hope to be
able to force a quick and violent solution of the . . .
problem',[67] and in November Heydrich was writing in alarm
to the Foreign Minister about the 'altogether undesirable'
situation in which the same young zealots threatened to
place the Reich.[68] In December Neumann had tried pleading
that he could not 'keep this movement within the bounds of
discipline', but was this time given Hitler's personal decision
that calm must be maintained.[69] Though SA, SS and Hitler
Youth organisations were flourishing in Memel early in
1939, the potentially explosive convening of the city's
Landtag was delayed on orders from Berlin, whilst the
wretched Neumann was summoned before *Gauleiter* Koch of
East Prussia in February and told that if trouble was not
avoided for the time being he would be shot.[70]

Yet restraint was for Hitler no more than a tactic. The
'young hotheads' were his as much as were the directives of
March and October 1938 in which he had ordered the
OKW to be ready to occupy Memel. Only the need to time
matters in the light of the international situation held him
back; certainly not morality, and certainly not the difficulty
of a task which he described as 'requiring only a registered
letter' to the rulers of Lithuania.[71] As early as 2 January
1939 the German Minister in Lithuania was told that
Neumann had been promised by Hitler that 'the matter
would be settled in that year', and that 'the end of March
or, even better, the middle of April was set as the desired
date'.[72]

The forecast could be the more confidently made since

European tension was producing favourable and familiar circumstances. When Chamberlain blithely assured questioners in the Commons that he had Hitler's word he would abide by the Memel Statute, he was using the only form of pressure the West could consider; despite clear warnings of a *coup* after Prague, Britain would still not predict her action in 'hypothetical circumstances'. On the other flank Estonia's pro-German leanings promised that she, if not Poland, would view seizure with equanimity. Moreover, frightened hints from Lithuania herself that concessions were possible — one journalist close to the Minister President, Mironas, suggested that even Memel might be ceded if his country's prestige and economic interests could be saved — inevitably encouraged Berlin to tighten the screw.[73] It needed only the frenzy of the German Memellanders, their eager swastikas and salutes when the news of 15 March came through, and the scene was set for the *dénouement* as before.

At 6.40 p.m. on the 15th a surprised Foreign Office in Berlin received the text of a speech made in Memel that morning by Neumann as he struggled to maintain control of his movement.[74] Complaining of Lithuanian violations of the Memel Statute and declaring that steps would be taken to secure the 'vital prerogatives' of the Germans there, it followed drafts prepared earlier that year in Berlin. It did not repeat their appeals to Hitler for reunification, but once the Czech affair had been settled the Fuehrer did not need asking.

On the 20th the Lithuanian Foreign Minister was received in Berlin by Ribbentrop and given the alternative of a solution by agreement or force; on his return to consult his Government he was pursued by scarcely veiled threats telephoned by Weizsäcker.[75] The required plenipotentiaries arrived back in Berlin on the 22nd, and the signing away of Memel was accomplished in the small hours of the 23rd. A communiqué issued by the Lithuanian Government revealing that threats had been used was withdrawn after a further 'phone call by Weizsäcker.[76] At 1.30 a.m. Ribbentrop was able to signal the news of success in reply to the testy inquiries of a seasick Hitler, who was already on his way to Memel on the pocket battleship *Deutschland*. It was the Fuehrer's last bloodless triumph.

It remained only for the jackal to ape its master. Italy had been informed of the march into Bohemia only at the last minute and to the accompaniment of spurious excuses. Mussolini, 'profoundly shaken', bitterly complained that 'every time Hitler occupies a country he sends me a message'. 'It is useless to deny that all this worries and humiliates the Italian people', wrote Ciano. 'It is necessary to give them satisfaction and compensation: Albania.'[77]

This did not mean that the invasion of Albania, where Italian influence was already predominant, was newly conceived. It had been planned long before, with the assassination of King Zog as a possible adjunct, and the fall from power in February 1939 of Stoyadinovitch, the accommodating crypto-fascist Premier of Yugoslavia, had temporarily produced an urgent target date of early April.[78] In fact the latest German action brought hesitation rather than encouragement, for with the fear that Berlin might now use the Croats in the role of the Slovaks to disrupt Yugoslavia and advance on the Adriatic, it became more necessary than ever not to offend Belgrade. It was only on 23 March, when Ribbentrop had assured him that Yugoslavia was of no interest to the Reich and when the news from Spain was encouraging, that Mussolini again decided to go ahead with the move which, in part anti-German, was to drive him closer to Germany. With the fall of Madrid on the 28th it became certain.

The Italian landings at Durazzo on Good Friday, 7 April, were covered by the usual diplomatic smoke-screen of 'restoring peace, order and justice'. Ciano had already told Perth that King Zog had been asking for Italian help to

attack Yugoslavia,[79] and the Ambassador, gullible to the
end,[80] proved a friend in time of need. The operation had, in
fact, been necessitated by King Zog's refusal to bow before
an ultimatum from Rome. As it went ahead, however,
British concern to keep close to Mussolini was more evident
than any indignation over this violation of the agreement to
preserve the *status quo* in the Mediterranean. Though the
Albanians briefly appealed for British help, and though the
British Minister on the spot telegraphed that events were
'wholly inconsistent with any . . . concern for the independence of Albania',[81] the Duce's reassuring messages to
London were not repudiated. In private Halifax left his
Ambassador's naïvety far behind,[82] but Ciano could write in
his diary on the 7th that 'the memorandum which Lord
Perth left with me in the course of a cordial visit might have
been composed in our own offices'. 'It is clear', he added
three days later, 'that the British protests are more for
domestic consumption than anything else.'

The Anglo-Italian agreement was left untouched, but
Whitehall had not lost its inventive skill. When Sir Percy
Loraine arrived in Rome to replace Perth at the end of
April, he brought with him credentials which made no
mention of Albania as part of Victor Emmanuel's empire.
The reason given was simple: the documents 'had been
signed on March 28th'. Honour was saved.

[1] *D.B.F.P.* iv, App. i.

[2] Hesse, op. cit., p. 62.

[3] *Livre Jaune Français*, no. 33.

[4] Hassell, p. 26. For Hitler's later, corroborating testimony, see *N.C.A.*
iii, pp. 572–580.

[5] *Ciano's Diplomatic Papers*, pp. 242–6; cf. *D.G.F.P.* iv, nos. 400 and
411, and Jodl's diary, *loc. cit.*

[6] *D.G.F.P.* iv, nos. 81 and 152.

[7] Coulondre, p. 252; *I.M.T. Proceedings*, pt. 12, p. 243 (evidence of
Gisevius); Dirksen, op. cit., pp. 228–9.

[8] *D.G.F.P.* v, no. 272.

[9] Cf. Feiling, pp. 385–6; Avon, *The Reckoning*, p. 36; and *D.G.F.P.* iv, no. 251.

[10] *D.B.F.P.* iii, no. 285.

[11] *F.R.U.S.* (1938), i, pp. 85–6.

[12] See *D.G.F.P.* iv, nos. 260, 262, 316, 317, 323.

[13] Cf. the letters of Chamberlain and Halifax concerning a speech by the Duke of Coburg at an Anglo-German dinner in February: *D.B.F.P.* iv, App. i.

[14] Bonnet, *Défense de la paix*, vol. ii, pp. 51–3.

[15] *D.B.F.P.* iii, no. 189.

[16] *F.R.U.S.* (1938), i, p. 112.

[17] *D.G.F.P.* iv, no. 383; Ribbentrop later 'cooked' the record of this talk with Coulondre: see ibid., vii, App. iii (L).

[18] See Coulondre, p. 225.

[19] *D.G.F.P.* iv, no. 387; author's italics. The British Foreign Office were also suspicious of the affair: see *D.B.F.P.* iii, footnote to no. 385.

[20] Baynes, vol. 2, p. 1532 ff., and *D.B.F.P.* iii, no. 315.

[21] *D.B.F.P.* iii, no. 325.

[22] Ibid., no. 496.

[23] *D.G.F.P.*, iv, no. 175.

[24] *D.B.F.P.* iii, nos. 403, 505 and 509.

[25] See ibid., iv, nos. 5, 41 and 98; *History of the Times*, vol. iv, p. 954 (record of a talk between Halifax and Dawson); Bonnet, vol. ii, p. 127; *F.R.U.S.* (1939), i, pp. 2–6.

[26] *Hansard*, 5th series, vol. 343 (House of Commons), col. 623.

[27] *D.B.F.P.* iii, App. ii.

[28] Ibid., no. 285.

[29] See ibid., nos. 328, 329, 333, 336, 340, 348 and 360.

[30] *Ciano's Diary, 1937–1938*, entry for 16 Nov. 1938.

[31] Feiling, p. 393.

[32] *Ciano's Diary, 1939–1943*, entry for 11 Jan. 1939.

[33] Ibid., entry for 12 Jan. 1939.

[34] Ibid., entry for 1 Jan. 1939.

[35] Ibid., entry for 23 Mar. 1939, and *D.G.F.P.* iv, no. 448.

[36] *D.B.F.P.* iii, no. 479; (Phipps to Halifax).

[37] *The Times*, 17 Dec. 1938.

[38] As late as June he was still working for a Franco-Italian settlement; see *D.D.I.* xii, no. 142.

[39] See *D.B.F.P.* v, nos. 76, 238, 298, 376 and App. i.

[40] See ibid., no. 369.

[41] *D.G.F.P.* iv, nos. 55 and 61.

[42] Ibid., v, no. 289.

[43] *Livre Jaune Français*, no. 48. Cf. *D.G.F.P.* iv, nos. 158 and 159, and *F.R.U.S.* (1939), i, pp. 34–5.

[44] See *D.G.F.P.* iv, nos. 68, 69, 72, 73 and 168.

[45] See *I.M.T. Proceedings*, pt. 2, p. 105, and *D.G.F.P.* iv, no. 184.

[46] Massey, op. cit., p. 276.

[47] *D.B.F.P.* iv, no. 118 and App. i; for the influence of his views see

ibid., no. 158 (Halifax to Roosevelt); for a rebuke by Halifax see ibid., vii, App. iv.

[48] Ibid., iv, no. 195.

[49] See Feiling, pp. 396-7, and for Henderson's influence the minute by Sir Orme Sargent on *D.B.F.P.* iv, no. 197. Also *F.R.U.S.* (1939), i, pp. 14-17 (Kennedy to Hull, 17 Feb.).

[50] *D.G.F.P.* iv, nos. 188 and 460.

[51] Ibid., no. 204.

[52] Ibid., nos. 198 and 199.

[53] Ibid., no. 202.

[54] See ibid., no. 228 and *Livre Jaune Français*, no. 77.

[55] Schmidt, p. 124.

[56] *D.G.F.P.* iv, no. 229.

[57] *D.B.F.P.* iv, no. 230.

[58] Ibid., no. 235.

[59] Ibid., no. 247.

[60] *D.G.F.P.* iv, no. 213.

[61] *D.B.F.P.* iv, no. 288.

[62] *D.G.F.P.* vi, no. 16.

[63] Coulondre, p. 266. Contrast Coulondre's own despatches with those of Henderson; e.g. *Livre Jaune Français*, no. 73.

[64] See *D.B.F.P.* iv, no. 418, and Zay, p. 47.

[65] *D.G.F.P.* v, no. 329 (Ribbentrop memorandum of 17 Mar. 1938).

[66] See ibid., v, nos. 356 and 425, and vi, no. 141.

[67] Ibid., v, no. 349.

[68] Ibid., no. 366.

[69] Ibid., nos. 369 and 370.

[70] Ibid., nos. 388, 390 and 392.

[71] Hassell, p. 26.

[72] *D.G.F.P.* v, no. 381.

[73] Ibid., and footnote.

[74] Ibid., no. 395.

[75] Ibid., nos. 399 and 400. Cf. Weizsäcker, *Memoirs*, pp. 177-8 for his later whitewashing of the affair.

[76] *D.G.F.P.* v, no. 403.

[77] See *Ciano's Diary, 1939-1943*, entries for 13 Mar. 1939 to 16 Mar. 1939.

[78] See *Ciano's Diary, 1937-1938*, entry for 27 Oct. 1938; and *Ciano's Diary, 1939-1943*, entries for 19 Jan. 1939, 6 Feb. 1939, 7 Feb. 1939, and 14 Feb. 1939.

[79] *D.B.F.P.* v, no. 72.

[80] See ibid., no. 132.

[81] Ibid., no. 129.

[82] See ibid., no. 138.

5 The Search for Security

Ne laissez pas abattre à l'est le bastion polonais, sinon la France serait en grand danger.

MARSHAL FOCH, *Mémorial*

Soviet Russia can scarcely become the ally of Germany so long as Hitler lives.

HALIFAX to PHIPPS, November 1938.[1]

THE German occupation of Bohemia and Moravia spread alarm and confusion throughout Europe. Julius Streicher was already declaring at Nuremberg that the act 'was only a beginning' and that 'greater achievements would follow'. 'We have so many open doors in front of us', observed one of Goebbels's lieutenants to Coulondre on 18 March, 'so many possibilities, that we don't know which way to turn.'[2]

In some fear bred an anxiety to please, and the Secretary-General of the Turkish Foreign Ministry assured the German chargé d'affaires in Ankara that his country would 'co-operate actively' in making the Balkan area 'more than ever an economic hinterland of Germany' and 'a reliable source of supplies in times of political crisis'.[3] Others waited to see where self-interest lay, and though a strong protest was despatched from Moscow, the German Embassy there observed that alternative lines of action were being kept open.[4] The new Pope and his Cardinal Secretary of State, for their part, continued in private to manifest an 'un-mistakably forthcoming attitude' towards the Third Reich, for in the Vatican, as for long in the private temples of Halifax's Anglo-Catholicism and Lothian's Christian Science, no outright condemnation on spiritual grounds of a régime of manifest and unparalleled barbarity could be allowed to intrude upon political considerations.[5]

It was in Poland and Rumania that the repercussions appeared greatest, however. The reduction of Slovakia to a state of vassalage was a serious blow to Warsaw, and the treaty of protection which provided for a zone of German military presence at once increased current tension and the potential threat from the south. For Bucharest, too, the possibility of German attack came nearer, and the hostile presence of Hungary in Ruthenia complicated strategic and minority problems as well as severing a vital railway link with Poland.

It was the Rumanian issue, in fact, which was to precipitate new and far-reaching undertakings by the West. From the beginning of the Czech crisis M. Tilea, the Rumanian Minister in London, had privately been begging Halifax to make at least a gesture which would help retrieve British prestige in Central and Eastern Europe. He now arrived on 17 March to declare that his country had received an ultimatum from Germany whereby her economy must become an auxiliary of the latter's, and with 'extreme urgency' asked Halifax to indicate what Britain's reaction would be to a fresh act of aggression. On the same day the news was conveyed from London to Moscow, Paris, Warsaw, Belgrade, Athens and Ankara, and by the time the Rumanian Foreign Minister declared on the 18th that there was 'not a word of truth' in the story, the process of involvement had begun.

Tilea had exaggerated, possibly deliberately, but his fears were not without foundation. Though the agreement which Dr. Wohlthat was negotiating in Bucharest on behalf of Germany recognised 'the necessity for Rumania to maintain economic relations with other countries', and though no ultimatum or armed threat was presented, Wohlthat himself acknowledged that 'far more than a commercial treaty in the usual sense was involved'. Such were its terms in the

1*a*. Halifax visits Goering, November 1937; Henderson on the left

1*b*. Hitler arrives in Vienna, 14 March 1938

2a. Hitler takes the salute at the Party Rally at Nuremberg, 12 September 1938

2b. Chamberlain departs for Godesberg, 22 September 1938. Sir Horace Wilson is
next to him

3a. Chamberlain and Hitler after their final talk at Godesberg

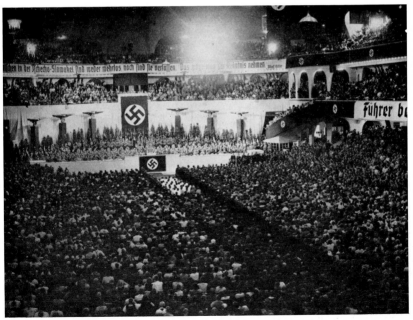

3b. Hitler speaks: the *Sportpalast* meeting, 26 September 1938

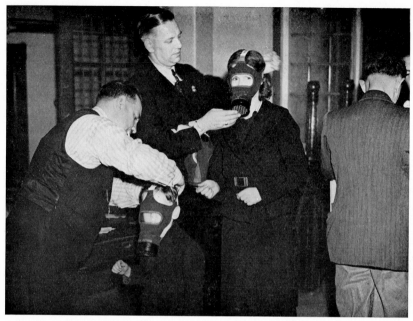

4*a*. Gas masks being fitted at Holborn Town Hall, 26 September 1938

4*b*. Bonnet, Daladier and Gamelin (l. to r.) in London for talks, 26 September 1938

5a. Departure for Munich from Heston, 29 September 1938. L. to r., Kingsley Wood, Hailsham, Chamberlain, Hore-Belisha, Burgin, Halifax

5b. Arrival at Munich airport: Chamberlain and Ribbentrop, with Henderson following

6a. Return from Munich: reading the Anglo-German declaration at Heston

6b. Return from Munich: Downing Street crowds, with two Ministers (Geoffrey Lloyd and Malcolm MacDonald) climbing the railings

7*a*. Return from Munich: Hitler's reception in Berlin

7*b*. Ciano, Halifax, Chamberlain and Mussolini in Rome, January 1939

8a. German troops enter Prague, 15 March 1939

8b. Beck (centre) arrives for Anglo-Polish talks in London, 3 April 1939

agricultural, mineral, oil and financial spheres that he was confident it would soon 'secure Germany the dominant position in Southeast Europe', and he employed hustling tactics to achieve the signing on 23 March.[6]

Moreover for the West confused suspicion was almost as effective as certainty, for, as Daladier insisted to the French Cabinet, 'the day Germany controls Rumanian oil supplies she will be in a position to wage war against all Europe'.[7] A further reason for prompt action also existed in the suspicion that the 'cynical and false' Beck might be seeking to deflect Hitler away from Poland by betraying his Rumanian friends. At 8.30 p.m. on the 18th a telegram from Paris arrived at the Foreign Office relating a conversation held that morning between the British Minister and Léger in which the latter had passed on alarming news concerning the Polish Foreign Secretary. Beck, it appeared, intended on a forthcoming visit to London to ask Britain for a guarantee and alliance in the knowledge that no such undertaking could be given; he would then be able to return home with this rejection, and persuade his government to seek an accommodation with Germany.[8] It was known that Léger and Beck were, in Bullitt's words, 'mortal enemies', and the former was about to clash bitterly with the Polish Ambassador over Poland's apparent unwillingness to aid Rumania.[9] Doubtless, however, Léger had good grounds for his warning, and his assessment of Beck's thinking was supported by his Ambassador in Warsaw.[10] Perhaps the chance to hasten the increased British commitment which he and Daladier looked for was also in his mind when he spoke.

Whatever the case, a new initiative was forthcoming from London. Though on the 19th Halifax rejected as premature Litvinov's suggestion of a meeting between Britain, France, Poland, Rumania and Russia to discuss common action, Chamberlain had already 'worked out a . . . pretty bold and startling plan . . . which I shall put to the Cabinet

E

tomorrow'.[11] Its need was underlined on the following day when details of Hácha's treatment in Berlin and fresh, French evidence of the threat to Rumania arrived at the Foreign Office. That night a proposal was sent to Moscow, Warsaw and Paris for a joint declaration that consultations would be held to decide on the steps necessary to resist 'a threat to the political independence of any European State'.[12] Some such move seemed all the more suitable on the 21st, since it was then learned that Rumania, though anxious not to provoke Germany by any pacts of assistance, would welcome a general declaration by the West on the *status quo*, while the Turkish Ambassador urged Halifax to think of co-operation with his country as well.[13] On the morning of the 22nd a message from King Carol himself indicated that a Hungarian attack on Rumania was expected soon, that 25 German divisions were on the Hungarian border, and that Bulgaria was also moving troops towards the Dobrudja.[14] Though in the event of a Bulgarian attack Rumania's allies in the Balkan Entente — Greece, Yugoslavia and Turkey — were bound to go to her aid, the same was not so in the case of aggression from Hungary or Germany, and there seemed every cause for alarm. The British Government realised that Tilea's news had been inaccurate, but were convinced of the general danger.[15]

Yet by the time the German–Rumanian economic agreement was announced on the 23rd the centre of attention had moved to Warsaw. In the first place this was due to the conviction of the West that Polish aid was the key to the protection of Rumania — doubly so in the light of the resistance of both to any idea of help from the Soviet Union. As Bonnet and Halifax agreed in London during their talks on the 21st and 22nd, it was essential 'to get Poland in', 'even', Bonnet added, 'to the extent of threats'.[16] The motive was again made clear, for instance, in the instructions sent by Bonnet to Noël on the 29th. An agreement with

Rumania and Poland was imperative, they ran, because 'on the one hand Polish military strength borders on Germany, and on the other the menace of German expansionist aims is pressing upon Rumania'.[17] In the words of the British military attaché in Berlin on the 25th:

Germany risks defeat only if confronted by a two-front war and a blockade. Such a blockade can only be *rapidly* effective if Germany's eastern front is on or close to her present frontiers and if she has to fight to gain and hold resources essential to her powers of resistance.[18]

Given the widely accepted thesis that Soviet military effectiveness could be defensive only, even the Polish short-comings in the air and in supplies[19] could be overlooked. The professional advice the Cabinet received, wrote Sir Samuel Hoare later, was that 'Poland was a more valuable ally than Russia'.[20]

For the moment, therefore, Litvinov's agreement, received on the morning of the 23rd, to sign Halifax's declaration as soon as France and Poland had promised to do so, was of secondary importance. More weighty was Beck's dislike of any public association with Russia and his argument that such an act would only provoke Germany; his own counter-proposal for a *secret* Anglo-Polish agreement arrived through Kennard on the evening of the 22nd, and was repeated by the Polish Ambassador on the 24th.[21] At the same time the Memel episode increased the feeling that Poland's own security was directly threatened. Familiar German complaints against the treatment of her minority in Poland were noted, and while Warsaw undertook partial mobilisation to prevent a *coup* in Danzig, ominous rumours began to filter through that she had been presented with far-reaching demands by Berlin.[22] Even *The Times* was proclaiming that events were 'a danger signal for all Europe, no single Power excepted'.[23] Thus, although the Rumanian crisis appeared to have passed its peak as demobilisation on either side of the frontier with Hungary gradually took place, it had led to a decisive moment. Not the least irony in the months ahead was the absence of Rumania from the list of countries, violation of whose independence was recognised as a *casus belli* by the Anglo-Polish agreement as ratified in August.

As tension between Poland and Germany increased, so did the pressure on the British Government to commit themselves openly. On the 28th Churchill, Eden and thirty-two others — nearly all Conservatives — tabled a motion in the Commons calling for the formation of a genuine National Government with full emergency powers, and neither Chamberlain's hint that moves were being planned which went 'a good deal further than consultation', nor a counter-motion by the latter's supporters, removed the widespread disquiet. Though the official Soviet reaction was becoming increasingly cold in the face of rebuffs, Maisky, the Ambassador in London, was assuring Sir Alexander Cadogan on the 29th that a British offer of military aid to Poland and Rumania 'might have far-reaching results (and) would increase enormously the confidence of other countries'.[24] Perhaps the decisive conversation of that day, however, was the one Cadogan, Halifax and Chamberlain had with Mr. Ian Colvin, the Berlin correspondent of the *News Chronicle*, for the latter had come hot-foot from Germany bearing somewhat premature evidence and the warnings of General Beck's circle to the effect that Hitler was determined to attack Poland and that the Polish Foreign Minister might be in German pay.[25] Something of the atmosphere in Berlin from which he had come may be gauged by a suggestion from the British military attaché which was also forwarded on the 29th, urging that London should welcome an early war as the only means of avoiding 'certain eventual elimination'.[26]

More than ever was Poland seen, in Halifax's phrase, as 'the key to the whole situation'. In the words of a Foreign Office memorandum of the 29th:

The absorption of Czecho-Slovakia has clearly revealed Germany's intentions . . . and there is every reason to suppose that the treatment applied [there] will be extended to other countries, notably Rumania and Poland. . . . It is [Germany's] purpose gradually to neutralise these countries, deprive them of their armies and incorporate them in the German economic system. When this has been done, the way will have been prepared for an attack on the West. . . .

Poland is no longer in a position to sit comfortably on the fence between the Soviet Union and Germany. . . . Circumstances would seem to dictate closer association with Russia, but there is much anti-Soviet feeling in Conservative and Catholic circles, and the Poles have not forgotten the Soviet invasion of 1921. . . . Poland has reached the parting of the ways.[27]

On the 30th, therefore, a fresh proposal was put to Warsaw and Bucharest in the name of the British and French Governments: if they were ready to defend their independence, the West would assist them, though in Poland's case a promise to aid Rumania and a reciprocal guarantee of Britain and France were required.[28] Even this was held to be too slow in the face of fresh alarms, however; on the evening of the 30th Kennard conveyed to Beck Chamberlain's enquiry as to whether he would accept an interim and unilateral guarantee of his country pending negotiations.[29] In the time taken to smoke a cigarette, as he liked to say later, Beck agreed. Though Greenwood, Alexander and Dalton for the Labour Party attempted to persuade Chamberlain that no announcement should be made until Russia had been brought in, the decision was made. In the Commons on the 31st the Prime Minister inaugurated a fundamental change, on the surface at least, of British foreign policy: a wide and binding commitment would be undertaken in Eastern Europe. If Poland's independence were 'clearly threatened' during the period of consultations, and she resisted, Britain and France would 'feel themselves bound at once to lend her all support in their power'.[30] At Newcastle on the same day, Eden was able to declare happily that it was 'unadulterated nonsense' to suggest that there was dissension in Government ranks over foreign policy.

Beck visited London from the 4th to the 6th April and made the most of the favourable position in which he had been placed. In the face of Chamberlain's suggestions concerning Poland's need for military supplies from Russia he maintained his view that any closer association with Moscow would provoke war; nor would he go beyond a promise of discussions with Rumania to provide for their mutual security. Reassuringly, however, Beck also informed his listeners that no written German demands had been presented to Poland, airily remarking that he 'did not propose to trouble His Majesty's Government with the various phases through which the Danzig question might pass'. It was finally agreed that a permanent and reciprocal agreement would be drawn up in which France should join. War by the West on behalf of other European countries might be included as an act which would incur Polish obligations; in the light of Germany's past methods of subversion, a case of indirect aggression was also to be allowed for.[31] Meanwhile a communiqué was issued which announced the new, mutual basis of the forthcoming pact, and extended the interim guarantee. It seemed at last everyone knew where they stood.

The first reason why this was not so was that the West were not informed as to the exact state of German–Polish relations. They had, of course, anxiously watched tension growing in Danzig since Munich, with student chauvinism from both nationalities, and the Danzig Senate increasingly avowing its Nazi allegiance by enacting anti-Semitic and other measures. Britain in particular, as a member of the League's Committee of Three on Danzig, had anxiously consulted the High Commissioner, Professor Burckhardt, in attempts to avoid being involved and humiliated in what appeared to be an inevitable crisis. The Foreign Office had also received, as early as November 1938, 'reliable information to the effect that Hitler . . . has plans for dealing with the Polish question . . . [possibly] based on the application of the racial principle . . . [after which] Poland would cease to have any right to expect free access to the sea'.[32] Neither Britain nor France, however, knew exactly what had taken place during the comings and goings between Berlin and Warsaw since that time. They did know that the problem was taking on a complexity to rival that of Bohemia.

'Free and secure access to the sea' for a resurrected Poland had been one of the concrete proposals contained in Wilson's somewhat maligned Fourteen Points. History, geography and the Polish majority in what became known as the Corridor* suggested that Danzig should provide that access, and despite the development of Gdynia, the former port had remained vital to the economy and independent existence of the Polish state. Gdynia was incapable of handling the other half of that proportion of Poland's foreign trade — about 78 per cent of the total — which she had come to share with Danzig, and was within shelling distance of the latter. If Danzig were made part of the Reich, in fact, the two arms of the German pincers would be only about 40 kilometres apart.

Given such factors, and the preponderance of Germans in Danzig itself — of its 400,000 inhabitants only about 15,000 were Poles — it is difficult to see what better and simpler solution could have been arrived at in 1919 than the creation of a Free City under the auspices of the League. But the proximity of East Prussia and the deep-rooted antipathy of the two peoples were strong irritants, and though German was recognised as the official language of the city in 1922, customs and foreign policy remained Polish interests, while

* Quite rightly, the Poles insisted that the Province of Pomorze, peopled mainly by their own countrymen, should not be termed thus; not only the Germans among contemporaries adhered to the word 'Corridor', however, and having acknowledged the fault it is convenient to follow suit.

the League's High Commissioner was empowered to call in Polish troops if disorder or aggression arose. It was not surprising, then, that disputes between Danzig and Warsaw had been a regular feature of the Geneva scene until the unexpected German–Polish treaty in 1934. Thereafter, however, the growing nazification of the city had been condoned by the Polish Government — never a whole-hearted member of the League — in the interests of good relations with Berlin, a course prompted by fear of Russia and by the conviction that the West would not stand firm against Hitler.*

The Nazi line after 1934 had been a mixture of soothing words and probing hints of change. Thus when a German–Polish agreement for improving the lot of each other's minorities was signed in November 1937, Hitler assured Lipski that no alteration would be attempted over Danzig.[33] He had, however, talked two years before of 'an idea, premature today', of an extra-territorial road and rail strip across the Corridor to East Prussia, and proposals by Beck in 1937 for a bilateral agreement to respect the *status quo* in Danzig were rejected as entailing 'recognition of the pertinent provisions of the Versailles treaty'.[34] 'Some day', remarked Neurath to Lipski, the city would have to return to the Reich, and Beck's response when he heard of it had been encouragingly equivocal.[35]

Relations appeared to prosper in 1938. Further re-assurances were given Beck by the Fuehrer in person in January,[36] the former bridled not one whit over the *Anschluss* in March, and both hunted happily at the expense of Czechoslovakia in September. In November the notes which Hitler drew up as a basis for *Wehrmacht* talks with Italy presumed that the Polish position would be no more than

* In March 1933 Poland had landed soldiers opposite the port of Danzig in response to Hitler's denunciations of the Corridor, and been rebuked by the West in consequence; in 1936 Poland had offered to support France if she moved against the militarization of the Rhineland, and whether she had been sincere or not, the lesson seemed a clear one.

'doubtful' in the planned eventuality of a German attack on Britain and France.[37] By then, however, gentle but firm suggestions which were to result in European war less than a year later had begun to emerge from Berlin. A solution of the Corridor and Danzig issues would give Poland less to fight for and less to fight with when the Reich attacked westwards, and until around May 1939 Hitler expected to achieve this situation by diplomatic bargaining, backed up if necessary by the creation of tension and fear. On 24 October, therefore, Ribbentrop suggested to Lipski that 'it was time to arrive at a general settlement of all possible points of friction between Germany and Poland'. Danzig should revert to the Reich, which would also obtain that extra-territorial corridor across the Corridor; Poland in return would be granted port facilities, have her 1934 treaty with Germany extended, and enter the secure fold of the anti-Comintern pact. It was further hinted that if an understanding were reached, Hungary might be allowed to swallow those dangerous Ukrainians in Ruthenia and a common policy could be followed against Russia.[38]

Beck's reply, when it arrived over three weeks later, was unsatisfactory, adducing reasons of history, economics, symbolism and domestic politics why Danzig must remain untouched, and again proposing a bilateral treaty to replace the League Statute.[39] Hitler therefore bent his own powers of persuasion to the task, and on 5 January entertained the Polish Foreign Minister at Berchtesgaden. Admitting that he had been deflected from 'a liquidation of Czechoslovakia' in September, he hinted enticingly at a future 'political solution' of that problem by 'all countries interested'. He also asserted that 'Germany would under all circumstances be interested in maintaining a strong, nationalist Poland', and suggested that though Danzig must return to Germany politically it could 'remain with Poland economically'.

Doubtless Hitler would have strangled Poland eventually, but he may well have been sincere in his offer at the time. In this case, however, Beck stalled again: he would like time to think the matter over, for Polish opinion made the question 'extremely difficult'.[40] He was no more forthcoming the next day when Ribbentrop hinted at co-operation against Russia.[41] When Ribbentrop visited Warsaw three weeks later, Beck was ready to agree that 'Poland has aspirations directed towards the Soviet Ukraine and a connection with the Black Sea', but was still 'not optimistic' about Danzig.[42]

By the time of the Prague *coup* the need to apply pressure of some kind on Poland had become apparent, but Hitler was still cautious. One might suspect his assurances to Attolico on 20 March that he 'had to be careful' over Poland since 'if Britain intervened in a general conflict Poland might quite possibly be found among Germany's enemies',[43] but the same language appeared in a directive to the army five days later:

The Fuehrer *does not* wish to solve the Danzig question by force however. He does not wish to drive Poland into the arms of Britain by this. A possible military occupation of Danzig could be contemplated *only* if L[ipski] gave an indication that the Polish Government could not justify voluntary cession of Danzig to their own people and that a *fait accompli* would make a solution easier for them.[44]

On the 21st, too, Ribbentrop had talked to Lipski of the essential need 'to bring German–Polish policy onto the right lines', inviting Beck to Berlin, promising a guarantee of the Corridor in return for his previous demands, and speculating 'that in such circumstances it would be possible to deal with the Slovak question to the satisfaction of all'.[45]

Yet there was never any hint from Berlin that 'the right lines' could be any other than those of Germany's own choosing, and when relations deteriorated over Memel Hitler cancelled a telegram which had been drafted to Moltke in Warsaw again urging a settlement.[46] Moreover his directive of 25 March (the date is significant in view of some suggestions that Hitler was provoked into attacking Poland only by Britain's guarantee*) had clearly shown that his restraint was of that variety found remarkable by A. J. P. Taylor, for it stated that if in the near future 'especially favourable political preconditions' appeared, Poland could be dealt with and 'so beaten down' that it would be of no political account 'for the next few decades'. Germany's frontier could then be extended 'from the eastern border of East Prussia to the eastern tip of Silesia'.

The Polish reply to Ribbentrop's latest urgings was delivered by Lipski on the 26th and was unsatisfactory. It repeated Warsaw's desire for good relations and offered to facilitate German transit across the Corridor, but did not give way on Danzig or the extra-territorial issue; Ribbentrop therefore repeated his own suggestions, flung in a 25-year non-aggression and frontier treaty for good measure, and warned that a Polish violation of Danzig's sovereignty would constitute a *casus belli*.[47] In his subsequent memorandum for Hitler, however, he still thought that Poland 'would like to get off as cheaply as possible', and that her proposal 'might not represent the Polish Government's last word'. His recommendation that a waiting game be played was therefore repeated to the President of the Danzig Senate, Greiser, on the 29th: a 'sphinx-like attitude' must be adopted. As Weizsäcker told the German embassy in Warsaw, they must

---

* In his *Memoirs* (vol. ii, pp. 214, 217 and 255), Captain Liddell Hart describes the new guarantee as 'a provocative gesture' and 'manifest provocation', and quotes his contemporary judgement of its ratification on 25 August as 'inevitably adding fuel to the flames'. This seems misleading and somewhat questionable; when he heard the news of ratification on the 25th, for instance, Hitler's reaction was to pause rather than to go faster into his attack. This does not mean that I question Captain Liddell Hart's argument that to defend Czechoslovakia in 1938 was a better military proposition than was supporting Poland in 1939. But given Hitler's general intentions, Britain *had* to stand somewhere or accept a perilous subservience. And whatever the military or political wisdom of doing so over Danzig, the guarantee did help focus a new national awareness of the danger, as well as bringing nearer, perhaps, the essential downfall of the very men who had negotiated it.

not enter into any further material discussions on the German offer and the Polish counter offer. We must prevent Poland from throwing the ball back to us, and then manœuvring us into the position of appearing to have let a Polish offer go unheeded.[48]

But for the moment nothing more was forthcoming, even though on the 27th Ribbentrop upbraided Lipski over outrages against Germans in Poland, and regretted that relations were 'deteriorating sharply'.[49] Beck's reply to the threats over Danzig, while repeating his desire for a friendly solution, returned the compliment as to a *casus belli*. As his train waited at Berlin on April 2nd on his journey to London, he was approached by a protocol official and on Ribbentrop's instructions asked if he had any wishes to make known; looking fixedly at Lipski, Beck politely indicated that there was nothing.[50]

This did not mean that the Foreign Minister was committed to an anti-German course, however, though events and the intransigence under pressure of Polish public opinion[51] made it impossible for him to yield for the moment. Between himself and the West he had drawn a veil of reticence and understatement, to say the least, on the subject of Germany's demands,[52] and when the truth began to emerge in April Halifax was moved to observe that his opposite number had been 'less than frank'.[53] The Poles have shown 'a most remarkable disinclination to tell us the truth', commented a Foreign Office memorandum on May 4th; 'at the time of the announcement of our guarantee . . . we merely knew that . . . the German Government had communicated *desiderata* regarding the return of Danzig, a motor road across the Corridor, and co-operation against Russia. We had no knowledge of the so-called concessions which accompanied these *desiderata*'.[54]

Doubtless Beck wished to keep open as many alternative lines of policy as possible, whatever the growing opposition to his equivocation from within his own country. He was, after all, fond of quoting Rule 3 of his beloved horse artillery: 'Don't give the order to gallop until the last moment, for once you have given it you cannot change direction', and on 23 March the American Ambassador in Warsaw had described Polish policy as

steering a careful course through confused events, hoping that by strictly minding her own business and through adoption of precautionary military measures to meet a possible challenge of her own frontiers, she will not incur Germany's forceful attention.[55]

It is significant that Beck's reaction to the British note of 20 March had been to propose a bilateral agreement, but a secret one, and though during the uneasiness which followed Munich there had been a slight *détente* with the Soviet Union, the celebrated Pilsudski–Beck balancing act between Germany and Russia had always had a distinct leaning towards the former. Noël and Léger had good general grounds for suspecting that closer ties with Germany would not be entirely unacceptable, especially if the West were flirting with the Kremlin; according to the French Ambassador, Beck agreed to the British guarantee with mixed feelings,[56] and on 7 April the semi-official *Gazeta Polska* went out of its way to affirm that no rigid bloc had been formed. In May the Polish Under Secretary of State in the Foreign Ministry, Arciszewski, was still hinting to Moltke that Beck would like direct talks, but was under pressure from public opinion and military circles to maintain the link with the West unimpaired. He added that the Foreign Minister had hurled away in anger a sheaf of congratulatory telegrams which had arrived after a firm speech he had made on 5 May: 'Even today M. Beck is still at heart an adherent of the old policy'.[57]

Whatever his deviousness, Beck certainly remained confident. His belief early in March that Hitler would not deceive him, that they spoke 'as man to man and soldier to soldier', was not dispelled by Prague and Memel. He was still sure that 'to weaken Poland would be to play Russia's game', and that Hitler, who was at bottom 'a timid Austrian who would not risk war against determined and strong opponents', would 'never consent to pay such a price for the Free City'. The hope of balancing Germany with Italy had gone, but even if tension increased, he would manage things. 'It did not take me ten days to fall on my feet again', he boasted to Gafencu of Rumania with reference to Ribbentrop's demands and the British guarantee. 'The Prague business is not going to be repeated. Hitler has found someone to talk to.'[58]

If the Polish partner in the new guarantees was, in some quarters, not wholehearted, the same was true of the other two. Having rushed in to avert apparent disaster, both the British and French Governments were left to contemplate their handiwork with some uneasiness. The Franco-Polish alliance of 1921 already called for rapid mutual aid against aggression, but there were many in France who had come to feel that a dangerously rigid commitment was involved and who coupled a desire for flexibility with the assurance that Poland would be bound to fight anyhow if France were to be attacked. Gamelin and Weygand for the army were joined by Noël and Bonnet in this matter. Few staff talks had taken place between the allies, and good feeling was not increased by the behaviour of Warsaw during the Munich crisis or the increased anti-Semitism which followed. That autumn Noël, though warning against the danger of throwing Beck towards Berlin, advised that the 1921 treaty should be revised, and Bonnet's eager agreement was known in London.[59] But though the Foreign Minister thought he could see 'sufficient loopholes' in the treaty to shelter France from the risk of war,[60] Poland had not proved receptive to any ideas of change by the time the March crisis arrived.

Nor did fresh ties do much to increase the enthusiasm or

determination of France, for the swift British guarantee all too clearly relied upon French troops for its effectiveness; there were those in office who would privately have echoed Marcel Déat's forthcoming question: 'pourquoi mourir pour Dantzig?'. The drafting of a new military agreement and political protocol with Poland in May was the occasion of some confusion and suspicion at the time and much specious pleading afterwards,[61] and French promises of relieving assaults in the West meant little. General Ironside saw the military plans of both countries that summer: 'The French have lied to the Poles in saying that they are going to attack', he wrote. 'There is no idea of it.'[62]

Though public determination over Poland was greater in Britain than in France, there, too, there were second thoughts in high places. The pressure of altered circumstances had to struggle with echoes of Austen Chamberlain's aside in 1925, that 'for the Polish Corridor no British Government ever will or ever can risk the bones of a British grenadier'.[63] As recently as September 1937 Eden had apparently told Burckhardt that his country was disinterested in Danzig,[64] and Halifax had declared to the same listener in the following summer that 'Danzig and the Corridor were an absurdity . . . probably the most foolish provision of the Treaty of Versailles'.[65] Berlin had been informed on both occasions, and even in the 1939 *volte-face* could find some elements of comfort. 'No sir', Chamberlain replied to a questioner in the Commons on 30 March who asked if war materials were to be withheld from Germany,[66] and neither National Service nor a Ministry of Supply was announced as a concomitant of the guarantee. The weeks that followed did not produce ratification of the new agreement, but did witness Poland's depression and alarm at the failure of her mission in London to obtain economic aid adequate to offset the strain of having to remain semi-mobilised. For all its sound reasoning, the Treasury fed the Nazi propaganda

machine with jeers, while Ironside returned from a special
mission to Poland to find that in military circles, too, there
was little interest in the new ally.[67]

More ominous still for the opponents of appeasement was
the reaction to the news of the guarantee in some quarters of
the British press. On the evening of 31 March Reuters
suggested that to guarantee Polish independence did not
mean that concessions over Danzig and the Corridor were
out of the question. 'Independence' was not the same as
'integrity' echoed *The Times* the next day, adding: 'The
new obligation does not bind Great Britain to defend every
inch of the present frontiers of Poland.'* With Munich in
mind it was extremely sinister, as Churchill was quick to
point out, and doubly so for those few who knew that
Dawson had been seen outside Chamberlain's room at the
House of Commons on the evening of the 31st.[68] Yet the
views expressed were not long without support. On 3 April,
for instance, *The Times* published a letter from Arthur
Bryant hailing the 'wisdom' of what it had written.

In fact, though the motive of Chamberlain and his closer
associates in undertaking a guarantee of Poland seemed
plain enough on the surface — Hitler must be stopped at all
costs — the matter was more complex, as Halifax's earlier
musings to Kennedy suggest.† There was the pressure of
public rage and the need to provide a positive answer to the
anti-Munich scorn which so worried Henderson; there was
the urge, in a world gone mad, to re-state in forceful terms
the moral basis of British foreign policy;‡ and there was the
bewildering and urgent impetus of the events, pleas and
rumours themselves. Was there also, one wonders, the
unconscious need to save oneself from another sell-out? Did

---

* Sir Alexander Cadogan expounded the opposite case in most
forthright terms to his diplomatic visitors; see *F.R.U.S.* (1939), i, pp. 105-6
(Kennedy to Hull, 31 Mar.).   † See above, pp. 93-4.

‡ See above, pp. 12-13. Professor Medlicott in *The Coming of War in 1939*
(1963) suggests that a more sanguine view of Britain's military strength
was also an important factor.

that joyless band sign the pledge, as it were, in part to erect a barrier between themselves and the tempting memories of past intoxications?

At the time the guarantee was criticised mainly on the grounds of its leaving the decision of peace or war for Britain in the hands of another country. In fact, given Hitler's general intentions it was the timing rather than the likelihood of British involvement in war which was affected, and in the event Warsaw behaved with extraordinary coolness and responsibility under pressure. Far more serious was the effect of the pledge to Poland, together with that to Rumania which followed, on the Soviet Union. Without Soviet participation, Western assistance in Eastern Europe could scarcely amount to much in practice. Yet Stalin was now protected from German attack by a belt of guaranteed intervening territory; not having had to commit himself beforehand, he could therefore watch the development of events and name his own terms, or at least sell himself to the highest bidder. Conversely, the new situation made a Soviet understanding all the more attractive to Germany. 'Aprés avoir poussé Staline vers Hitler à Munich', wrote Coulondre later, 'c'est maintenant Hitler que l'on pousse vers Staline.'[69]

The guarantee of Rumania came about in muddled fashion considering the original alarm over that rich prize, and the aim of bringing Poland into it was never achieved.* When it was suggested to Chamberlain that public sentiment and military circles in Poland were so much more anti-German than Beck that the latter could be pushed harder and more openly in this matter, the Prime Minister merely confessed: 'I don't know much about conditions in Poland'.[70] It was an apt comment on a great deal of his foreign policy.

---

* Poland and Rumania were already tied by a treaty which sprang from the Soviet danger. Rumania now interpreted it as covering the case of German aggression as well, and Beck was content to offer vague assent in order to avoid anything more definite which would offend not only Germany but his Hungarian friends as well. See *D.B.F.P.* v, no. 278.

Rome rather than Berlin impelled the new move. Alarms over fresh Italian assaults had followed immediately on the heels of the Albanian episode, with Léger again prompting British involvement as hard as possible by passing on rumours of a possible *coup* against Gibraltar '*par acquit de conscience*'.[71] At midnight on the same day, 8 April, the Greek Premier summoned the British Ambassador in Athens to say that he had reliable information of an attack on Corfu planned for the 10th to 12th, and asked if an indication of British intentions might be forthcoming.[72] Though the news was not accurate, an attack upon Greece was indeed one of the schemes being revolved in Mussolini's mind during this period, at times taking second place to the possibility of disrupting Yugoslavia from within and annexing Croatia.[73]

A Mediterranean threat was bound to produce a more instinctive and immediate response in London than any confused rumblings in Central or Eastern Europe could do. It spoke with a nineteenth-century tongue even the 'inner Cabinet' could understand. Though Perth protested that, since Mussolini had said as much, no attack could be contemplated,[74] Halifax had already asked France whether she would join in giving a guarantee to Greece; anti-Italian firmness from London had long been Daladier's aim, and he agreed immediately, remarking that they 'had to deal with gangsters who merely sought to throw dust in their eyes'.[75] The Greek issue, in fact, now took precedence over Rumania in the view of the British Government, even though the Secretary-General of the Rumanian Ministry for Foreign Affairs arrived in London on the 10th to urge that there should be an early declaration of willingness to help defend his country. M. Cretzianu insisted that to seek Russian assistance before war broke out would be political suicide for any Bucharest administration, and stressed the need for a guarantee in order to strengthen the position of his Foreign Minister, Gafencu, before the latter visited Berlin on the

18th,* but Halifax was not encouraging. The participation of the West would in his opinion have to await the successful outcome of talks between Rumania and Poland, and the Foreign Minister did not comment when his visitor expressed anxiety as to the interpretation of Polish 'independence' in the light of her existing frontiers.[76]

Daladier now thrust London forward, however. On the 12th Halifax was handed the text of a declaration which the French Premier intended making on the afternoon of the following day, announcing a guarantee of Rumania as well as Greece. In vain did Halifax protest that Rumania was in no immediate danger and that 'if we now give her an unconditional guarantee ... we throw away the lever which we have for bringing Poland and Turkey into a wider arrangement'.[77] Phipps could only report on the morning of the 13th that Daladier 'feels that this is the best and indeed the only way of averting a general conflagration. If this be not done at once Germany will present an ultimatum to Rumania *within a few hours* and we shall again be presented with a *fait accompli*'.[78] Phipps was told to urge delay on Daladier and to report before the Cabinet met in London at 11 a.m., but the Admiralty, concerned for their oil supplies, were also pressing for a guarantee, and Attlee and Dalton added the promptings of the Labour party in a private talk with Chamberlain that morning.[79] At 1.35 p.m. a telegram to Paris announced that 'in the interests of solidarity' Britain would conform.[80] That afternoon Chamberlain informed the House that

in the event of any action being taken which clearly threatened the independence of Greece or Rumania and which the Greek or Rumanian Government respectively considered it vital to resist with their national forces, His

---

* Gafencu was having to be all things to all men, assuring Berlin that he was endeavouring to avoid 'being involved in the British encirclement policy' and, later, that he had been unable to refuse the unilateral guarantee thrust upon him. *D.G.F.P.* vi, nos. 180 and 195.

Majesty's Government would feel themselves bound at once to lend . . . all the support in their power.[81]

In the new situation which had arisen Ankara appeared to fill the role of Warsaw further north. To Halifax Turkey was 'the key to Balkan solidarity',[82] the best agency, for instance, for persuading Rumania to reach an accommodation with Bulgaria over the Dobrudja which would enable the latter to be drawn away from the Axis and into the Balkan Entente. In return the apparent threat to Greece made Turkey more receptive, and on 12 April Halifax followed up enquiries as to whether Ankara would therefore participate in the forthcoming guarantee by declaring that 'in principle' Britain was ready for a separate, reciprocal pledge with Turkey against Italian depredations.[83] On the 13th he added that a guarantee against Germany, too, 'would naturally follow' if Turkey again reciprocated and joined in the new obligation to Rumania. Though the reply indicated that in a purely Western conflict Turkey would remain neutral, co-operation seemed likely regarding South-eastern spheres,[84] and on 12 May a joint communiqué bound the two countries to support one another, pending a final agreement, 'in the event of an act of aggression leading to war in the Mediterranean area'.

The momentum of negotiations was not sustained, however. Although von Papen — now German Ambassador to Turkey — worked in vain to reduce disturbing Italian bellicosity in the area,[85] the passing of the immediate crisis allowed other, awkward considerations to come into play. Rumania and Yugoslavia, the latter struggling with her Serb/Croat negotiations and both apprehensively watching the reactions of the Axis and Hungary, urged that it would be fatal if the new agreement were to cover the Balkans as well as the Mediterranean, and Bulgarian intransigence increased rather than diminished. Turkey's own anxiety not to get out of step with Moscow also retarded matters, and her demands for British arms supplies and financial aid to offset the repercussions of a break with Germany could not easily be met.[86] Though France reached an agreement with Ankara whereby she ceded the Sandjak of Alexandretta in the interests of a Mediterranean understanding, the machinery of British diplomatic and economic control seems to have been unable to stand the unnatural burden of negotiations and commitments which accumulated during the spring and summer of 1939. As August opened with Halifax's draft of an agreement still awaited,[87] the Ambassador in Ankara reported 'a feeling of disappointment and disillusionment which is growing and harmful'. Matters had not been settled when the storm burst towards the end of the month.

The main embarrassment in the affair had, of course, been the apparent contradiction it raised with Chamberlain's overriding desire to stay close to Mussolini. Even while the new guarantees and negotiations were emerging, Halifax had assured the Italian chargé d'affaires that he would try to soothe the British public's hostility and that the hard words that would have to be used should not be taken too seriously.[88] Moreover Daladier was soon being harassed again to come to terms with the Duce, and after Halifax had failed to move the defendant in May from his stubborn reiteration that 'Italy was now in Germany's hands',[89] Chamberlain tried a personal letter in July. Again, however, the plea that 'Mussolini was the one man who could influence Hitler to keep the peace' met with the insistence that only Anglo-French determination and solidarity would split the dictators.[90]

It is interesting to note that in taking this line London was not now following the advice of her Ambassador in Rome. On the fear that French participation in the Turkish agreement would alienate Italy, Loraine had commented in May that good relations could not 'be obtained by minor concessions — which are unlikely to be requited — in matters of major interest to our own policy'.[91] And when, after the signing of the Pact of Steel, Mussolini had the effrontery to demand to know whether the Anglo-Italian agreement had not been negated by Britain, Sir Percy noted:

Whether the policy of complete identification with Germany is that of Signor Mussolini interpreted by Ciano or that suggested by Ciano to Mussolini is henceforth immaterial....
I fear the die is cast and that the only argument is the visibility of overwhelming physical strength.[92]

Perhaps the Prime Minister wished Perth back at his old post as he read such irritating advice.

Chamberlain and those near him still did not see that the man who mattered now was not Mussolini but Stalin. Here, as with Hitler, one's questions must ultimately disappear into the impenetrable recesses of a dark mind — in this case with no secret documents to make the approach easier — but the brooding search for advantage can be sensed in outline, if not plotted in detail.

Munich had appeared to confirm all the fears and misgivings which for Litvinov had accompanied an advocacy of collective security against the dictators.[93] 'The policy of Litvinov has suffered a complete fiasco', wrote the Counsellor of the German Embassy in Moscow. 'There is no escaping the idea that the Soviet Union will have to reconsider her foreign policy [and] ... a more positive attitude ... towards Germany might be possible....'[94] 'The real point', declared Molotov on 6 November 1938, 'is that ... the "democratic" States, although they deplore the "excesses" of the Fascist States ... have a still greater fear of the working-class movement ... and think that fascism is a good antidote....'[95] To Coulondre in Moscow, Litvinov's Assistant Commissar, Potemkin, burst out: 'My poor friend, what have you done? As for us I do not see any other outcome than a fourth partition of Poland'.[96]

Stalin still preferred to wait, but in a speech to the Eighteenth Communist Party Congress on 10 March he made the trend of his thoughts clear enough. Though he declared that the Soviet Union would support victims of aggression, he added that she would not 'be drawn into conflicts of warmongers who are accustomed to have others pull the chestnuts out of the fire for them', and accused the West of being 'eager not to hinder the aggressors . . . not to hinder Germany, say . . . from embroiling herself in a war with the Soviet Union'.[97] Despite the new guarantees which followed, there were plenty of signs that these were half-hearted; on 27 March the German Embassy in Moscow was still able to report 'unusual mistrust as to the real intentions of the Western Powers towards the Soviet Union'.[98] Thus, in the unexpectedly advantageous position in which he found himself, shielded by Poland and Rumania yet sought after by both sides as tension over Danzig increased, Stalin could push his price as high as he liked. In particular, that further element of cover which was needed for Leningrad would be sought with the utmost determination through an extension of territory into the Baltic States. Since the West could only offer the risk of war without gain as opposed to Hitler's gain without war, the presence, eventually, of any sincerity on the Soviet side in their negotiations with the former must be open to question. The Italian Ambassador in Moscow, for one, was convinced by June that successive and excessive Soviet demands were being put forward in the hope that they would prove unacceptable.[99]

It was not surprising, then, that the Western negotiators found themselves having to endure 'a humiliating experience'. 'Time after time', wrote one of them in July, 'we have taken up a position and a week later have abandoned it. . . . Our need for an agreement is more immediate than theirs. . . . The Russians have . . . at least two alternative policies, namely . . . isolation [or] . . . accommodation with Germany . . . and have good reason to assume that we shall not dare to face a final breakdown in negotiations.'[100]

Yet the same writer observed that 'we should perhaps have been wiser to pay the Soviet price at an earlier stage', and the tardiness to which he referred reflected, in Britain's case especially, an underlying reluctance and under-estimation on the part of the West. It was not that warnings were lacking to point the grim alternative. From Moscow Coulondre had indicated the strong possibility of a Russo-German *rapprochement*, and he was producing more urgent evidence to the same effect from Berlin in May, June and July.[101] The same kind of rumour was passed on by Henderson to London,[102] as were the direct warnings of Germans like Goerdeler and Erich and Theo Kordt. Even Goering gave out clear hints at times.[103]

Many, however, would still have agreed with the Foreign Office minute which was written on one of the warning telegrams in May: 'Inherently improbable',[104] while others who accepted the possibility were the readier to do so since they concurred with Henderson that 'a settlement with Germany and Italy will be easier . . . if the Russian negotiations end in some quite anodyne agreement'. Fear of a war which did not involve Russia and left Soviet power supreme at its conclusion was balanced by the alarming thought of a commitment which might place a Soviet finger on the trigger. The half-heartedness displayed by Chamberlain in the Commons and in his private correspondence harmonised with the considered opinions of some professional advisers, and in May a Foreign Office memorandum on the possibility of alliance weighed as heavily on the 'disadvantages' as on the 'advantages' side. 'There are indications', it ran, 'that the real Soviet policy is to get us involved and then to try to keep out herself.' It went on to stress the likelihood of a pact infuriating Germany and alienating Italy, Japan, Spain, Portugal, Finland, Yugoslavia and the Vatican, the proof it would seem to offer for the German cry of 'encirclement', and the danger of splitting British opinion if a war had to be fought purely to defend Russia. Besides, it added, 'it is unlikely that on land [Soviet] military effort could be of very much effect'.[105] With such considerations being allowed to outweigh the urgency and peril of the moment, and remembering the West's record at Munich and after, there is an indirect sense, already suggested by Coulondre, in which the British Government in particular contributed to the Nazi-Soviet pact.* This in no way detracts, of course, from the utter cynicism and barbarity of the signatories, and should not cause the ultimate fate of Eastern Poland, the Baltic States and Bessarabia to be forgotten.

After the false start occasioned by the British rejection of a conference and Poland's refusal to be associated with Russia in a declaration of resolve, negotiations had begun again on 14 April. On that day Maisky indicated Soviet willingness to join in assistance to Rumania, while Halifax despatched to Moscow the suggestion that 'a positive declaration' in the same sense might be made as regards all Russia's neighbours.[106] Though Litvinov returned a pointed question as to what practical measures Britain herself envisaged taking, he was ready with a counter-proposal; it was to begin a period of complex manœuvring which must be seen against the background of rising tension over Danzig and the secret Russo-German negotiations which will be described later.

---

* Though France sought a pact with the Soviet Union more eagerly than Britain, Daladier was also doubtful of the political and military reliability of Moscow; according to Léger, Bonnet, too, like Sir Eric Phipps, was personally cool; see F.R.U.S. (1939), i, pp. 29–31 and 248–51. The British mixture of scepticism and casualness was conveyed to Washington in reports by Kennedy on 6 and 17 Apr. After seeing Halifax on the 6th, he wrote: 'The general feeling is that Russia cannot be of any help at all outside her own borders. They are going to try and go along with them, but are not very hopeful of any results.' On the 17th Kennedy saw Chamberlain who 'felt he could make a deal with Russia at any time, but was delaying until he got the Balkan situation straightened away, because . . . to bring Russia in before the Balkan deals were all completed might cause trouble'. Ibid., pp. 113–14 and 139–40.

For the sake of clarity, the frustrating process as seen from the West may be divided into six stages:

1. *17 April to 14 May.* Litvinov's proposal of the 17th was for an alliance between Britain, France and the Soviet Union in which they would guarantee to assist against European aggression each other and the 'Eastern European States situated between the Baltic and Black Seas and bordering on the U.S.S.R.'. The allies were to sign an agreement on the details of military aid at the same time as the political document, and were to agree not to conclude a separate peace without the others' consent; the Polish-Rumanian treaty was to be declared to be operative in cases of aggression from any quarter, or to be revoked as directed against Russia alone.[107] The document breathed Soviet suspicions that the West would never act militarily to check Hitler, or would use Russia then leave her in the lurch, and the three-week delay before an answer was forthcoming may have been decisive in Stalin's mind. The tour of goodwill and reassurance undertaken by Potemkin in Eastern and South-eastern Europe in the interval may have marked a last, desperate effort by Litvinov to get his policy through.[108] The West had still not replied, however, when on 3 May it was announced that Molotov had taken Litvinov's place.

London had meanwhile been twisting and turning to avoid offending the susceptibilities of Poland and Rumania and to avoid a thoroughness of commitment to Russia which would have been anathema to those in power.[109] Paris on the other hand, though agreeing that Poland could not be named as being under Soviet protection and insisting that the latter should guarantee the states on Germany's Western flank, was far more anxious for the arrival of the big battalions to deter the lunatic in Berlin. Bonnet not only urged that there must be a triple alliance, but 'in the heat of the conversation' showed his suggestions to the Soviet Ambassador,[110] and with obvious dissension in the Western camp Soviet intransigence was further ensured. Sir William

Seeds, the British Ambassador in Moscow, fumed at such a 'gross and deliberate error of tactics or . . . foolish amateurish-ness of a politician',[111] for when he finally presented Molotov with the British reply on 8 May he was subjected to an uncomfortable and 'relentless cross examination' which included questions on the discrepancy of French and British views. His brief was a thin one, anyway, for it admitted that the Soviet proposal was 'logically complete', arguing only that it 'took too little account of practical difficulties and would require too long a time for its negotiation'. 'The time was not yet ripe', it added, for so 'comprehensive' a measure; the most it could suggest was that the Russian offer of willingness to help East European states might be made contingent upon prior Western action. Ominously, Molotov let fall the cryptic observation that Soviet policy 'was liable to be altered if other states changed theirs'.[112] On 14 May the British proposals were rejected as not covering, and indeed being likely to provoke, an attack on the U.S.S.R.; the original Soviet terms were repeated, with the addition of Latvia, Estonia and Finland by name among those states which had to be guaranteed.[113]

2. *14 May to 31 May*. As Churchill, Lloyd George and the Labour Party led a growing clamour in the Commons for the speedy conclusion of an alliance,[114] as there arrived further promptings from France[115] and an offer from Eden to go to Moscow to clinch matters in place of the reluctant Halifax,[116] the Government sought unhappily for a fresh solution. Maisky was no more than a puppet, of course, and encouraging talks he had with Vansittart in London and with British delegates at Geneva[117] meant no more than Chamberlain's assurance in the Commons on the 24th that an agreement was in sight. Though a new British draft was prepared whereby mutual guarantees would operate in the case of direct attack or following aid for another state which had asked for help, Halifax told Daladier on the 20th that 'it was unlikely that His Majesty's Government would be

able to accept such a draft', and that an alliance 'might well provoke Germany to violent action' as well as 'divide opinion in Britain'. The exasperated Frenchman, on the other hand, found the document 'quite acceptable', and 'could not understand Britain's difficulties'.[118] Even Beck had only minor changes to suggest, though the Rumanian position remained as distant and non-commital as before.[119]

The feebleness of the British approach was revealed to Ambassador Kennedy when Halifax returned from Geneva a few days later. The Foreign Secretary privately passed on his decision that the Russian terms would have to be accepted; 'but', reported Kennedy, *'in order that the humiliation will not be too great in having to step down from their original plan and accept the Russians' plan*, they have decided to put it under the cloak of the League platform of anti-aggression and bring in Poland and Turkey and all the rest under the same canopy'.[120]

On 27 May, therefore, Molotov was offered a fresh Western (meaning British) suggestion. A tripartite pact was conceded to cover direct attack, war in fulfilment of existing pledges, or war when responding to a request for aid from a state whose neutrality was threatened. The last category was intended to cover 'e.g. the Baltic States, Holland and Switzerland'; like Poland and Rumania they were to be reassured by a clause whereby assistance would be undertaken 'without prejudice to the rights and position of other Powers'. Action was also to be declared to be 'in accordance with the principles of Article 16, paragraphs 1 and 2, of the Covenant of the League of Nations',* because, said Halifax with gay invention, British public opinion would want the League connected with the undertaking in some way or other.[121] Molotov remained frosty. 'My words', wrote Seeds,

---

* The paragraphs concerned were anodyne generalisations and condemnatory steps against aggression; para. 3 of Art. 16 and Art.17, which would have invoked the frightening prospect of fellow members having to grant a passage for troops, etc., were deliberately left aside.

'seemed not to be heard or understood, although . . . the interpretation was excellent',[122] and the reference to the League was particularly criticised as involving the interminable delays of Geneva.

On the 29th, moreover, Molotov insisted that for the sake of security some states would *have* to be guaranteed, if necessary against their wishes, and that a military agreement must accompany the political one in order to avoid another 'paper delusion' like the Franco-Soviet pact.[123] He repeated his demands in a speech on the 31st. Threateningly, he added that commercial negotiations with Berlin might soon be reopened,[124] though experienced observers like Seeds and the former American Ambassador in Moscow, William Bullitt, still felt that a yielding response would only raise the price all the quicker.[125]

3. *2 June to 22 June.* The Soviet position was restated with additions in a note of 2 June.[126] It demanded that there should be no League of Nations reference and no clause safeguarding the rights of other states, while eight countries were to be guaranteed by name whether they liked it or not: Belgium, Greece, Turkey, Rumania, Poland, Latvia, Estonia and Finland. France was quick to point out the omission of Holland and Switzerland from this list, and Poland and the three Baltic states insisted that they should not be mentioned; Latvian and Estonian non-aggression pacts with Germany on 7 June underlined the possibility of their being pushed into the other camp altogether.

Wearily, therefore, London produced another draft, the caution of which was calculated in French eyes to fill the Russians with 'the darkest suspicions'.[127] As usual, however, Paris had to take second place, and it was substantially the British contribution which Seeds, his French colleague M. Naggiar, and the newly arrived Foreign Office expert, William Strang, put to Molotov on the 15th. Consultations were proposed should a threat to the independence or neutrality of another state involve also the security of one of the signatories, but the principles of the League were still mentioned, even if its procedure was not to be involved. The 'without prejudice' clause was also inserted again, though Seeds was told it could be dropped under pressure, and the 'no separate peace' pledge was still missing.[128] Why, one wonders, was the League reference still to be insisted upon, and was it not too late to include as a bargaining tactic items which were recognised as dispensable? Should not someone more senior than Strang have been despatched on a mission where much 'face' and publicity were involved? And as the French asked, what conclusion would the West have drawn if they themselves had proposed a 'no separate peace' clause and had it refused? The probable insincerity of the other side does not exempt the British Government from criticism over its handling of the issue. Its too little and too late advances remind one of the commitment of troops to the Dardanelles enterprise twenty-four years before.

As it was, secret German advances were improving the Soviet position daily, and on 16 June Molotov insisted that unless the Baltic states were included Russia would not help where Western obligations were concerned.[129] He was no more satisfied on the 21st when he was offered a rush of mainly French-inspired concessions which hinted or promised to give way over the League, no separate peace, and the reserved rights of other states, whilst suggesting mutual aid in the case of 'aggression . . . which, being directed against another European State, thereby constituted a menace to the security of one of [the three signatories]'.[130] With some justification, Halifax was 'bewildered' when the demand for the naming of the eight countries was repeated. Had the Soviet Union been sincere at this point, they had been given, though grudgingly, adequate satisfaction. Even Maisky — the gloss of his memoirs years away — could offer only one, prophetic explanation: perhaps the published list was necessary, he said, to cover 'a sort of Monroe doctrine in Eastern Europe'.[131]

4. *27 June to 17 July.* Again the West gave ground. Despite a scornful article in *Pravda* on 29 June by Zhdanov, a member of the Politburo, and the reiterated opposition of Finland and Holland to being involved in any guarantees, fresh proposals drawn up on the 27th were presented in Moscow on 1 July. A list could be published, or preferably added in a secret protocol, if it included Holland and Switzerland, and in that case mutual aid would be rendered over 'another European State whose independence or neutrality the contracting country concerned felt obliged to defend against aggression'.[132] Molotov's negative, barely sweetened by the acceptance of an unpublished list, refused on the thinnest of grounds an increase on eight; it also demanded that indirect aggression must be included to cover Hácha-like episodes, being defined as 'an internal coup d'état or a reversal of policy in the interests of the aggressor'.[133] The West was invited, in other words, to draw a curtain of legality over Soviet expansion (defensive preparedness, Moscow might have termed it) in Eastern Europe.

On 8 and 9 July, Seeds delivered what Halifax described as 'the limit of British concessions'. The omission of Holland, Switzerland and Luxemburg would be accepted, as would the words 'indirect aggression' in the secret protocol; this would only cover, however, 'action accepted by the State in question *under threat of force* by another Power and involving the abandonment by it of its independence or neutrality'.[134] To this, Molotov replied that cases not involving a threat of force must be covered, that the word 'indirect' must be published, and that a military agreement must be signed with the political one.[135] Since by now the neutral states of Eastern Europe were much alarmed, Halifax in return, reverting to his own definition of 'indirect', asked that it should be published, and though Seeds announced on the 17th that technical talks could begin at once he also conveyed the observation that 'Britain's patience was well-nigh exhausted'. Molotov merely repeated his previous stipulations.[136]

5. *17 July to 27 July.* Only despair over Danzig and the urgings of the French kept things alive a little longer, though Stalin himself was still not quite in a position to cut loose altogether. In response to the pleas of Bonnet, London agreed to simultaneous military and political agreements, though there could be no surrender over an interpretation of indirect aggression which, said Halifax, amounted to 'naked, immoral interference' in the internal affairs of other states.* Even here, firmness was impaired by French press leaks which hinted at their own readiness to accept Russia's definition, an attitude M. Naggiar scarcely concealed in Moscow.[137] Reluctantly, Britain then agreed to the Soviet demand that military talks should begin immediately, before the indirect aggression issue had been settled. Molotov would still not sign a joint statement on progress, however. On the 27th he found that Halifax's draft gave 'too optimistic an impression'.[138]

6. *12 August to 21 August.* Despite fresh storms in the Commons on 31 July, a sense of urgency now seemed to leave the British Government, though not the French. For logically sound reasons Strang was recalled as no longer being needed, an invitation to Moscow to participate in trade talks was delayed since the August holidays must come first, and a military mission of gallantry rather than renown was despatched to Russia by the slowest route possible. In London the *Wehrmacht* attachés observed 'a surprising scepticism in British military circles about the forthcoming [Soviet] talks', and got the impression that they were to be conducted 'mainly to obtain for once a picture of the real

* Students of post-war politics may not be surprised at an honest indiscretion by Mr. R. A. Butler in the Commons on 31 July which caused trouble in Moscow. The Under Secretary clearly hinted that the U.S.S.R. wished to 'encroach on the independence of the Baltic States', but that Britain had refused. *Hansard*, 5th series, vol. 350 (House of Commons), cols. 2094–2100.

fighting strength of the Soviet Army'.[139] In complete contrast to those of his French colleague, in fact, Admiral Ernle-Erle-Drax's instructions read: 'Until such time as the political agreement is concluded, the Delegation should go very slowly with the conversations'.[140] Only on 15 August were these orders to be reversed by Halifax, and Soviet sabotage made the change of academic interest only.

At the first military meeting on the 12th, the British delegation alone could produce no written credentials as to their powers to negotiate. When this embarrassment had been overcome two days later, Voroshilov in effect demolished the proceedings by asking, reasonably enough, whether the West had obtained the consent of Poland and Rumania for Soviet troops to cross their territories in time of war, and on the 17th he announced that there must be an adjournment until an acceptance was forthcoming. Though neither Halifax's nor Seed's telegrams at this time show any knowledge of how close disaster was upon them,* a barrage of urgent British and French demands fell upon Warsaw. Bonnet even authorised General Doumenc in Moscow to give Poland's agreement in advance, in the common interest. But Beck and the Polish Army were alike unmoved. 'Avec les Allemands, nous risquons de perdre notre liberté. Avec les Russes nous perdons notre âme.'[141]

The military talks were adjourned *sine die* after no further progress had been made on 21 August. That evening, it was announced that Ribbentrop would be arriving on the 23rd to sign a German–Soviet non-aggression pact. The West was left to seek security in its own resolution.

* A warning of the forthcoming Russo-German agreement was sent by the British Ambassador in Washington on the evening of 17 August. For some reason his telegram was not received by the Foreign Office until the 22nd, as were the details by air-mail. *D.B.F.P.* vii, no. 41.

[1] *D.B.F.P.* iii, no. 285.

[2] Coulondre, p. 259.

[3] *D.G.F.P.* vi, no. 32.

[4] Ibid., no. 51.

[5] Ibid., nos. 28 and 65.

[6] See ibid., v, nos. 293 and 306; and vi, nos. 30, 42, 47, 78 and 131. Also *F.R.U.S.* (1939), i, pp. 79-80.

[7] Bonnet, vol. 2, p. 155.

[8] *D.B.F.P.* iv, no. 405.

[9] *F.R.U.S.* (1939), i, pp. 83-5 (Bullitt to Hull, 21 Mar.).

[10] See Noël, p. 283.

[11] Feiling, p. 401.

[12] *D.B.F.P.* iv, no. 446.

[13] Ibid., nos. 457 and 472.

[14] Ibid., no. 467. Cf. Bonnet, vol. 2, p. 157.

[15] See *F.R.U.S.* (1939), i, pp. 90-2 (Kennedy to Hull, 22 Mar.).

[16] *D.B.F.P.* iv, nos. 458 and 484.

[17] Bonnet, vol. 2, pp. 168-70.

[18] *D.B.F.P.* iv, no. 522.

[19] See ibid., v, no. 12 for reports from the military and air attachés in Warsaw.

[20] Templewood, p. 344. Cf. Liddell Hart, ii, p. 221.

[21] *D.B.F.P.* iv, nos. 485 and 518.

[22] See ibid., no. 523, and *Livre Jaune Français*, nos. 84 and 86.

[23] *The Times*, 24 Mar. 1939.

[24] *D.B.F.P.* iv, no. 565.

[25] See ibid., no. 566; Wheeler-Bennett, *The Nemesis of Power*, pp. 436-7; Dalton, p. 237; Colvin, pp. 298-311.

[26] *D.B.F.P.* iv, App. v.

[27] Ibid., App. iv.

[28] Ibid., nos. 538 and 561.

[29] Ibid., no. 568, and *Polish White Book*, no. 68.

[30] *Hansard*, 5th series, vol. 345 (House of Commons), col. 2415. For the brusque treatment of the U.S.S.R. which was involved, see Dalton, and I. Maisky, *Who Helped Hitler?* (1964), pp. 107-8.

[31] *D.B.F.P.* v, nos. 1, 2, 10 and 16.

[32] Ibid., iii, no. 301; (Strang to Kennard).

[33] *D.G.F.P.* v, no. 19.

[34] See ibid., nos. 1 and 7.

[35] See ibid., nos. 13 and 16.

[36] Ibid., no. 29.

[37] Ibid., iv, no. 411.

[38] Ibid., v, no. 81, and *Polish White Book*, no. 44.

[39] *D.G.F.P.* v, no. 101.

[40] Ibid., no. 119.

[41] Ibid., no. 120.

[42] Ibid., no. 126; Beck's remark about the Ukraine betrayed vanity and unrealism if true; he was capable of both, though the record of the conversation is Ribbentrop's and therefore suspect.

[43] Ibid., vi, no. 52.

[44] Ibid., no. 99.

[45] Ibid., no. 61.

[46] Ibid., nos. 73 and 88.

[47] Ibid., no. 101, and *Polish White Book*, no. 63.

[48] *D.G.F.P.* vi, no. 159.

[49] Ibid., no. 108.

[50] Ibid., no. 148.

[51] For the comments of the British Ambassador on Polish public opinion see *D.B.F.P.* iv, no. 605, and v, no. 266; at times in Poland there was open hostility to Beck as pro-German.

[52] See Noël, pp. 269, 288 and 319, and *D.B.F.P.* v, no. 46.

[53] *D.B.F.P.* v, no. 268.

[54] Ibid., no. 361.

[55] *F.R.U.S.* (1939), i, pp. 96–7.

[56] Noël, p. 333.

[57] *D.G.F.P.* vi, no. 429. For the supporting opinion of the Italian Ambassador in Warsaw, see *D.D.I.* xii, no. 43.

[58] G. Gafencu, *The Last Days of Europe* (1947), pp. 37, 42 and 44, and *F.R.U.S.* (1939), i, pp. 117–9 (Bullitt to Hull).

[59] Cf. Noël, pp. 247–57; Bonnet, vol. 2, pp. 138–44; and *D.B.F.P.* iii, footnote to no. 407.

[60] Noël, p. 259.

[61] Cf. Bonnet, vol. 2, pp. 222–4; L. B. Namier, *Europe in Decay*, pp. 70–2; Beck, pp. 198 and 345; *F.R.U.S.* (1939), i, pp. 189–91 (Bullitt to Hull).

[62] *The Ironside Diaries*, entry for 26 July 1939; cf. Churchill, op. cit., pp. 343–4 and 357.

[63] Quoted in F. P. Walters, *A History of the League of Nations* (1952), vol. 1, p. 284.

[64] *D.G.F.P.* v, nos. 4 and 5.

[65] Ibid., no. 37.

[66] *Hansard*, 5th series, vol. 345 (House of Commons), col. 2216.

[67] *The Ironside Diaries*; entry for 24 July 1939. Cf. *D.B.F.P.* vi, nos. 498 and 492 for the Treasury's role and its effect as seen from Warsaw, and Beck, pp. 210–11.

[68] See Dalton, p. 244.

[69] Coulondre, p. 264.

[70] Dalton, p. 248.

[71] *D.B.F.P.* v, no. 96.

[72] Ibid., no. 97.

[73] See *Ciano's Diary, 1939–1943*, entries for 21 Apr. 1939, 12 May 1939, and 26 May 1939.

[74] See *D.B.F.P.* v, no. 132.

[75] Ibid., no. 103.

[76] Ibid., no. 37.

[77] Ibid., nos. 49 and 144.

[78] Ibid., no. 53.

[79] Dalton, pp. 247–8.

[80] *D.B.F.P.* v, no. 57.

[81] *Hansard*, 5th series, vol. 346 (House of Commons), col. 13.

[82] *D.B.F.P.* v, no. 144.

[83] Ibid., nos. 128 and 138.

[84] See ibid., nos. 155, 157, 191, 199, 286, 310 and 311.

[85] See Papen, p. 448.

[86] See *D.B.F.P.* vi, no. 320.

[87] It was sent on 4 Aug.; see ibid., no. 552.

[88] *D.G.F.P.* vi, no. 182.

[89] *D.B.F.P.* v, nos. 569 and 570.

[90] Ibid., vi, nos. 317 and 428.

[91] Ibid., v, no. 462.

[92] Ibid., no. 653.

[93] For examples of Litvinov's earlier urgings and fears, see Degras (ed.), *Soviet Documents on Foreign Policy*, vol. 3, pp. 256, 262, 266 and 276.

[94] *D.G.F.P.* iv, no. 476.

[95] Degras, p. 308 ff.

[96] Coulondre, p. 165.

[97] Degras, p. 315 ff.

[98] *D.G.F.P.* vi, no. 112.

[99] *D.D.I.* xii, no. 201.

[100] *D.B.F.P.* vi, no. 376; (Strang to Sargent, 20 July).

[101] See Coulondre, pp. 165, 171 and 205; and *Livre Jaune Français*, nos. 123, 135 and 155.

[102] See *D.B.F.P.* v, no. 552, and vi, App. i.

[103] See ibid., v, nos. 377 and 413, and vi, App. i; Coulondre, p. 270; B. Dahlerus, *The Last Attempt* (1947), p. 45; Kordt, pp. 313-19.

[104] *D.B.F.P.* v, no. 413; for Loraine's similar reaction, even after Litvinov's dismissal, see ibid., no. 372.

[105] Ibid., no. 589. The same views found some support in the press: see the *Daily Mail* for 21 Mar. 1939. See also Lord Strang, *Home and Abroad* (1956), p. 167.

[106] *D.B.F.P.* v, nos. 166 and 170.

[107] Ibid., no. 201.

[108] See Beck, p. 201.

[109] See *D.B.F.P.* v, no. 247 and, for an example of Chamberlain's reluctance in public, *Hansard*, 5th series, vol. 346 (House of Commons), col. 115.

[110] Ibid., nos. 252, 277, 350 and 351.

[111] Ibid., no. 533.

[112] Ibid., nos. 389, 397, 421 and 436.

[113] Ibid., no. 520.

[114] See, for instance, the debates of 19 May: *Hansard*, 5th series, vol. 347 (House of Commons), cols. 1809-1883. Churchill and others were informed of developments by the Soviet Ambassador at this time: see Maisky, pp. 125-6.

[115] *D.B.F.P.* v, no. 528.

[116] Avon, *The Reckoning*, p. 55; cf. Maisky, pp. 141-3.

[117] *D.B.F.P.* v, nos. 527, 581, 582, 621.

[118] Ibid., nos. 556, 576 and 578.
[119] Ibid., nos. 586 and 595.
[120] *F.R.U.S.* (1939), i, pp. 259–60 (Kennedy to Hull, 24 May); author's italics.
[121] See *D.B.F.P.* v, nos. 609 and 624.
[122] Ibid., no. 657.
[123] Ibid., nos. 648 and 670.
[124] Degras, pp. 332 ff.
[125] *D.B.F.P.* v, nos. 681 and 719.
[126] Ibid., no. 697.
[127] See ibid., vi, nos. 3, 20 and 25.
[128] Ibid., no. 35.
[129] Ibid., no. 73.
[130] Ibid., nos. 75, 76, 89, 94, 112, 113 and 123.
[131] Ibid., no. 135.
[132] Ibid., nos. 146, 151, 158, 159 and 171.
[133] Ibid., nos. 207, 225, 226 and 227.
[134] Ibid., nos. 252 and 253; author's italics.
[135] Ibid., nos. 279, 281 and 282.
[136] Ibid., nos. 298, 329 and 338.
[137] Ibid., nos. 346, 357, 358, 378 and 405.
[138] Ibid., nos. 414, 435, 465 and 473.
[139] *D.G.F.P.* vi, no. 753 (Dirksen to Ribbentrop, 1 Aug.).
[140] *D.B.F.P.* vi, App. v.
[141] See ibid., vii, nos. 90 and 91, and Bonnet, vol. 2, pp. 279–90.

6 Danzig: Western Fears and Nazi Reality

We could not say Boo to Beneš last year till we were on the abyss of war. And we can't say Boo to Beck this year. . . . Generally speaking we seem to learn nothing.

HENDERSON to HALIFAX, 16 August 1939.[1]

Further success can no longer be won without bloodshed. . . . We cannot expect a repetition of Czechia. There will be war. Our task is to isolate Poland.

HITLER to his generals, 23 May 1939.[2]

FROM London and Paris the Danzig issue had appeared more ugly as the summer wore on. Whether the Germans in the Free City were acting on their own initiative or were receiving orders as well as encouragement from Berlin, it seemed increasingly unlikely that an explosion could be avoided before the year was out. Hitler's birthday on 20 April had been the occasion of new displays of armed might in Berlin, and Forster had conferred the freedom of Danzig on the Fuehrer. Eight days later, in a brilliantly malicious speech which sneered at Roosevelt's appeal for assurances as to German intentions towards the rest of Europe, Hitler denounced the 1934 pact with Poland and the Anglo-German naval agreement. The Anglo-Polish agreement had abrogated the former, he declared, while the latter was meaningless since the British Government were now encircling the Reich and were 'governed by the opinion that England ... must always take up an attitude hostile to Germany'.[3] Many were relieved that the speech had contained no ultimatum, but some also noticed what Phipps called its 'uncanny silence' concerning Russia. And if Hitler had hoped that a Polish climb-down might follow he was disappointed; Beck's address in reply, though conciliatory, was firm over the sovereignty of Danzig and transit facilities across the Corridor.*

The activities of Nazi youth and para-military formations in Danzig increased during May, and the signing of the German–Italian 'Pact of Steel' on the 22nd appeared to underline Henderson's warning that Hitler was determined, 'by hook or by crook, to obtain before September some settlement which gives him the substance of his claim'.[4] There were rumours of German soldiers infiltrating into Danzig in plain clothes, and a Polish customs post on the East Prussian border was destroyed. In June special *Wehrmacht* exercises practised the manning of the West Wall, while SA units in Danzig, encouraged by bellicose speeches from the visiting Goebbels, were known to be preparing defensive positions under cover of darkness.[5] The danger appeared acute at the end of the month in particular, when several sources, the American Embassy in Warsaw among them, suggested that Forster had been authorised to demand an immediate return to the Reich over the weekend 1 to 2 July;[6] though nothing happened, the resemblance to the 'May scare' of 1938 had been uncomfortable, and the sense of crisis increased. Military activity in the Free City became still more open and provocative, and Lt.-Colonel Count von Schwerin brought to London fresh warnings from the German opposition that Hitler meant to succeed by September.[7] The visit of a German warship to Danzig at the end of August and the Tannenberg celebrations on the 27th were awaited with renewed anxiety.

The new month immediately brought fresh trouble. Polish troop trains passing through Danzig were the subject of German protests, and when Warsaw prohibited the import of herrings and margarine from the Free City Forster threatened to open the Danzig–East Prussian border

* Though see above, p. 127.

as an alternative commercial outlet. On the 4th Polish customs officers on that border were told that the Danzig Senate would not permit them to carry out their duties after the 6th. That night an abrupt Polish ultimatum demanded that the order be revoked by the evening of the 5th, and while the President of the Senate complied, a counter-protest from the Free City authorities reached Warsaw on the 7th.[8] Moreover *Gauleiter* Forster flew to see Hitler on the 8th, and on the following day Germany added her own warning over what had happened. Though Beck confidently replied on the 10th that any further and unwarrantable interference by Berlin would be considered an act of aggression, the event made him anxiously seek on the same day a 'very early' conclusion to the alliance negotiations with London, with the undermining of Polish rights in Danzig recognised as a clear *casus belli*.[9]

Talks on the customs issue began between Greiser and Chodacki, the Polish representative in Danzig, on 16 August, but the recall of German reservists and the absence from their posts of several German ambassadors were familiar and ominous signs that the worst was not over. In Basle Professor Burckhardt passed on to British and French diplomats an account of a disturbing interview he had had at Berchtesgaden on the 11th. Hitler had apparently been speechless with rage over French press reports that he had lost a war of nerves over the customs ultimatum, and though Burckhardt found his host 'nervous, pathetic, almost shaken at times', the threat of force was harsh and clear:

If the slightest incident happens now I shall crush the Poles without warning in such a way that no trace of Poland can be found afterwards. I shall strike like lightning with the full force of a mechanised army. . . . I will hold the West with 74 divisions, the rest will be hurled against the Poles.

Laughing hysterically over the pathetic air forces which might oppose him, Hitler had gone on to demand 'a free hand in the East'. 'If each time I take a step necessitated by history I find England and France in the way, what can I do?' He would be as patient as possible, but Polish atrocities against their German minority were becoming intolerable.[10]*

It was the minority dispute which now came to the forefront of Nazi propaganda, in fact. Weizsäcker spoke sharply to Coulondre and Henderson on the 15th of the Poles 'running amok', seeking, as Coulondre was quick to recognise, an issue less likely than Danzig to invoke Western pledges.[11] There were further customs and frontier incidents, however, as well as the arrest of some German Nazis in Poland. The Silesian disputes of the past were aired anew. On the 19th Halifax passed on to Chamberlain in Scotland fresh indications that a German attack would take place between the 25th and 28th of that month, and even the Prime Minister's optimism was at last somewhat impaired.[12] He hurried south in time to learn of the forthcoming German–Soviet pact.

The problem he and his Government now had to face had already been complicated by events in the Far East. In May

* For some reason, however, the most startling of Hitler's remarks to Burckhardt was not included in the Western reports from Basle. Hitler stated that he would conclude an agreement with the Soviet Union, defeat the West, and then turn back against Russia, securing the Ukraine to nullify the effects of a blockade as in 1914–18: 'Alles was ich unternehme, ist gegen Russland gerichtet; wenn der Westen zu dumm und zu blind ist, um dies zu begreifen, werde ich gezwungen sein, mich mit den Russen zu verständigen, den Westen zu schlagen, und dann nach seiner Niederlage mich mit meinen versammelten Kräften gegen die Sowjetunion zu wenden. Ich brauche die Ukraine, damit man uns nicht wieder wie im letzten Krieg aushungern kann.' C. J. Burckhardt, *Meine Danziger Mission* (1960), p. 348. Was this a genuine indiscretion or a calculated mixture of threat and bait for Western consumption? Was it, in fact, passed on through as yet unpublished channels? If not, why not; or if so, what was its reception? Beck, thanks partly to British reticence, did not obtain a full report of the meeting, and the United States chargé d'affaires in London found that the official reaction to the talk was that 'it has thrown no new light on Hitler's intentions': *F.R.U.S.* (1939), i, pp. 215, 219. Oddly enough, Burckhardt himself apparently laid stress on the more favourable passages of his interview when relating it at the time.

the triumphant Japanese had interfered with British traffic on the Yangtze, and on 14 June had blockaded the British concession at Tientsin; owing to their restrictions, there was only 10 days supply of rice in Shanghai by 19 August. With inadequate arms, a still-quiescent America and the growing danger in Europe, humiliation had perhaps been inevitable. Halifax had long before been 'frankly at a loss' as to what could be done.[13] A Foreign Office memorandum of 3 August confessed that

The more one reflects on the situation the more one is obliged to conclude that no satisfactory solution can be found that does not recognise some 'new order' in Eastern Asia in which Japan plays a dominant part.[14]

The trouble was that weakness in one hemisphere was likely to have grave effects in the other. The Berlin Embassy had informed London in June that 'our experiences at Tientsin are making a considerable impression in confirmation of the idea that we shall do nothing about Danzig',[15] and from Rome Loraine added that 'any compromise . . . will be hailed as a British humiliation and will confirm the impression . . . that His Majesty's Government . . . always give way rather than risk . . . the use of force, however grave the provocation'.[16] Conversely, Sir Robert Craigie argued from Tokyo that a firm stand over Danzig which led to Hitler climbing down would 'have the best possible deterrent effect on Japanese extremists',[17] and this way round, at all events, a clear and viable choice of policy did seem open to Chamberlain. It was one, however, that he had done his best to avoid between April and the journey he was now making back to London and the moment of inescapable decision.

Whether the West would stand firm or would seek a fresh accommodation with Germany depended essentially upon Britain in the summer of 1939; though Daladier was less

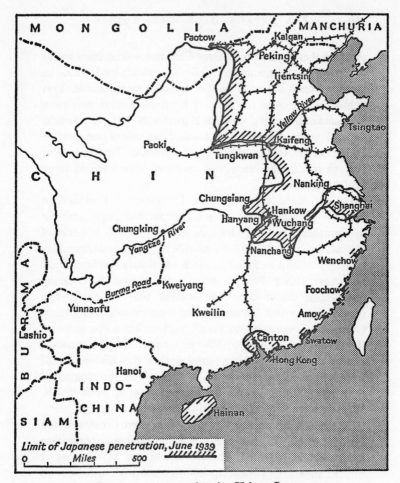

Limit of Japanese penetration, June 1939

0   Miles   500

3 Japanese penetration in China, June 1939

yielding than he had been over Czechoslovakia, Paris could
do little more than anxiously follow London's lead. Many in
Europe hoped it would be the strongest one possible. Von
Schwerin's message has already been mentioned, and even
Weizsäcker suggested through Burckhardt that peace would
depend upon Britain maintaining 'un silence menaçant'.[18]
Daladier, too, was quick during the week-end scare early in
July to call for an 'energetic reaction' which would force
Hitler to retreat.

Of the ambassadors, it was Sir Howard Kennard in
Warsaw who urged the same course most strongly, striving
to counteract the pro-German and anti-Polish hysteria of
Henderson in Berlin and the pliable tendencies of Chamberlain and Wilson in London. 'It is absolutely fundamental,'
he wrote, 'that Poland must fight rather than make
concessions under menaces', adding that all confidence
would disappear if Britain pushed forward as a mediator.[19]
German provocation and Polish moderation under pressure
should not be obscured by Nazi propaganda, and Kennard's
chargé d'affaires, Norton, writing that the Embassy staff
were 'appalled' by Henderson's failure to see this, suggested
that resignations would be forthcoming if, as a result,
Warsaw were to be abandoned as Prague had been.[20]

At times it did appear that the lesson of earlier events had
been learned. In the face of bitter Labour opposition
Chamberlain warmed French hearts by announcing a
limited measure of conscription on 26 April* and, though
Henderson tried to soften the words involved, a warning
that Britain would fight over Danzig was leaked, as if by
accident, to the Germans in May.[21] The July scare in
particular produced a firm reaction. In a speech at Chatham
House on 29 June, Halifax acknowledged that

---

* Captain Liddell Hart also opposed the measure, of course, on
grounds which he persuasively repeats in his *Memoirs* (vol. ii, chap. 5).
The technical disadvantages of the move may perhaps have been offset
by its symbolical value to a greater degree than he will allow.

if the security and independence of other countries are to disappear, our own security and independence will be gravely threatened. We know that, if international law and order is to be preserved, we must be prepared to fight in its defence. . . . The threat of military force is holding the world to ransom, and our immediate task is . . . to resist aggression. I would emphasise that to-night with all the strength at my command, so that nobody may misunderstand it.[22]

Chamberlain, too, reinforced the warning in the Commons shortly afterwards, and Coulondre and Henderson were both doing so to Weizsäcker as fresh tension gathered in the middle of August.[23] Even Bonnet had sent Ribbentrop an unambiguous statement of resolve, and the personal appeals which Chamberlain and Halifax sent Mussolini on 5 July and 19 August went out of their way to make it clear that 'any attempt to impose on Poland a unilateral settlement which she felt bound to resist would bring Britain immediately to her assistance with all her forces'.[24]

Yet in reality the British Government was scarcely more straightforward and dependable an ally than Beck himself was reputed to be. There was bound to be anxiety, of course, as to the behaviour of a state to whose fate one was now tied, and it was not reassuring when the League's Commissioner in Danzig passed 'highly critical' remarks about Polish policy,[25] nor when the customs ultimatum of 4 August and the warning to Germany of the 10th were despatched without consulting the West. Halifax expressed his uneasiness in a telegram to Kennard on 3 May which was obviously intended to influence the speech Beck was to make in reply to Hitler on the 5th:

I should not expect the Polish Government to abandon all hope of negotiation unless they were convinced that it afforded no possibility of averting a threat to Polish independence. . . . And I have no doubt that if [they] wished to establish that there 'clearly' was such a threat, they would naturally desire to consult with His Majesty's Government and would therefore do so *before* taking any irrevocable action.[26]

On several occasions Halifax also endeavoured to get a precise statement from Beck as to what German actions would be considered intolerable and what steps the Polish Government would then take. He did not succeed, however, in obtaining anything more definite than the assurance that Warsaw's reaction would be 'proportionate to the action taken either by the Danzig authorities or the Reich', though Beck did suggest that military necessity might well have to override the desire to consult.[27] One could only hope, as Halifax remarked to Daladier and Bonnet, that 'safety lay in the fact that, in the event of trouble, Poland would obviously be the first to suffer, and to suffer disastrously'.[28]

Anxiety could easily lead into more devious paths, however. If Beck had been 'less than frank' over the German offers and demands, Halifax passed on to Beck only 'the general drift of a summary' of Hitler's outburst to Burckhardt in which the Fuehrer had demanded 'a free hand in the East'.[29] A Foreign Office official who wrote to Eden in May had good reason to believe that appeasement was 'rearing its ugly head again' in 10 Downing Street,[30] and throughout the month the correspondence columns of *The Times* provided a forum for men like Lords Rushcliffe and Noel-Buxton, Sir Arnold Wilson and Sir John Marriott, who, like Bonnet, wished it to be so. They had no more fervent a supporter than the Ambassador in Berlin.

In fairness to Henderson it could be said, as Churchill did of Chamberlain, that he was acting 'in perfect sincerity according to his lights ... to save the world from awful, devastating struggle'. It remains astonishing that he had still not learned the lesson of Vienna, Munich and Prague; the 'mission' for which, in his own words, he had been 'specially selected by Providence'[31] (Eden and Vansittart were always ready to acknowledge ruefully that they, too, as

well as the Almighty, had had a hand in the mistake)
degenerated into narcissism and short-sightedness. He was
able in the summer of 1939 to minimise in his own mind
Hitler's bellicosity, to suggest that the latter might be
pushed into war through the free hand given his subordinates
and that 'the last word in Germany is always with the
army'.[32] To Henderson, the Danzig and Corridor issues
were 'so easily' capable of a solution through 'the just
settlement' of Germany's grievances; danger lay only in the
stupidity of the Poles or the temptation for the West to
rebuke and thus annoy Hitler.[33] There had been 'quite a
deal of Polish provocation', he wrote, and he 'greatly
doubted' whether Germany's treatment of her Polish
minority had been 'nearly as bad' as the reverse case. Why
could Britain not learn to coerce Beck as she had done
Beneš? If fighting began, 'it would be the stupidest of wars'.[34]
Halifax's gentle rebukes had no effect on the tone or content
of such communications; as Henderson's gloom increased he
could only hope that Mussolini would come forward at the
last minute to propose a repetition of Munich.[35]

To this siren song the Nazis added blandishments of their
own. Hints were frequently passed to London — via
Forster in conversation with Burckhardt, for instance —
that Berlin would be as patient as Warsaw allowed; that if
only the current dispute could be settled, a 'big peace
gesture' might well be forthcoming from Hitler; that
difficulties could be dealt with on a man-to-man basis
between the Fuehrer and some prominent, German-speaking
Englishman.[36] An additional and somewhat bizarre instrument for this purpose of isolating Poland was found in the
Swedish industrialist, Birger Dahlerus, a friend of Goering's
who was in touch with Halifax. In all sincerity and innocence
he brought together Goering and a party of British business-
men early in August, and while the latter restated their
country's new-found determination, the Field-Marshal
suggested that Four-Power talks might soon be the only

solution to the Vansittart-like stupidity and obstinacy of the Poles.[37]

In return, there were those in Britain who displayed sufficient eagerness for an understanding to bolster Ribbentrop's conviction that Poland would be left to fight alone. In May an ex-Conservative M.P. known to be close to Sir Horace Wilson had made private enquiries in Berlin as to German *desiderata* in financial, commercial and colonial fields,[38] and the former Labour M.P. Charles Roden Buxton followed in August with the suggestion that in return for German recognition of the Empire, autonomy for Bohemia and Moravia, and the prospect of disarmament talks, Britain might end her 'encircling' alliances, return Germany's colonies, and 'recognise East Europe as [her] natural living space'.[39] The Ambassador, too, who had been sent back to Berlin after the Prague episode 'to soften the blow' of the conscription announcement, had been dropping hints of a settlement, though insisting — and deploring — that British public opinion was ready to fight for Poland. On 15 May, Henderson again chose a markedly personal interpretation of how best to serve his country by telling Weizsäcker that if the worst happened and war came, it 'would be conducted defensively by the Western Powers'.[40]

The fear that Britain was secretly preparing to sell the pass became a public outcry, especially in France, towards the end of July, when it was rumoured that R. S. Hudson, Secretary of the Department of Overseas Trade, had offered Dr. Wohlthat during the latter's visit to London a loan of £1,000 million in return for a disarmament agreement. The denial given by Chamberlain in the Commons was true — the German Embassy suspected their French counterpart of deliberately fostering alarm — though the desirability of an economic and commercial arrangement had been discussed in general terms.[41] But other talks which had taken place, unnoticed ones between Wohlthat and Sir Horace Wilson, would have provided a far greater shock had their contents been known. According to one German report, Wilson did more than advocate secret and high-level contacts between the two countries ('the Fuehrer had only to take a sheet of paper and jot down his points; the British government would be ready to discuss them'); he suggested that they should cover colonial, disarmament and economic matters, that they could lead to mutual declarations of non-interference in each other's spheres of interest, and that non-aggression pledges could 'make Britain's guarantees to Poland and Roumania superfluous since, as a result of such a declaration, Germany would not attack these States, and they could not therefore feel that their national existence was threatened by Germany'. Such naïvety, to say the least, may seem scarcely credible, though a second German account again insists that the theme of the talk was how Britain could 'rid herself of her commitments vis-à-vis Poland'. Sir Horace's own official record certainly made somewhat less startling reading, and he has subsequently questioned the accuracy of the other versions.[42]

On 3 August Wilson saw the German Ambassador, and — again, according to the latter — confirmed his previous suggestions, specifically mentioning Danzig as a suitable subject for a British non-intervention pledge.[43] He was also anxious to know how his talk with Wohlthat had been received in Berlin, but Dirksen was not to know the answer to this until he returned home on leave. 'Herr Wohlthat's report', he then learned, 'had been interpreted . . . more as a picture of the general mood, and *my report of my conversation with Wilson had been taken as a further sign of Britain's weakness.*'[44]

The fear that Chamberlain and Wilson, left to themselves, might easily produce a second Munich was made plain in the House of Commons on 2 August as Churchill, Greenwood and others strove in vain to get the Prime Minister to bring forward the date of reassembly after the summer recess from 3 October to 21 August.[45] There would not be a peaceful four-power settlement, however. Poland would fight alone rather than surrender, and by August Hitler had little desire to be cheated of a conquest by force a second time.

In April the Fuehrer had still been undecided. On the 3rd Keitel had ordered that Operation 'White', an attack on Poland, was to be made possible 'any time as from September 1st', but a more detailed directive issued by Hitler on the 11th stated that relations should 'continue to be based on the principles of avoiding any disturbances'. A 'final settlement' might be necessary 'should Poland adopt a threatening attitude', and Warsaw's diplomatic isolation might be achieved in the 'not too distant future'; but for the moment, 'White' was 'only a precautionary complement' to the build-up against the antagonism of the West.[46] To a stream of Balkan visitors during that month Hitler mixed stern warnings with the happy thought that 'the greatest merit in the eyes of history was to achieve success without having to resort to the last expedient'.[47]

On the other hand Ribbentrop was confidently asserting that in the event of a German-Polish conflict 'not one British soldier would be mobilised', and Goering, for all his later anxiety, spoke in the same sense.[48] Moltke, too, was remarking in Warsaw that in three months' time Poland, as well as the West, would be too tired to fight for Danzig; then the matter would be settled.[49] Moreover the German Army were far more confident of a quick victory over a probably isolated Poland than they had been over Czechoslovakia in 1938 (Ribbentrop talked glibly of three days being enough to annihilate the Polish forces[50]), and a conflict of honour in that direction to restore the depredations of 1919 had long been relished. 'Now we have a treaty with Poland,' observed the wife of General von Seeckt to Ambassador Dodd in 1936, 'but we are going to take [the Corridor] in spite of the treaty. Danzig is not a free city. It is our city.'[51]

Despite the private waverings of Beck, it became clear early in May that neither bribery nor bullying was likely to move Poland in the near future. The official reply to Hitler's denunciation of the pact of 1934, delivered on 5 May, marked the beginning of a stern silence from Warsaw, as from Berlin:

It is clear that negotiations in which one State formulates demands and the other is to be obliged to accept these demands unaltered, are not negotiations in the spirit of the Declaration of 1934 and are incompatible with the vital interests and dignity of Poland.[52]

The growing resolve to smash Poland was also fostered by fresh proof of Italian subservience. Despite the shock of Prague and a certain uneasiness over the way in which Ribbentrop was speaking of Danzig, it was too late for Mussolini to change sides. 'After all,' he remarked in March, 'we are not prostitutes.'[53] The Albanian episode, too, though anti-German in spirit, drove the Duce still closer to Berlin, while Ribbentrop, Brauchitsch and other German visitors early in May talked reassuringly of peace for at least four or five years.[54] It was possibly the news of Anglo-Turkish moves towards a pact which gave Mussolini the final push, however; on 7 May he ordered Ciano to offer the startled Ribbentrop an immediate military alliance, without waiting any longer for the Japanese. The Nazi Foreign Minister returned home jubilant, declaring to Weizsäcker that 'Poland was no longer a problem',[55] and despite the warnings of Attolico, Rome allowed itself to be committed in advance to terms which gave Germany all the latitude she needed. On 22 May the Pact of Steel was signed, and the two countries pledged each other support should one 'become involved in warlike complications with another Power or Powers'. Mussolini's hopes of restraining Hitler thereby, his memorandum of 30 May urging the Fuehrer to delay the inevitable conflict with the West perhaps until 1942, were no more than a vain and belated mimicry of shrewdness. The facile pleasures of snubbing Western diplomats and of laying their stolen documents at the feet of the Nazis still meant more than the cares of responsible diplomacy.[56]

Hitler's thinking was still not fully clarified, but the tortuous reasoning and speculation which accompanied a harangue to his generals on 23 May did not hide his new decision to strike. The Reich, he said, must win living space or decline: 'It is not Danzig that is at stake.* For us it is a matter of expanding our living space in the East and making food supplies secure. . . .' At the same time he advanced the consideration that Poland would always be on the side of Germany's enemies, the main one being England, at whom a 'smashing blow' must one day be delivered. The decision was therefore 'to attack Poland at the first suitable opportunity', having first isolated her diplomatically. Though 'it must not come to a simultaneous showdown with the West', England's intervention could not be ruled out entirely; in that event 'declarations of neutrality could be ignored', and 'a lightning attack on Holland' would become necessary.[57]

By July and early August the usual military and diplomatic preparations were being made. Ambassadors like Dirksen in London and Moltke in Warsaw were forbidden to return to their posts, and any awkward advice they might wish to offer — the London Embassy, for instance, continued to insist that Britain would fight — was ignored.[58] Propaganda material which would offer a pretext for aggression was gathered in, and Hungary was driven into line after daring to suggest that her support could be counted on only in a general conflict, not in an attack on her Polish friends.[59] The growing anxiety of Italy was also ignored. With Attolico providing urgent warnings that Ribbentrop was convinced force could be used in August with impunity, Mussolini began to think in terms of a Danzig plebiscite and a meeting of 'interested Powers'; but wavering suggestions for a Brenner meeting with Hitler to concert policy in these directions met with polite evasion, even though it seems that

* Goering once confirmed this in an aside to Lipski: Beck, p. 205.

Italian interference came as a nasty shock.[60] On 2 August the Italian military attaché in Berlin received the clearest hint from Admiral Canaris that force was being planned, and the jeers with which Ciano had greeted his Ambassador's alarm were silenced as the Duce spoke fervently of the need to convince Hitler to preserve peace.[61]

On 11, 12 and 13 August, Ciano learned for himself the real meaning of Nazism and lost his enthusiasm for the Axis partnership even more swiftly than Ribbentrop had turned his hopes of England into hatred.[62] At Salzburg he heard Ribbentrop declare that neither Danzig nor the Corridor would suffice: ' "Not that any more", he said, gazing at me with his cold metallic eyes. "We want war." '

'The decision to fight is implacable', wrote Ciano privately. '[Ribbentrop] rejects any solution which might give satisfaction to Germany and avoid the struggle. I am certain that even if the Germans were given more than they ask for they would attack just the same, because they are possessed by the demon of destruction. . . . I am becoming aware of how little we are worth in [their] opinion.'

Hitler confirmed this impression on the two following days. Echoing Ribbentrop's 'information and psychological know-ledge', he declared his 'unshakable conviction that neither England nor France would embark on a general war'. Poland must and would be attacked before the rain and mud of autumn, and liquidated in preparation for 'the inevitable clash with the Western democracies'; Italy would not be needed in so local a conflict, but should similarly smash Yugoslavia, the Axis covering each other in turn as they eliminated all 'false neutrals'. Though the details of the move were still withheld from Ciano, Hitler left no doubt as to the immediacy of the crisis. 'The last date for the beginning of the operation is the end of August. . . . Action will be rapid, decisive and implacable.'

The German press reported the meetings as reaffirming Axis solidarity, though Attolico and Magistrati, the Italian

Counsellor in Berlin, were soon hinting that their country would not be dragged into what was certain to be a wide-spread war. Mussolini was left to waver between the logic of military unpreparedness and the desire for cheap glory; between the urgings of Ciano, Attolico and Magistrati that Germany's unilateral decision had released Italy from any obligation, and concern for his own and Fascism's martial honour.[63]

Meanwhile Hitler moved on alone. At the Obersalzberg on the 14th he assured his generals that the political and military situation was favourable, and reminded them that 'any success involved taking risks'. General Halder entered the salient points of the address in his notebook: the 'conviction of Poland's isolation strengthening from day to day', the proof offered in the shape of Britain's refusal to grant her full financial aid and the tapped telephone calls to Poland which revealed that 'England was continuously putting on the brakes'.[64] For the OKW, who considered 25 August to be the best date to strike, there would be 48-hours' notice; meanwhile on the 15th, the Nuremberg rally was cancelled and fresh orders were given to those ships which needed to be positioned in good time. On the 19th Ribbentrop's special agent in Danzig, Veesenmayer, warned that in the customs talks Poland appeared 'ready to give way'. His suggestion that Forster should 'increase the demands still further, so as to make agreement impossible' was therefore approved on the 20th, with the instruction that he must so contrive matters that 'the responsibility for the breakdown ... and for all the consequences fell upon Poland'. And when the spotless Weizsäcker, who drafted this reply, enquired also about more radical plans still which he had heard of, he was curtly referred to Heydrich. Clearly, it was the turn of the thugs.[65]

There was still one decisive diplomatic move to be made, however, and despite frequent warnings from his embassies in Moscow and Berlin the news of it astonished Ciano, as well as the West, when it burst upon the world late on 21 August.[66] The Molotov–Ribbentrop pact, coming when Forster was shouting that the hour of returning to the Reich was at hand, appeared to seal Poland's fate.

Relations between Russia and Germany, for long tensely watched by each other and the rest of Europe, suddenly seemed to have assumed an impossible shape. The theme of expansion at the expense of the lesser breeds of the East had, after all, been deeply rooted in Germany long before the appearance of Nazism, while from *Mein Kampf* onwards Hitler's hatred of Bolshevism, reaffirmed in the anti-Comintern propaganda which made such good reading in the West, had been met with equal vituperation from Moscow. For Nazis like Rosenberg, the eventual conquest of the Baltic States, Ukraine, and more was almost a *sine qua non*. Yet the idea of co-operation, now proclaimed as an unscrupulous and advantageous tactic by two dictators, was not an entirely strange one.[67] The treaty of Rapallo had shown the outcasts of 1918 ready to seek economic ties with each other, and von Seeckt's co-operation with the Red Army was something an important section of the German Army would gladly renew. Even Goebbels was perhaps the more able to perform the required somersault when he remembered the strong socialist emphasis of his own, early brand of National Socialism, while Stalin had secretly urged Berlin to negotiate as recently as 1937.

Despite the shock of Munich, no significant change in Nazi–Soviet relations had been made until the spring of 1939. Though the Soviet Ambassador in Berlin announced in January a desire 'to begin a new era in economic relations', and though in return Goering and his planners were anxious to increase the supply of Russian raw materials, Ribbentrop was still counting on a German–Polish under-standing. Publicity was allowed to cause the cancellation of the visit to Moscow of an economic negotiator in January, and it was decided to mark time in credit discussions in March.[68]

After the elimination of Czechoslovakia, however, matters moved forward, it would seem on Soviet initiative. Moscow's unwillingness to adopt a firmly hostile line had been observed during the crisis, and on 17 April, the same day on which Litvinov's proposal for a tripartite pact was being put to London, the Soviet Ambassador in Berlin asked Weizsäcker point blank what he thought of relations between their two countries, observing that ideological differences need not prevent an 'increasing improvement'.[69] In May, as the chilly British response to Litvinov's proposal at last arrived in Moscow, the Russian advances became more marked. Their chargé d'affaires in Berlin, Astakhov, sought a resumption of trade talks on the 5th, and on the 17th he told Schnurre, the German economic negotiator, that there were 'no conflicts in foreign policy' between them, and that Western hopes of Soviet agreement 'would hardly materialise'. Molotov himself suggested to Schulenburg in Moscow on the 20th that economic discussions would only make sense if a 'political basis' for them could be found.[70]

At this stage, Hitler's response was cautious. It was appreciated in Berlin that such hints might well be directed towards exacting a higher price from the West or playing off Germany against Japan, and on 26-27 May Weizsäcker told Schulenburg that 'the attitude of complete reserve... still stands', adding that an offer might only be met by a 'peal of Tartar laughter'.[71] The key to the change which now took place must therefore be sought only partly in the approaching attack on Poland — tension was not particularly high at the end of May — and only partly in the need to forestall a Soviet-Western agreement. More immediate were the indications that Japan would not, after all, hasten to join the newly-signed Pact of Steel, and the feeling in consequence that there was less to be lost through the offence a Nazi-Soviet *rapprochement* would give in Tokyo.

On 27 May, Ambassador Oshima, to his personal regret, had to tell Ribbentrop that his government wished to reserve its position in the event of a war between the Axis and the West. 'The Japanese attitude', wrote Ribbentrop on the following day, 'is beginning to be regarded with distrust in Berlin and Rome.'[72] With the sickly state of Anglo-Russian talks well known through his Embassy in London, Hitler therefore decided to explore the Soviet offers further. On the 30th Schulenburg was told that careful initiative was now approved, and Weizsäcker warmly agreed with Astakhov that political dogma need not stand in the way of better relations.[73] The courtship had begun in earnest, and the German press was forbidden by Goebbels to continue with anti-Soviet material. Astakhov, on his side, hinted clearly through a third party at a non-aggression pact, and on 6 June Ribbentrop tartly informed a Japanese diplomat that since agreement could not be reached with Tokyo it would be sought, and obtained, in Moscow.[74]

As Hitler moved forward, however, Stalin coolly moved back; no doubt his confidence in his position was increased by the knowledge of German–Japanese difficulties and of German earnestness which he was obtaining from his master-spy in Tokyo, Richard Sorge. The intimation, given by Berlin on 17 June, that Schnurre could come to Moscow to negotiate a trade agreement was enough to enable Molotov to reject the considerable Western concessions he was offered on the 21st, but not enough to prevent him asking endless questions about the political motives behind the Nazi move, and Hitler in turn ordered that feelers be withdrawn.[75] The Soviet ones were therefore advanced again. On 18 July, the day after Seeds had made clear Britain's refusal to comply over the rapacious interpretation of 'indirect aggression', a Russian trade official, Babarin, astonished Schnurre by bringing a list of points to be cleared up, after which he was empowered to sign a commercial agreement. The news that talks were being resumed in

Berlin was announced by Moscow on the 22nd, and Schulenburg was ordered to resume soundings at the same time: 'The period of waiting stipulated for you ... [has] expired'.[76]

Perhaps the decisive moment in this grim relationship took place four days later in the unlikely, lush setting of Ewest's restaurant in Berlin, where Schnurre dined Astakhov and Babarin till the small hours. There were no impediments between the Baltic and the Black Sea to an arrangement, said Schnurre. German policy was aimed against Britain, not Russia, and events necessitated a speedy decision as to where Moscow stood. Britain, after all, could offer only war, whereas Germany could offer neutrality and an 'understanding on mutual interests'. Though Astakhov in return gave the impression that Stalin was still undecided, he agreed on the need for a *rapprochement*, and that Danzig and the Corridor would have to be solved in Germany's favour. It was all sufficiently encouraging for Schulenburg to be ordered to follow up the talk with speed, especially in the light of new Danzig tension and the secret knowledge that Britain and France were to go ahead with military talks in Moscow.[77] Ribbentrop himself repeated Schnurre's offer to Astakhov on 2 August, and 'dropped a gentle hint at an understanding on the fate of Poland'. When the Soviet response over the following week continued to balance encouragement with an infuriating caution, even the role of suppliant had to be adopted.[78]

On the 14th, with Hitler in full spate to his uniformed audience and Voroshilov posing his Western fellow delegates an unanswerable question, Schulenburg was ordered to seek an interview with Molotov on the morrow; he was to urge that relations were at 'an historic turning point', that 'English agitation for war' and the Danzig crisis made 'speedy clarification' imperative, and that Ribbentrop be allowed to come to Moscow.[79] At 6.40 a.m. on the 16th the decoded response was telephoned to Ribbentrop at Fuschl: Molotov welcomed the idea of a visit, but thought it required 'adequate preparation' and that any non-aggression pact needed discussing 'in concrete terms'. Schulenburg was therefore told to see Molotov again. A non-aggression pact of 25 years' duration with a joint guarantee of the Baltic States was offered, and Ribbentrop could arrive any time from the 18th onwards with full powers to sign; speed was essential since 'serious events' might occur 'any day' as a result of Polish provocation. Again, however, the news of the morning of the 18th was that 'thorough preparation' was suggested, as well as a 'special protocol defining the interests of the contracting parties in this or that question of foreign policy'.[80] Stalin was making his price clear.

Urgent new instructions from the Obersalzberg were therefore despatched to Schulenburg on the evening of the 18th in which a protocol defining spheres of interest was accepted and Ribbentrop's journey was sought with redoubled fervour. When it was learned on the evening of the 19th, and in more detail at 7 a.m. on the 20th, that Molotov, though handing over the draft of a non-aggression pact, was still proposing a week's delay between the signing of a trade agreement* and Ribbentrop's visit, his desire for action within a week forced Hitler to intervene personally.[81] In a telegram to Stalin, despatched at 6.45 p.m. on the 20th, the Fuehrer accepted the Soviet draft agreement, while almost pleading that his Foreign Minister should be received on the 22nd, or at the latest the 23rd. The Polish situation had 'become intolerable'; the crisis might break any day.[82] At 7.55 on the evening of the 21st the eagerly awaited reply arrived in Berlin, and the full text of what Stalin had said was with Hitler at 10.30: Ribbentrop would be welcome on the 23rd, and a communiqué heralding the agreement could be released in triumph.[83]

The pact was signed in Moscow on the night of the 23rd–24th. In an atmosphere of great conviviality, Stalin agreed

* It had been signed in Berlin at 2 a.m. that morning.

with Ribbentrop that only the stupidity of others allowed England to dominate the world, though he warned that she would fight 'craftily and stubbornly'. Ribbentrop for his part, dizzy with success, promised to help improve Soviet–Japanese relations, and assured his hosts that the anti-Comintern pact had always been aimed at the West. It is interesting to note that at the end of the proceedings it was Stalin who anxiously and privately swore that Russia 'would not betray its new partner';[84] in the light of what Hitler had said to Burckhardt earlier in the month,* his fears were well founded.

The agreement itself was worded in sinister fashion. It did not contain that escape clause in Russia's other non-aggression pacts whereby an attack committed on a third party by one signatory absolved the other from her obligations, and it talked, not of being attacked, but of becoming 'the object of hostile action'. The secret protocol spelled out what had been implied. In the event of 'a territorial and political transformation' in the Baltic States and Poland, the Nazi–Soviet spheres of influence would meet on the northern border of Lithuania and along the Rivers Narev, Vistula and San.† Soviet interest in Bessarabia was also acknowledged. As for Poland, only 'the course of further political developments' would show whether its maintenance as an independent state was desirable; in any case, this would be settled in 'friendly understanding'.[85]

While Japan declared all negotiations with Germany at an end (the Hiranuma cabinet resigned on the 27th), Molotov prepared his cynical explanations for the Supreme Soviet and Hitler, having 'used Beelzebub to drive away the devil', rejoiced.[86] Already, on Tuesday 22 August at the Obersalzberg, he had gloated over the master-stroke to his assembled generals as he explained his 'decision to act':

* See below, p. 175.
† The River Pissa was added to the list on the 25th and Lithuania went to Russia later.

I had already made this decision in the spring, but I thought that I would first turn against the West in a few years, and only after that against the East. But the sequence of these things cannot be fixed. . . . I wanted first of all to establish a tolerable relationship with Poland in order to fight first against the West. But . . . it became clear to me that, in the event of a conflict with the West, Poland would attack us.

His own, unique presence and that of Mussolini made it imperative to fight sooner rather than later, and it was necessary 'to test the military [machine]'. 'Iron nerves, iron resolution' would triumph, though 'the probability was still great' that the nonentities of the West would not intervene. It would be a short war. 'If Herr von Brauchitsch had told me that I would need four years to conquer Poland I would have replied: "Then it cannot be done." ' His only fear, in fact, was that 'at the last minute some swine or other will yet submit to me a plan for mediation':*

I shall give a propagandist reason for starting the war, no matter whether it is plausible or not. The victor will not be asked afterwards whether he has told the truth or not. . . . Close your hearts to pity. Act brutally. . . . The stronger man is right. The greatest harshness.

Goering swore that the *Wehrmacht* would do its duty. In his notebook, General Halder recorded: 'Probable start: Saturday morning.'[87]

* Field-Marshal von Manstein has since denied that this last phrase was used. He agrees, however, that the tone of the speech was 'certainly that of a man whose mind was finally made up'. Manstein, *Lost Victories*, p. 28.

[1] *D.B.F.P.* vii, no. 37.
[2] *D.G.F.P.* vi, no. 433.
[3] *D.G.F.P.* vi, no. 277, and Baynes, vol. 2, pp. 1605 ff.
[4] *D.B.F.P.* v, nos. 541 and 542.
[5] See ibid., vi, no. 155 (Shepherd to Halifax).
[6] Ibid., nos. 170, 175 and 186; cf. *Dirksen Papers*, no. 29.

7 *D.B.F.P.* vi, no. 269.

8 Ibid., nos. 550 and 565.

9 See *D.G.F.P.* vii, no. 10, and *D.B.F.P.* vi, no. 613.

10 *D.B.F.P.* vi, no. 659.

11 See *D.G.F.P.* vii, nos. 64 and 66, and *Livre Jaune Français*, no. 199.

12 See *D.B.F.P.* vii, no. 83, and Feiling, p. 414.

13 *D.B.F.P.* viii, no. 277.

14 Ibid., ix, App. i. Cf. ibid., no. 365 for an example of the specific humiliations involved for Britain.

15 Ibid., vi, no. 180.

16 Ibid., ix, no. 244.

17 Ibid., no. 323.

18 Ibid., vi, no. 36.

19 Ibid., v, nos. 290 and 266.

20 Ibid., no. 301.

21 Cf. ibid., nos. 431, 489 and 513, and *D.G.F.P.* vi, no. 377.

22 *Documents concerning German-Polish Relations and the Outbreak of Hostilities* (Cmd. 6106, H.M.S.O., 1939), no. 25.

23 *D.G.F.P.* vii, nos. 64 and 66. In his *England, 1914-1945* (p. 449), A. J. P. Taylor somewhat misleadingly states that 'the British Government sent no new warning to Hitler'.

24 *D.B.F.P.* vi, no. 234, and vii, no. 79, and *D.G.F.P.* vi, nos. 602 and 603.

25 *D.B.F.P.* v, no. 336.

26 Ibid., no. 346.

27 See ibid., nos. 459, 558 and 677.

28 Ibid., no. 569.

29 See ibid., vii, no. 4.

30 Avon, *The Reckoning*, p. 53.

31 Henderson, *Failure of a Mission*, p. 13.

32 *D.B.F.P.* v, no. 604 and vi, no. 337.

33 Ibid., v, App. i, and nos. 727 and 281.

34 Ibid., vi, App. i, and vii, nos. 116, 37 and 49.

35 See ibid., vi, no. 481, and Bonnet, vol. 2, pp. 254-6.

36 See, for instance, *D.B.F.P.* vi, nos. 353 and 621, and Burckhardt, p. 320.

37 See B. Dahlerus, *The Last Attempt* (1947).

38 *D.G.F.P.* vi, nos. 368 and 380.

39 Ibid., vii, no. 87.

40 See *D.D.I.* xii, no. 249, and *D.G.F.P.* vi, no. 385.

41 Cf. *D.B.F.P.* vi, no. 370; *D.G.F.P.* vi, no. 716; *Dirksen Papers*, nos. 16 and 29; and *Hansard*, 5th series, vol. 350 (House of Commons), cols. 1025-8.

42 Cf. *D.G.F.P.* vi, no. 716; *Dirksen Papers*, no. 13; Hesse, *Hitler and the English*, p. 68; *D.B.F.P.* vi; no. 354, and M. Gilbert and R. Gott, *The Appeasers* (1963), p. 226.

43 *Dirksen Papers*, no. 24.

44 Ibid., no. 29, and Dirksen, *Moscow, Tokyo, Berlin*, pp. 241–2; author's italics.

45 *Hansard*, 5th series, vol. 350 (House of Commons), cols. 2425–2520.

46 *D.G.F.P.* vi, nos. 149 and 185; cf. no. 211, and E. von Manstein, *Lost Victories* (1958), p. 22.

47 Ibid., nos. 227, 234, 262, 271, 295 and 296.

48 Ibid., nos. 209 and 237.

49 *Livre Jaune Français*, no. 128.

50 Burckhardt, p. 294.

51 *Ambassador Dodd's Diary*, entry for 12 Nov. 1936, and see Wheeler-Bennett, *The Nemesis of Power*, pp. 228 and 441.

52 *D.G.F.P.* vi, no. 334.

53 See *Ciano's Diary, 1939–1943*; entries for 19, 20, and 21 Mar., and 16 Apr. 1939. This was not the first time the harlot simile had been used about Italian policies, nor the last; Mussolini himself described his people in 1940 as being 'like a whore, always on the side of the winner'.

54 Ibid., entry for 9 May 1939; and *Ciano's Diplomatic Papers*, p. 284.

55 Weizsäcker, p. 184.

56 See *D.G.F.P.* vi, no. 426 and 459; *D.D.I.* xii, no. 59; and *Ciano's Diary*, entries for 27 May 1939, and 8 June 1939.

57 *D.G.F.P.* vi, no. 433; the harangue was muddled as to whether Poland, the West, or both together could or should be engaged, and it spoke of the need to prepare for a 10 or 15 years' war, a statement Hitler appeared reassuringly to contradict in August.

58 See ibid., vi, no. 674, and vii, nos. 58, 130 and 287; and *N.C.A.* iv, pp. 1035–7, and vi, pp. 932–4.

59 See ibid., vi, nos. 712 and 784, and vii, no. 46.

60 See *D.D.I.* xii, nos. 367, 443, 535, 647, 662, 717 and 731; and Hassell, p. 55.

61 *D.D.I.* xii, no. 750, and *Ciano's Diary*, entries for 28 July 1939, 9 Aug. 1939, and 10 Aug. 1939.

62 The account of these days is based on *D.G.F.P.* vii, nos. 43 and 47; *D.D.I.* xiii, nos. 1, 4 and 21; *Ciano's Diary* for 11, 12, and 13 Aug. 1939, and 23 Dec. 1943; and Schmidt, p. 132. *Ciano's Diplomatic Papers*, pp. 297–303, duplicate some of this material.

63 See *D.G.F.P.* vii, no. 146; *D.D.I.* xiii, no. 47; and *Ciano's Diary* for 13, 15 and 20 Aug.

64 *D.G.F.P.* vii, App. i.

65 Ibid., nos. 119, 139, 153 and 155.

66 Cf. *Ciano's Diary* for 21 Aug. 1939; and *D.D.I.* xii, nos. 53, 187 and 451; and xiii, nos. 55 and 69.

67 See Wheeler-Bennett, op. cit., and W. Laqueur, *Russia and Germany* (1965). For an example of Hitler's anti-Bolshevik propaganda, see Baynes, vol. 1, pp. 692 ff.

68 *D.G.F.P.* iv, nos. 483, 488 and 495.

69 Ibid., vi, no. 215.

[70] Ibid., nos. 332, 406, 414 and 424.
[71] See ibid., nos. 437, 441, 442 and 446.
[72] Ibid., no. 447, E. Presseisen, *Germany and Japan* (1958) chap. vii.
[73] See ibid., nos. 446, 451 and 458.
[74] Ibid., no. 529.
[75] Ibid., nos. 543, 583, 588 and 628.
[76] Ibid., nos. 685 and 700.
[77] Ibid., nos. 729, 731 and 744.
[78] Ibid., nos. 758, 760, 766, 772 and 779, and vii, nos. 18 and 50.
[79] Ibid., vii, nos. 51 and 56.
[80] Ibid., nos. 70, 73, 75, 79 and 105.
[81] Ibid., nos. 111, 113, 125 and 132.
[82] Ibid., no. 142.
[83] See ibid., nos. 152, 158 and 159.
[84] Ibid., no. 213.
[85] Ibid., no. 229.
[86] See ibid., no. 262; Degras, pp. 363 ff.; and Hassell, p. 66.
[87] *D.G.F.P.* vii, nos. 192 and 193, and App. i.

7 War for Danzig and more

Les Allemands n'ont donc pas tort, lorsqu'ils prétendent que Dantzig n'est en soi qu'une question secondaire. Ce n'est pas seulement le sort de la Ville Libre, c'est la servitude ou l'independance de l'Europe qui est l'enjeu de la partie actuellement ouverte.
COULONDRE to BONNET, 30 April 1939.[1]

GERMAN preparations were now moving fast towards the climax planned for 25–26 August. The complete military subservience of Slovakia was obtained in advance, and the decision to strike on the 26th was confirmed at an OKW conference on the 23rd. Allegations of Polish atrocities against their German minority were increased in number and violence, the old battleship *Schleswig-Holstein* slid into Danzig harbour on its courtesy visit, and the Greiser–Chodacki customs talks were sabotaged according to Veesenmayer's plan when Poland was forced by outrageous demands to withdraw from the discussion on the 24th.[2] It is unwise to talk simply of 'inevitable' wars, and two of the main postulates on which Hitler based his plans were about to be destroyed. On the other hand he was determined and now ready to destroy Poland; his *Blitzkrieg* preparations, as well as the 'face' involved, created a momentum of their own which reinforced his inclination to run whatever risks the use of force entailed; and Poland, a stage in the drive eastwards, was also an adjunct to the decision to turn against the West at a later moment of Germany's own choosing. If war within a few years was not 'inevitable', Hitler was doing his best to make it so.

Meanwhile London and Paris had maintained the appear-

G

ance of firmness in the face of the Nazi–Soviet pact, though far from agreeing with Beck that 'it did not make much difference to the situation'.[3] Halifax was too late in trying to moderate his first, angry reaction to the news, and through the medium of a 'subservient and very frightened M. Potemkin' Seeds accused a savage Molotov of 'an act of bad faith' on the evening of the 22nd.[4] And despite fresh evidence from Burckhardt that 'the last moment had arrived' over Danzig, a Cabinet statement on the same day reaffirmed Britain's pledges to Poland: on Thursday the 24th Parliament would meet to pass an Emergency Powers (Defence) Bill, and precautions involving the call-up of key personnel would be taken.

At the same time, however, everything possible was done to avert a showdown. The line between London and Rome began to work overtime, and Halifax reinforced his own suggestion to the Poles that they should offer to negotiate by repeating Mussolini's urgent promptings to the same effect. Beck's reply that anything other than informal, social contact between Lipski and, say, Goering 'would be interpreted in Berlin as a sign of weakening' was not a welcome one.[5] In Paris Bonnet was busy suggesting to the Committee of National Defence on the 23rd that in the light of the Nazi–Soviet pact it would be wise for France 'to reconsider her attitude and profit by the respite thus gained to increase her military strength'. And though Gamelin asserted that the army was ready, it was evident that no offensive was contemplated which might offer the Poles real assistance.[6]

The French rôle had become an entirely secondary one, however. What mattered was the reaction of Britain, and when Chamberlain now despatched a personal appeal to Hitler it was to Rome, not to Paris or to Warsaw, that he took care to furnish detailed and early information of the fact. The message was sent to Henderson at 9.50 p.m. on the 22nd, repeating the warning that Britain would fulfil her

obligations but urging an end to all incitement and speedy
German–Polish negotiations to reach a settlement which the
Powers would guarantee.[7] It was delivered to Hitler at
Berchtesgaden by the Ambassador at 1.15 p.m. the next day.
Cringingly, the messenger suggested that the Fuehrer, 'who
had taken ten years to win over Germany, would have to
give England a longer period of time' and that 'he personally
had never believed in an Anglo-French–Russian pact'. It
did nothing to stem the angry reproaches against Britain's
unwarranted support for the vicious and stupid Poles, or the
warning that if further military measures were taken by
London, Germany, too, would mobilise in full. As the door
closed behind Henderson's back Hitler slapped himself on
the thigh and laughed. 'Chamberlain won't survive that
conversation', he crowed; 'his Cabinet will fall this evening.'
Presumably he expected a more yielding one still to take its
place, though nothing could further demonstrate his state of
maniacal unreality.[8]

A few hours later Henderson was summoned to receive
the text of Hitler's reply. The latter made it clear that 'at the
next instance of Polish provocation he would act' (the
Gestapo already had one planned, with the use of Polish
uniforms). The former was heartbroken. 'As you know,' he
wrote to Halifax later, 'I have held from the beginning that
the Poles were utterly foolish and unwise. But there it is, and
perhaps Providence regards war as necessary to teach us not
to do it again.' Now, according to the German record, he
could only assure Hitler that hostility to Germany in Britain
was merely 'the work of Jews and enemies of the Nazis', and
that war between the two would benefit only the 'lesser
races' of the world.[9] The message he was given to pass on to
Chamberlain had his sympathy, for it spoke of Germany's
interests 'laid down by . . . history and deriving from vital
economic prerequisites', interests of a 'national-political and
psychological character' which could not be renounced and
which included Danzig and the Corridor. The crime of

Versailles and the brutal behaviour of the Poles would be answered, whatever the cost; if Britain continued to take military measures Germany would mobilise immediately.[10] The only hopeful news received by London on the 23rd to offset this rebuff was Loraine's confident judgement that Italy would not fight, and Mussolini's tempting suggestion that if Britain could get Poland to renounce Danzig he, too, would press Berlin to preserve peace.[11]

On Thursday 24th Parliament reassembled in London to hear speeches from Chamberlain and Halifax in which the determination to stand by Poland and the hope of a negotiated settlement were repeated.[12] Henderson, in opposition to Kennard, was urging that Lipski should ask to see Hitler, but Halifax privately rejected Mussolini's suggestion that Warsaw might be coerced.[13] Even when Lipski had an amiable talk with Goering it seemed that nothing could prevent war, for while the Danzig Senate appointed Forster their Head of State a calm Beck reported that the Polish Army was partially mobilised. Most Western journalists were leaving Berlin, and Henderson found Attolico in despair. Few believed that the appeals of Roosevelt and the Pope could avert disaster.

The feeling that war might be imminent produced some belated French and British preparations on Friday the 25th, and Halifax suggested that it was time for the two countries to concert the procedure to be adopted should their guarantee be invoked. But in marked contrast to the growing determination of their country, the weakness of the Foreign Secretary and his Prime Minister was far from dispelled. The former still envisaged no more than a fixed time limit for Germany to halt her troops and agree to discuss matters, and a Foreign Office memorandum of the same day thought in terms of allowing Danzig to choose its political allegiance in return for an international guarantee of Poland's frontiers and economic rights in the former Free City.[14] When at 1.30 p.m. Hitler produced the move which he expected would ensure British neutrality as he struck at dawn the next day, it did indeed test the susceptibilities of Chamberlain and his circle to the full. The Fuehrer summoned Henderson to make one last, magnanimous offer to the British Government and people.

Polish provocation, said Hitler, had become intolerable, and 'in the interests of quiet and order and European peace' he had therefore determined to remove the 'Macedonian conditions' on Germany's eastern border. The Danzig and Corridor questions must be solved, and though war now would be more horrible than that of 1914–18 Germany's agreement with Russia made her task relatively easy. Afterwards, however, he wished 'to approach England once more with a large, comprehensive offer'. He would pledge his recognition of the British Empire, place the power of the Reich at its disposal, and 'accept a reasonable limitation of armaments'. All he wanted in return was a fair colonial settlement and a recognition of the Axis and Russo-German friendship; he, an artist who wished only to return to contemplative pursuits, offered blessings in place of futile, bloody conflict. The performance was calm and earnest. Only a refusal to pledge in advance a negotiated settlement with Poland seemed to detract from its sweet reasonableness.[15]

It was certainly enough to convince Henderson, who promised to fly back to London the following morning to deliver it in person. Despite the fact that his Embassy had by now acquired a detailed report of Hitler's bloodthirsty exhortation to his generals of the 22nd, Henderson urged London and Lipski that the offer should be taken 'very seriously', and that an exchange of populations might also help solve the Polish issue. Kennard pleaded that for Beck or Lipski to seek an interview with Ribbentrop or Hitler 'would be too much like Canossa', but Halifax was already joining Bonnet in backing the idea of a population exchange.[16] Unfortunately Warsaw continued to reaffirm its determination not to see its rights eroded, and Daladier insisted that the only way to convince Hitler was for British troops — 'a regiment with bagpipes would do the trick' — to land in France.

Hitler's own anxieties had mounted during that Friday afternoon. A personal message had been despatched to Mussolini (the Duce was still not given the details of his ally's timetable) explaining away the shock of the Soviet pact and clearly hinting that action would be taken in response to intolerable Polish provocation in the very near future. But the final decision to strike on the following morning had been postponed at midday, and though Attolico found the Fuehrer jubilant that his Soviet treaty would enable him to crush Poland with ease, Schmidt noticed that his master awaited the Duce's reply 'with unconcealed impatience'.[17] With the *Wehrmacht* already secretly mobilised and waiting for the order, tension in the Berlin Chancellery increased. At 3.02 p.m. Hitler appeared before the waiting generals at the doors of the Music Room, pale and somewhat theatrical, to give his decision. '*Fall Weiss*.' The attack was on.[18]

At about 4.30, however (though the exact time is uncertain and may have been later), it seems that news reached Berlin that the Anglo-Polish treaty was about to be ratified, despite the blow of the Molotov–Ribbentrop pact and the lure of the Fuehrer's new offer. The five months of waiting were in fact ended soon after 5.30 in London when the two countries agreed to support each other against 'any action by a European Power which clearly threatens, directly or indirectly, the independence of one of [them]'. Only in a secret protocol was it to be made clear that Germany was the Power referred to and that Danzig was included within the category of indirect aggression, but the news was enough to shake Hitler. He sat brooding at his desk until Coulondre was announced at 5.30. It seemed that his thoughts were elsewhere as he delivered the assurance that he had no wish

ever to fight France unless she were so foolish as to aid and
abet the Poles, and he hurriedly brought the interview to
an end.[19] Attolico was waiting outside with Mussolini's
reply.

He brought, in Schmidt's words, 'a bombshell'. Though
the Duce fully approved the Soviet pact and the need to
answer Poland, he could only support Germany in a general
war if he received supplies of military and raw materials,
for his own preparations had been aimed, as agreed, at war
in 1942. Gone was the total solidarity of the twin movements
of European regeneration. Gone, too, in more practical
terms, was the much-needed help of the Italian Navy in the
Mediterranean. An A.D.C. who was present saw that 'the
Fuehrer was considerably shaken'.[20] By the time a request
for details of what was required had been telephoned to
Rome at 7.40 p.m., the decision had been taken to halt the
attack in the face of this second great surprise. Keitel came
running out from Hitler's study shouting to his adjutant, and
at 7.30 Halder noted: 'No opening of hostilities.'* According
to Keitel Hitler had said 'I need time for negotiations', and
to Goering he observed that the cancellation was temporary
only, 'to see whether we can eliminate British intervention'.[21]
In the week which followed, the isolation and destruction of
Poland remained his main hope, though under strain there
was to be a hint that for the moment a Polish climb-down
would also be acceptable. The third alternative was to
proceed regardless of the risk. It was in the nature of Nazism
that it should be the one finally taken.

During Saturday the 26th it became clear in Berlin that
there was no hope of bringing Italy to the starting post in the
near future. After urgent prompting from Ribbentrop, Ciano

* Though later entries in his notebook offer conflicting and sometimes
impossible times for the moment of cancellation. The change of plan
threw into some confusion those conspirators in Germany who were
trying to influence Brauchitsch and Halder. See Wheeler-Bennett, op.
cit., and *I.M.T. Proceedings*, Pt. 12, pp. 244–6.

telephoned Attolico with the details of Italian requirements at 12.10 p.m. The Foreign Minister had by now sufficiently overcome his master's 'furiously warlike' mood of the previous morning to be able to produce a list that was 'enough to kill a bull', and Attolico added the assertion that delivery must precede hostilities. The most Hitler could do was ask that his ally should pin down Anglo-French forces by threatening propaganda and military movements, declaring at the same time that he 'did not shrink from solving the Eastern question even at the risk of complications with the West'. The Duce promised to cooperate as asked, and corrected Attolico's exaggerated date of delivery for all supplies apart from AA guns. But he could still only bemoan his state of mind 'at finding myself compelled by forces beyond my control not to afford you real solidarity at the moment of action'.[22]

At the same time the British Government was doing everything possible to win Mussolini to the cause of peace, deliberately concealing the extent of their contacts in that direction from Poland and France. François-Poncet, in fact, was soon to complain bitterly from Rome of the lack of trust and coordination between allies, but the idea that they alone could manage the Duce had long been a belief of Chamberlain and his circle, and fresh warnings from Léger against Italian duplicity must have appeared to confirm its wisdom.[23] Loraine had already reported that the Italians would avoid any incidents likely to involve their forces in the Middle East, and on the same day he conveyed the outline of Hitler's 'magnanimous offer' to the British Empire to the other angry and indignant Axis partner.[24] Despite the skill and success of such manœuvres, however, they were not conducive to trust and harmony between Britain and her own allies. Poland's fears of a sell-out, for instance, were amply demonstrated by the speed of her Ambassador's *démarche* to Halifax following hints in *The Times* on the 26th that a compromise solution, possibly involving the surrender of Danzig and the Corridor, had been discussed in Berlin.

From Paris, Hitler still appeared implacable. Using all the eloquence at his command Coulondre delivered during the day a personal letter from Daladier to Hitler in which the French Premier urged that a 'friendly and equitable settlement' could be found, recalling to a fellow soldier the horrors of the previous conflict and warning that the only victors in another would be 'the forces of destruction and barbarism'. Only when the terrible fate of women and children in war was mentioned did Hitler seem to hesitate. Murmuring that he had often thought of that, he went into a corner with Ribbentrop; he came back with his face hard, again insisting that the Poles must bow to his will.[25] That day the Tannenberg celebrations planned for the 27th were cancelled and fresh troop movements and communications interference were reported.

As he made use of the delay to obtain diversionary Russian military manoeuvres on Poland's eastern frontier,[26] Hitler was still working to obtain Britain's acquiescence. He had as yet received no reply to his official offer, and during the night of the 26th–27th Goering brought Dahlerus to him as a secondary means through which to achieve the same result. Lovingly running over the details of his military power, screaming dementedly of his determination to build U Boats and planes for victory, the Fuehrer also suggested a territorial settlement whereby peace could be preserved: Poland could keep Gdynia and a corridor to it through the Corridor, with economic rights in Danzig and a German guarantee of her frontiers.[27] Since London already had some knowledge of the postponement of the Nazi assault, this fresh sign of second and more reasonable thoughts was likely to prove tempting indeed.

Dahlerus arrived in Downing Street to see Chamberlain, Halifax and Cadogan on the afternoon of the Sunday the 27th. The desperate hope in the Prime Minister's heart

again led him towards betrayal, dishonour, and perhaps
overthrow by an angry nation, for he indicated to his visitor
that while Poland would fight for the Corridor she might
possibly concede Danzig and an extra-territorial corridor,
subject to international guarantees.[28] It was agreed, and
confirmed by telephone to Goering, that Dahlerus should
return to Germany ahead of Henderson with an outline of
Britain's answer to Hitler's earlier offer. It rejected the idea
of German aid for the Empire but promised talks on other
issues once the current crisis had been solved on a fair and
honourable basis. The official reply was still only in the
drafting stage. Hore-Belisha found it 'fulsome, obsequious
and deferential'.[29]

There were one or two other encouraging signs during the
day. It was learned that Beck had agreed to consider the
possibility of a population exchange, and at 2.45 p.m. Ciano
telephoned Halifax to recommend a positive reply to Hitler's
offer and to promise Italy's cooperation in the search for
peace.[30] A Foreign Office memorandum written by
Kirkpatrick and approved by Halifax suggested that 'the
German Government are wobbling', that 'we have an
unexpectedly strong hand' with which to be 'conciliatory in
form [but] absolutely firm in substance'.[31]

The strain was indeed beginning to tell on Hitler.
According to one member of his entourage he now 'wanted
to replace the "big Polish solution" by the "small one" '.[32]
The Fuehrer repeated the idea at a conference in the
Chancellery at 5.30 p.m., the outline of which Colonel Oster
passed on to Halder:

Minimum demands: return of Danzig, settling of Corridor
question. Maximum demands: 'Depending on military
situation.' If minimum demands not satisfied, then war.
Brutal! . . . War very difficult, perhaps hopeless. . . .

Hitler looked exhausted and haggard. His voice was a croak,
and he kept himself closely surrounded by his SS advisers.[33]

When Goering telephoned him with the latest news from Dahlerus in the small hours of the 28th, he declared himself satisfied with the British reply providing it tallied with this advance information, and the Swede hurried off to the British Embassy with the good news.[34]

But Hitler's nerve was not broken. Mussolini, who knew his man, was prepared to urge peace 'in forcible terms' to Mackensen in Rome, but in a fresh letter to his fellow-dictator did not dare venture so far.[35] The Fuehrer's reply to Daladier's letter, handed to Coulondre during the afternoon of the 27th, was polite but uncompromising,[36] and operational plans against the West were prepared during the day. The decision to use Slovak territory in preparation for a 'Polish attack' was finally put to the authorities in Bratislava, and at 10 p.m. Ribbentrop telephoned Mackensen with orders to deny all rumours of a *détente* since the situation was deteriorating hourly: 'The armies are on the march'.[37] The British Consul in Danzig noticed that a scarlet-and-gold tribune had been erected in the market-place, with loud-speakers in the streets. At 10.46 p.m. Beck informed Kennard that further mobilisation measures would have to be taken, though the final, public stage would still be withheld.

Hitler's new line of thought was passed on to Halder by Brauchitsch on the afternoon of Monday, 28th:[38]

Attack starts September 1st. Fuehrer will let us know at once if we are not to strike. . . . Fuehrer very calm and clear. . . . Plan: we demand Danzig, corridor through Corridor, and plebiscite on same basis as Saar. England will perhaps accept, Poland probably not. *Wedge between them!*

and a more detailed timetable was forthcoming on the following day:

Basic principles: raise a barrage of demographic and democratic demands. . . . 30.8. Poles in Berlin. 31.8. Blow up. 1.9. Use of force.

The plan would have stood considerable chance of success had Chamberlain, Simon, Hoare, Halifax and Wilson been backed by the public opinion of twelve months before. Their main concern was still to make the Poles see reason, and American aid in this had been sought when direct pressure appeared awkward and inadequate. Though Halifax thought it 'more than possible' that Hitler might strike on the 29th and warned Mussolini that Britain would then fulfil her obligations,[39] he was still urging Warsaw to agree to direct negotiations. At 4 p.m. on the 28th, twenty minutes after the Berlin Embassy had passed on the news that the German Army would be in a position to attack on the Wednesday night, Beck's acceptance at last arrived.

At 10.30 that evening, 'fortified by half a bottle of Champagne' and greeted by a guard of honour, Henderson delivered the official British reply to Hitler. Firmer than the draft which had appalled Hore-Belisha, it insisted that only a settlement which safeguarded Poland's 'essential interests' could be accepted. It also passed on the Polish agreement to direct negotiations and implied that, once the crisis was over, economic assistance would be forthcoming to help transform the German economy from a warlike to a peaceful basis.[40] Henderson personally guaranteed that Chamberlain could carry public opinion in a policy of friendship for Germany, and, to Vansittart's horror when he read it, replied to a question of Hitler's that he did not think even an Anglo-German alliance impossible. For his part Hitler was calm, but obdurate. Neither Britain, France, nor Poland had yet fully mobilised, and the neutrality of the Low Countries had been freshly reaffirmed by the West as well as Germany. A quick victory in the East, and at most a shadow war in the West seemed more and more possible. To Henderson he demanded parts of Silesia as well as Danzig and the whole of the Corridor, and still talked of annihilating Poland, wild and awkward remarks which Halifax took care to withhold from Warsaw.[41] 'In two months', Hitler assured

Weizsäcker the following evening, 'Poland will be finished; then we shall have a great peace conference with the Western Powers.'[42]

To Poland the situation on Tuesday the 29th offered little comfort. Press and public remained, by secret German testimony, amazingly calm, but traffic through Danzig had been stopped, there was news of Russian troop movements in the East, and German forces were entering Slovakia. The possibility that the West might waver seemed more likely than ever, and Beck felt the need to insist that his Government could not think of accepting the demands Hitler had put forward in March.[43] At 4 p.m. he informed Kennard and Noël that he would have to proceed with general mobilisation if Poland's existence was not to be entirely jeopardised, but allowed himself to be persuaded to postpone so provocative an action until the following day when Hitler's reply to the British note might have been received.[44] As a result, Polish military preparations were by no means complete when Germany invaded three days later.

In London, on the other hand, it was a day of qualified optimism. At 7 a.m. Dahlerus telephoned that a satisfactory settlement now seemed possible to Hitler and Goering, and in the evening the latter tore a map out of an atlas to shade in the plebiscite areas envisaged in the Fuehrer's forthcoming and generous offer.[45] Halifax on the telephone to Ciano and Chamberlain in the House of Commons both blended hope with their anxiety. And though at 12.30 p.m. Attolico had his suggestion of a conference contemptuously brushed aside by Ribbentrop, it was known in London at 7 p.m. that Mussolini was strongly recommending to Hitler that the British note offered the basis for an entirely satisfactory settlement of the issues at stake.[46] Shortly afterwards Dahlerus reported that Chamberlain's speech had been well received, and Henderson found a 'noticeable relaxation of tension' in the German press.[47]

At 7.15 p.m. the Ambassador arrived at the Chancellery to receive Hitler's reply to the British note. The communication he was given accepted direct negotiations, 'though sceptical', and protested that no diminution of Poland's vital interests had ever been intended; but the demand for Danzig and the Corridor was as firm as ever, and it was laid down that a plenipotentiary from Warsaw had to arrive in Berlin on the following day. Hitler himself stormed at the manner in which Britain presumed to bargain over Germany's vital interests, and gave his own game away by declaring that negotiations were bound to fail. Amazingly the worm turned, though it made no difference, and Henderson shouted back in defence of British honour.[48] When he read the German note to Lipski later that evening, however, he was still ready to press for an acceptance of the ultimatum concerning a plenipotentiary, and though Halifax found this item 'unacceptable', he, too, suggested to Warsaw that night that there was some promise in the document as a whole.[49]

Confusion in the face of Hitler's mixture of brutality and reasonableness was evident in the West and in Rome on the 30th. While Mussolini postured ('Not being able to wage war,' noted Ciano, 'he makes all the necessary preparations so that in case of a peaceful solution he may be able to say that he would have waged it'[50]), Coulondre despatched a note which was to impress the French Cabinet on the following day: 'The trial of strength is turning in our favour. . . . Hitler is preoccupied to escape from the dead end he has got himself into'.[51] Hopes of a German military *coup* against the Nazi régime also revived in some quarters.

At 10 Downing Street the ubiquitous Dahlerus found the atmosphere sombre. After a telephone conversation with Goering, however, he was able to report that it was 'nearly certain' that Hitler would demand only Danzig and would accept a plebiscite for the Corridor, with a transit strip for the loser. It was a shrewd bait, and when Halifax insisted that the manner in which the proposals were put would be vital another phone call to Goering produced the reassuring answer that the Fuehrer's draft would be no more than a 'basis for discussion'; it only required someone to come from Warsaw to fetch it. Dahlerus left for yet another air flight between the two capitals carrying assurances of the British desire for a settlement, and Chamberlain despatched a telegram promising Hitler that the official reply would not be long in following.[52] Kennedy saw the Prime Minister that evening: 'Frankly,' he reported, 'he is more worried about getting the Poles to be reasonable than the Germans.'[53]

Others remained entirely sceptical, however. Beck informed Kennard around noon that general mobilisation would begin at midnight, with the necessary placards on the streets around 4.30 p.m., and Daladier refused an invitation Phipps was told to extend 'as from himself' to visit London that afternoon or the next day. The French Premier thought all the evidence pointed to a German intention to dismember Poland; perhaps he also thought it was beginning to suggest a British desire to repeat the Sudeten episode.[54]

At midnight Henderson brought his reply to Ribbentrop. The British Government found the immediate arrival of a Polish negotiator 'impracticable', but looked forward to examining Hitler's detailed proposals to see 'how far they are compatible with the essential conditions [already] stated'. In the meantime they urged a temporary *modus vivendi* over Danzig, and, with tragic irony, a German approach to Moscow to obtain the latter's agreement to participate in an international guarantee of a Polish-German settlement.[55]

There followed an interview so furious that Schmidt, who was the third person present, thought the two men would come to blows. At top speed, according to Henderson, though at a reasonable pace according to Schmidt, (and why, indeed, should essential propaganda be obscured?) Ribbentrop read aloud in German the Fuehrer's new and detailed proposals. Henderson certainly picked up the gist of them, which arrived in London at 9.30 the next morning, but he did not ask for Schmidt to translate. To his astonishment (though in the event it was of no account) Ribbentrop then refused to hand over the actual text on the grounds that the failure of a Polish representative to appear during the day invalidated the whole exercise. The reasonableness of this was argued on both sides in the most forceful manner, but Henderson left empty-handed. When he woke Lipski to suggest that the latter should ask to see Ribbentrop to learn the terms for himself, he was told that Warsaw's opinion and authority would have to be sought first. For a sick and desperately anxious man it had been a foul night.[56]

The proposals which he had heard were indeed startling at first sight; Schmidt 'felt himself back in Geneva' when he read them. They included the recognition of Danzig as German and Gdynia as Polish — both to be demilitarised; a plebiscite in the Corridor after twelve months under international supervision, the area concerned being smaller than that hastily indicated by Goering to Dahlerus; a corridor through the Corridor for the loser of the plebiscite and an exchange of populations thereafter; and international investigation of any further minority complaints.[57] Here was Hitler's 'barrage of demographic and democratic demands', calculated to do more than win London's approval. 'I needed an alibi,' he remarked later, 'especially with the German people, to show them that I had done everything to maintain peace.'[58]

The diplomatic activity, official and unofficial, on the last day of European peace was intense. At 1.30 on that morning, Thursday, 31 August, Goering was reading the details of Hitler's proposal to Dahlerus, perhaps part of the same calculated drama as Ribbentrop's behaviour shortly before; Dahlerus in turn telephoned them to Ogilvie-Forbes in the British Embassy, and took round a copy dictated by Goering at 8 a.m. as an additional precaution. The Swede

found Henderson tired and dispirited, however, for the
Ambassador had already seen Attolico and the news was
grim: Weizsäcker had said that unless a gesture were made
within the next few hours the *Wehrmacht* would march, but
Lipski was not making himself available to those who
desperately wanted to know Warsaw's reaction to Hitler's
offer.[59] Von Hassell, too, had arrived at Henderson's
breakfast table at Weizsäcker's prompting, and a phone call
to Goering again produced the assurance that all might be
saved if the Poles would promise to send a negotiator at
once.[60]

The unfortunate Lipski became the target for everyone's
pleading and harrying; even Coulondre temporarily abandoned his policy of firmness at all costs and joined forces with
the rest, in imitation of his Foreign Minister's concurrent
behaviour in Paris.[61] Henderson informed Weizsäcker of
what was being done, begging that no precipitate German
action should spoil things,[62] and sent Dahlerus and Ogilvie-
Forbes to spur Lipski on with the details of the bargain now
open to his country.[63] When the Polish Ambassador's
distrust and resentment had been made plain Henderson
then allowed Dahlerus to telephone Sir Horace Wilson for
all the Nazi intelligence services to hear, praising the 'liberal'
German offer and declaring that it was 'obvious to us' that
the Poles were entirely responsible for obstructing negotiations. Wilson cut him off abruptly, and Halifax despatched
a rebuke to his Ambassador, but the damage had been
done.[64] Who was 'us', one wonders? And did Henderson
know what was being said, with all its implications? He had
consciously weakened his Government's position over Spain,[65]
Austria, the Sudetenland, and Czechoslovakia, despite what
he called his 'exceptionally high sense of duty'. Had it been
the same now, it would at least have been consistent.

At 11 a.m. Ciano was on the telephone to Halifax to ask
whether London could not, in this extremity, persuade
Warsaw to surrender its rights in Danzig. But Halifax's first

reaction was unfavourable, and despite Loraine's support
for the Italian proposal he confirmed his negative later in
the day.[66] Kennard was instructed, however, to join Noël in
pressing Beck to inform Berlin of his acceptance of direct
discussions and to order Lipski to receive the new proposals;
Kennard's own advice to the contrary was having to give
way before that of Henderson.[67]

Beck was being forced by the mood of his country to be
more unyielding than he personally may have desired. He
would tell Lipski to inform the Germans that the British
proposals were accepted, but he would not send for a
document which experience showed 'might be accompanied
by some sort of ultimatum'. By the time Halifax had returned
to the charge it was too late. Through their interception and
decoding service the Nazis were aware of Lipski's new,
but limited, instructions long before he managed to see
Ribbentrop at 6.30 that evening. The Ambassador then
simply delivered a note stating that his Government were
'favourably considering' the proposal for direct talks, and
that a formal answer would follow 'within the next few
hours'.[68]

Meanwhile a last effort by Mussolini to repeat his Munich
triumph had appeared, offered its temptations to the West,
and gone drifting away down the stream of events. When
the proposal for a conference to revise those Versailles
clauses which were troubling Europe had arrived by phone
from Ciano to Halifax at 12.50 p.m., it had been Chamberlain who had anxiously summoned Corbin to obtain the
French reaction, and Daladier who had insisted to Phipps
that he would rather resign than accept this invitation to
'a second Munich'. Yet by the evening the positions had to
some extent been reversed. Bonnet had made the best use he
could of Coulondre's jubilant note which had now arrived
in Paris, and after the Ministerial Council had met assured
Phipps that his Government 'now quite realised that it
would not be possible to decline the Italian proposal

offhand'. Corbin, on the other hand, now found Chamberlain far less pressing. The Prime Minister had not been unaware of the dangers involved in the proposal, and it would seem that during the afternoon counsels of caution had prevailed.[69]

The one success of the day took place in Rome that evening after Ciano had learned with alarm that telephone communications with Britain had been cut off by the latter. It was the moment of truth for Fascist bombast. The Duce agreed that war looked far too close and that Ciano should 'commit an indiscretion': Loraine was informed that Italy would not fight 'whatever Berlin says'. According to each other's reports the Ambassador and Foreign Minister were 'on the verge of tears' and 'moved by the deepest emotion' respectively. London knew at 11 p.m.[70]

For the rest, it was wasted effort, though Attolico, Henderson, Dahlerus, Hassell and others did their best in Berlin, vainly hoping that Goering might restrain his master. At 7 p.m. Hitler abruptly informed Attolico that it was too late to do anything,[71] and at 9.15 Weizsäcker handed over the full text of Hitler's proposals to Henderson with the information that they were now to be considered terminated by the neglect of others.[72] The German troops had been ordered to take up their positions at 6.30 that morning, and instructions for the assault were released by OKW at 4 p.m. Since all peaceful means of ending an intolerable situation had been exhausted, ran Hitler's Military Directive No. 1, force would be used. In the West the responsibility for opening hostilities must be left to Britain and France, and even then the *Wehrmacht* would stand on the defensive until further orders. In the East, the attack would begin at 4.45 the next morning.[73]

Poland was invaded at dawn on Friday 1 September. The SS had already created incidents on the border to provide one last, transparent excuse, the SA in Danzig were ready, and the *Schleswig-Holstein* opened up from the harbour with her big guns. At 5.40 a.m. Berlin radio broadcast the text of the Fuehrer's proclamation to his army in which blood-thirsty persecutions and frontier violations on the part of Poland were blamed for the war — though German diplomats were instructed to avoid the word 'war', and to describe events as 'engagements brought about by Polish attacks'. Hitler also got off a private explanation to Mussolini in which he showed why he did not 'want to expose [the latter] to the danger of assuming the role of mediator',[74] though this did not prevent an Italian declaration of neutrality later in the day.

At 10 a.m. Hitler drove through silent streets to address the Reichstag and assured his audience that if victory were not forthcoming he would not survive the outcome. Goering took Dahlerus to see him on his return. With staring eyes, the Fuehrer screamed and gesticulated as he proclaimed his unshakeable determination to smash his enemies. Here, then, was 'Germany's destiny'. His breath was foul.[75]

In London the Foreign Office knew from Kennard by 8.30 that Cracow and other cities were being bombed and that the German Army had crossed the frontier. Count Raczynski arrived at 10.30 with similar information, expecting a swift implementation of the Anglo-Polish treaty and aid from the air if possible. Halifax was sympathetic rather than decisive, but at least he did not conceal his doubts when the German chargé d'affaires explained that it was only a case of shooting back at the aggressive Poles. Nor did a series of now-fatuous telephone calls from Dahlerus in Berlin receive much sympathy during the day when they offered a similar interpretation,[76] and at 2 p.m. it was known that Beck was breaking off all relations with Berlin. Even Henderson at last saw hope only in an 'inflexible determination on our part to resist force by force'.

The action expected of the West was not forthcoming, however. Bonnet was still clutching at the idea of an Italian-

sponsored conference, and as well as sending a fulsome
reply on the subject to Ciano had the temerity to sound
Beck through Noël. 'We are in the thick of war as the result
of unprovoked aggression', Beck replied. 'The question
before us is not that of a conference but the common action
which should be taken by the Allies to resist.'[77] And though
British forces were mobilised and a War Cabinet was being
formed which included Churchill, Chamberlain had nothing
final to announce to the Commons that evening, however
forthrightly he denounced Hitler and Nazism. He could
say, however, that Henderson had been instructed to
convey a warning to Berlin:

Unless the German Government are prepared to give His
Majesty's Government satisfactory assurances that [they]
have suspended all aggressive action against Poland and are
prepared promptly to withdraw their forces from Polish
territory, His Majesty's Government . . . will without
hesitation fulfil their obligations to Poland.[78]

The French Cabinet also issued a firm statement during
the evening, and Coulondre followed Henderson to present
a similar communication to Ribbentrop at 9 p.m. But when
the British and French Ministers at the Vatican suggested
that the Pope, too, should make known his grief that Hitler
had plunged the world into war less than 24 hours after His
Holiness's appeal for peace, the Cardinal Secretary of State
refused. The grounds were to become familiar: it would
'involve specific intervention in international politics'.[79]
Poland's own staunch Catholicism was not decisive.

The anguish of Poland and of those concerned for Britain's
honour continued throughout the following day. Delay
stemmed from Paris above all. Bonnet persisted with the
idea of a conference and the French Army begged for more
time to prepare for battle, while there was some confusion in
London as to whether or not the assent of the Chamber
would have to be awaited before Daladier could declare
war.[80] 'We shall be grateful for anything you can do to

infuse courage and determination into M. Bonnet', telegraphed Halifax to Phipps during the morning, but he soon
learned that a 48-hour limit was still being proposed for any
ultimatum that might be presented at Berlin.[81]

Moreover the hope of obtaining a conference still had
some hours before it died altogether. To Hitler's annoyance
and 'yielding to French pressure', Mussolini had enquired
again through Attolico at 10 a.m. whether such a move
would be acceptable if the armies could stop 'where they are
now'. In turn Ribbentrop had played for time by asking for
confirmation that the West's declarations of the previous
evening were not ultimata, in which case Hitler would
reply 'in a day or two'.[82] A series of frantic visits and
telephone calls between Rome, London and Paris then
confirmed that no ultimata had been delivered, though
Halifax made it clear to Ciano and to a dissident Bonnet
that Britain must demand a prior withdrawal of German
troops. Meanwhile, of course, those troops moved deeper
into Poland, and fresh appeals for help in warding off the
overwhelming strength of the *Luftwaffe* were received
through Kennard.[83]

The Cabinet met in London at 4.30 p.m., and at Hore-
Belisha's urging it was unanimously agreed that an ultimatum should be presented to Germany, expiring at
midnight.[84] But the decision reached neither Berlin nor the
British public. Cadogan did attempt to convince Bonnet by
telephone of the need to draw the line at midnight, but the
latter held out for a delay of two more days and coolly
denied that the Polish Ambassador in Paris had asked for
any assistance.[85] In Halifax's words, the position was 'very
embarrassing to His Majesty's Government', and he confirmed to Ciano that there could be no conference without a
German withdrawal. Despite better news from Paris,
however,[86] Prime Minister and Foreign Secretary were still
prepared to betray their Cabinet, and to the widespread
amazement and disgust of Members, it was of the continued

possibility of a conference that Chamberlain spoke when he
rose in the Commons at 7.44 p.m. If German troops would
withdraw, he said, the Government 'would be willing to
regard the position as being the same as it was before the
German forces crossed the Polish frontier',[87] and Halifax
sent the text to Henderson for him to pass on to Dahlerus
and Goering. Greenwood 'spoke for England' in the
Commons, and hard words were used on the telephone to
Corbin by some of his friends in London.

But the time for wriggling was almost over. At 8.50 p.m.
Ribbentrop informed Attolico that there would be no
withdrawal of German forces, and at 9.30 Loraine reported
that Mussolini was abandoning his efforts.[88] The violence of
the Commons' reaction was further brought home to
Chamberlain and Halifax when a Cabinet deputation
waited upon them at Downing Street with the determination
to tolerate no further delay. 'Right gentlemen, this means
war'; as the Prime Minister acquiesced a histrionic crash of
thunder sounded outside.[89] At Corbin's suggestion a direct
telephone call from Chamberlain to Daladier then by-passed
Bonnet at last, and though a deadline was still not agreed,
its early settlement came a stage nearer.[90] After Raczynski
had again called to voice his country's suspicions and
appeals, Halifax insisted to Bonnet at 10.30 that the British
ultimatum would have to expire by noon, even if France had
to delay another 24 hours. He received the reluctant
assurance that Paris, too, would act during the 3rd.[91] At
12.25 a.m. Henderson was instructed to seek an interview
with Ribbentrop at 9 that morning; Coulondre was to
follow him three hours later.

Some approached the point of no return with reluctant
steps. At 10 p.m. Dr. Hesse had arrived from the German
Embassy to see Sir Horace Wilson, bringing an invitation
from Ribbentrop to a secret meeting with Hitler 'to discuss
the whole position, heart to heart'. Wilson refused and
reiterated his Government's position, but according to the

German report he still assured Hesse that if there were a
withdrawal London 'would be prepared to let bygones be
bygones'.[92] Bonnet, too, went on trying, and had Ciano
wakened to see 'if we could not at least obtain a symbolic
withdrawal of German forces'. Ciano threw the message in
the waste-paper basket and went back to bed.[93]

Henderson delivered the British ultimatum at the German
Foreign Office at 9 a.m. It gave Hitler until 11 a.m.,
British Summer Time, to announce his withdrawal from
Poland. Ribbentrop would not deign to receive the Ambassador and Schmidt, who was to stand in his place and had
overslept, only just arrived in time by slipping in at a side
door as Henderson went in at the front. The interpreter took
the document over to where Hitler and Ribbentrop waited
in the Chancellery. They read, and there was silence; then,
with a savage look at Ribbentrop, Hitler asked: 'What now?'
Outside the room Goering muttered: 'If we lose this war,
then God have mercy on us.' Goebbels stood alone in a
corner; he looked downcast and absorbed with his thoughts.[94]
Between them, these men, their movement, and the nation
which had spawned and followed them had brought war
to an unhealthy Europe. The timing and circumstances had
been to a certain extent fortuitous. The responsibility was
not.

---

[1] *Livre Jaune Français*, no. 113.

[2] *D.G.F.P.* vii, nos. 165, 172, 176, 182, 214, 237, 244, 254 and App. i.

[3] *D.B.F.P.* vii, no. 123.

[4] Ibid., nos. 136, 144 and 165.

[5] Ibid., nos. 166 and 180.

[6] Cf. Bonnet, vol. 2, pp. 302–8; Gamelin, vol. 1, pp. 24 ff.; and Namier,
Diplomatic Prelude (1948), pp. 290–8.

[7] *D.B.F.P.* vii, nos. 142, 145, 174 and 177.

[8] Ibid., no. 200; *D.G.F.P.* vii, no. 200; Weizsäcker, p. 203.

[9] *D.B.F.P.* vii, nos. 257 and 248, and *D.G.F.P.* vii, no. 200. Note the
complete hypocrisy of Henderson's *Final Report* (Cmd. 6115), para. 11.

[10] *D.B.F.P.* vii, nos. 208 and 211.

[11] Ibid., no. 192.

[12] *Hansard*, 5th series, vol. 351 (House of Commons), cols. 2–10.

[13] *D.B.F.P.* vii, nos. 222 and 241.

[14] Ibid., nos. 278 and 307.

[15] Ibid., nos. 283 and 284.

[16] See ibid., nos. 286, 293, 314 and 357.

[17] *D.G.F.P.* vii, no. 266 and App. i; *D.D.I.* xiii, no. 259; Schmidt, pp. 143–6.

[18] Hofer, p. 191.

[19] *Livre Jaune Français*, no. 242.

[20] *D.G.F.P.* vii, no. 271 and App. i.

[21] *I.M.T. Proceedings*, pt. 11, p. 5, and pt. 2, p. 166.

[22] See *D.G.F.P.* vii, nos. 299, 301 and 307, and *Ciano's Diary, 1939–1943*, entries for 25 Aug. 1939, and 26 Aug. 1939.

[23] See *D.B.F.P.* vii, no. 496.

[24] See ibid., no. 327, and *Ciano's Diary*, for 26 Aug. 1939.

[25] *Livre Jaune Français*, nos. 253 and 261, and Coulondre, pp. 290–1.

[26] See *D.G.F.P.* vii, nos. 360, 383, 446 and 496.

[27] Dahlerus, pp. 56–9.

[28] *D.B.F.P.* vii, footnote to no. 349.

[29] Dahlerus, pp. 73–5 and Hore-Belisha, p. 220.

[30] *D.B.F.P.* vii, no. 373.

[31] Ibid., no. 397.

[32] Hesse, p. 79.

[33] *D.G.F.P.* vii, App. i.

[34] Dahlerus, pp. 78–9.

[35] *D.G.F.P.* vii, nos. 341, 349 and 350.

[36] Ibid., no. 354.

[37] Ibid., no. 362 and 357.

[38] Ibid., App. i.

[39] *D.B.F.P.* vii, no. 409.

[40] Ibid., no. 426.

[41] Ibid., nos. 450, 455 and 461.

[42] Weizsäcker, p. 208.

[43] *D.B.F.P.* vii, no. 487.

[44] See ibid., nos. 473 and 482, and Noël, pp. 462–5.

[45] *D.B.F.P.* vii, nos. 458 and 459, and Dahlerus, pp. 83–4.

[46] See *D.B.F.P.* vii, nos. 467 and 476; *D.G.F.P.* vii, nos. 411 and 417; and *Hansard*, 5th series, vol. 351 (House of Commons), cols. 111–16.

[47] *D.B.F.P.* vii, nos. 478 and 486.

[48] Ibid., nos. 490, 493, 502 and 508.

[49] Ibid., nos. 495, 505 and 510.

[50] *Ciano's Diary, 1939–1943*, entry for 30 Aug. 1939.

[51] Coulondre, p. 298.

[52] *D.B.F.P.* vii, nos. 514, 519 and 525, and Dahlerus, pp. 98–9.

[53] *F.R.U.S.* (1939), i, p. 392.

[54] *D.B.F.P.* vii, nos. 521 and 528.

[55] Ibid., nos. 543 and 547.

[56] Ibid., nos. 574 and 575; Schmidt, pp. 150-3; Hesse, p. 81.

[57] *D.B.F.P.* vii, no. 622.

[58] Schmidt, p. 153.

[59] *D.D.I.* xiii, no. 487, and *D.B.F.P.* vii, nos. 577 and 578.

[60] Hassell, pp. 67-71, and *D.B.F.P.* vii, no. 581.

[61] Coulondre, pp. 300-1.

[62] *D.G.F.P.* vii, no. 466.

[63] Dahlerus, pp. 100-3, and *D.B.F.P.* vii, nos. 587 and 597.

[64] *D.B.F.P.* vii, nos. 589, 591, 592 and 628.

[65] See *D.G.F.P.* iii, nos. 372 and 601.

[66] *D.B.F.P.* vii, nos. 580 and 627.

[67] Ibid., nos. 596, 618 and 628.

[68] Ibid., nos. 608, 609 and 632; *D.G.F.P.* vii, nos. 475 and 476; Dahlerus, p. 106.

[69] *D.B.F.P.* vii, nos. 604 and 634; Bonnet, vol. 2, pp. 340-2; Zay, pp. 81-2.

[70] *D.B.F.P.* vii, no. 621, and *Ciano's Diary*, entry for 31 Aug. 1939.

[71] *D.G.F.P.* vii, no. 478 and *D.D.I.* xiii, no. 507.

[72] *D.B.F.P.* vii, nos. 619 and 622. The German radio had broadcast the proposals at 9 p.m.

[73] *D.G.F.P.* vii, no. 493.

[74] Ibid., nos. 500, 504 and 512.

[75] Dahlerus, pp. 119-20.

[76] See *D.B.F.P.* vii, no. 651.

[77] See ibid., vii, nos. 649 and 693; Noël, p. 475; *Livre Jaune Français*, no. 343.

[78] *D.B.F.P.* vii, no. 664.

[79] Ibid., no. 687. Cf. S. Friedländer, *Pius XII and the Third Reich* (Chatto & Windus, 1966).

[80] See ibid., nos. 697 and 736, and Bonnet, vol. 2, p. 316.

[81] *D.B.F.P.* vii, nos. 699 and 708.

[82] *D.G.F.P.* vii, nos. 535, 539 and 541; *Ciano's Diary*, entry for 2 Sept. 1939.

[83] *D.B.F.P.* vii, nos. 709, 710, 716 and 720.

[84] Hore-Belisha, pp. 225-6.

[85] *D.B.F.P.* vii, no. 718.

[86] Ibid., nos. 727, 728 and 730.

[87] *Hansard*, 5th series, vol. 351 (House of Commons), cols. 126-33.

[88] *D.G.F.P.* vii, no. 554; *D.B.F.P.* vii, no. 739.

[89] Birkenhead, p. 447.

[90] Cf. *D.B.F.P.* vii, nos. 718, 740 and 747.

[91] Ibid., nos. 741 and 751.

[92] Ibid., ix, App. iv, and *D.G.F.P.* vii, no. 558. In his memoirs, (p. 85), Hesse recalls Wilson adding that Hitler would have to make a public apology.

[93] *Ciano's Diary*, entry for 3 Sept. 1939.

[94] Schmidt, p. 158.

Chronological Table

1933	January	Hitler becomes Chancellor of Germany.
	February	Japan leaves League of Nations.
	October	Germany leaves League of Nations and Disarmament Conference.
1934	January	German–Polish pact.
	July	Abortive Nazi *putsch* in Austria; murder of Dollfuss.
	October	Murder of Alexander of Yugoslavia and Barthou.
1935	January	Saar plebiscite.
	March	Hitler announces conscription and a military air force.
	May	Franco-Soviet and Czecho-Soviet pacts.
	June	Anglo-German naval agreement.
	October	Abyssinia invaded by Italy.
1936	March	Rhineland reoccupied by Germany.
	July	Austro-German agreement.
		Spanish Civil War begins.
	November	Rome–Berlin Axis announced.
		Germany and Japan sign anti-Comintern pact.
1937	May	Chamberlain becomes Prime Minister.
	July	Japanese begin advance into China.
	September	Mussolini visits Germany.
	November	Italy joins anti-Comintern pact.
		Hitler's 'Hossbach' survey.
		Halifax visits Hitler.
1938	4 February	Ribbentrop replaces Neurath as Foreign Minister.

12 February	Schuschnigg visits Hitler at Berchtesgaden.
20 February	Resignation of Eden.
9 March	Austrian plebiscite announced.
11 March	Schuschnigg forced by Berlin to resign.
12 March	German occupation of Austria.
13 March	Annexation of Austria proclaimed.
28 March	Konrad Henlein's destructive Sudeten tactics approved by Hitler.
16 April	Anglo-Italian agreement negotiated.
28–29 April	Daladier and Bonnet in London.
3–9 May	Hitler in Italy.
20–22 May	Scare over Czechoslovakia.
23 July	Lord Runciman 'invited' to Czechoslovakia.
7 September	*The Times* follows the lead of the *New Statesman* in suggesting the cession of the 'Sudetenland'.
	Beneš offers to meet the Sudeten German demands.
8 September	Talks between Prague and the Sudeten German Party broken off by latter.
13 September	Rioting in Sudetenland.
15 September	Chamberlain visits Hitler at Berchtesgaden.
18 September	Daladier and Bonnet in London.
19 September	Anglo-French advice to Beneš to cede areas containing 50 per cent or more Germans.
20 September	Czech refusal.
21 September	Anglo-French ultimatum to Beneš; accepted.
22 September	Hodža resigns as Premier of Czechoslovakia.
22–23 September	Chamberlain visits Hitler at Godesberg.
25 September	Daladier in London.

26 September	Sir Horace Wilson to Berlin.
	Hitler's *Sportpalast* speech.
	Foreign Office communiqué promises Britain and Russia will aid France if she stands by the Czechs.
27 September	British Fleet mobilised; Chamberlain broadcasts to the nation.
28 September	Hitler accepts Mussolini's proposal of Four-Power talks.
29–30 September	Four-Power agreement at Munich.
30 September	Polish ultimatum to Czechoslovakia.
5 October	Beneš resigns.
2 November	Vienna award gives southern Slovakia and part of Ruthenia to Hungary.
10 November	Fresh and systematic persecution of Jews in Germany.
16 November	Anglo-Italian agreement ratified.
6 December	Franco-German declaration of friendship.

1939	5 January	Beck visits Hitler at Berchtesgaden.
	6 January	Chamberlain and Halifax in Rome.
	6 March	Ruthenian administration dismissed by Prague.
	9 March	Slovak administration dismissed by Prague.
	13 March	Tiso in Berlin.
	14 March	Slovak Diet votes for independence.
	14–15 March	President Hácha in Berlin.
	15 March	Germany occupies remainder of Bohemia and Moravia.
		Hungary begins occupying Ruthenia.
	19 March	Britain rejects Soviet proposal for Five-Power talks on Rumania.
	20 March	Lithuanian Foreign Minister in Berlin.
	21 March	Ribbentrop–Lipski talk on Danzig.
	23 March	Lithuania cedes Memel to Germany.

23 March	German–Rumanian economic agreement.
31 March	Provisional Anglo–French guarantee of Poland announced.
4–6 April	Beck in London.
7 April	Italian seizure of Albania.
13 April	Anglo-French guarantee of Greece and Rumania.
14 April	Anglo-French negotiations with the Soviet Union recommence.
17 April	Soviet proposal for a tripartite alliance with West.
28 April	Hitler denounces Anglo-German naval agreement and German–Polish pact.
3 May	Litvinov replaced by Molotov as Soviet Foreign Minister.
8 May	Britain rejects Soviet proposal for tripartite alliance.
12 May	Provisional Anglo-Turkish pact announced.
22 May	Pact of Steel signed in Berlin.
23 May	Hitler addresses his generals on Danzig and Poland.
30 May	Nazi–Soviet negotiations for improved relations begin in earnest.
14 June	Japanese blockade British concession at Tientsin.
29 June	Halifax speech at Chatham House.
1–2 July	Scare over Danzig.
18–21 July	Dr. Wohlthat in London for economic talks.
4–6 August	Danzig–Polish customs crisis.
9–10 August	Mutual German–Polish warnings over Danzig.
11 August	Professor Burckhardt visits Hitler.
11–13 August	Ciano visits Hitler and Ribbentrop.
12 August	Anglo-French-Soviet military talks begin in Moscow.

14 August	Hitler addresses his generals on forthcoming action against Poland.
	Soviet question regarding passage of troops through Poland and Rumania halts military talks.
16 August	Danzig–Polish customs talks begin.
20 August	Hitler urges Stalin to receive Ribbentrop in the immediate future.
21 August	Anglo-French-Soviet military talks suspended.
	Forthcoming Nazi–Soviet pact announced.
22 August	Hitler addresses his generals on the need to fight.
	Britain reaffirms its pledge to Poland.
23 August	Nazi–Soviet pact signed in Moscow.
	Chamberlain's personal appeal delivered to Hitler; Hitler replies.
	Mussolini suggests Britain persuade Poland to surrender Danzig.
24 August	Danzig–Polish customs talks broken off.
	Parliament reassembles in London.
25 August	Hitler offers lasting friendship with British Empire.
	Anglo-Polish agreement signed.
	Mussolini informs Hitler that he cannot participate in a general conflict.
	German invasion of Poland, ordered for 26th, postponed.
26 August	Daladier personal appeal to Hitler.
27 August	B. Dahlerus in London with hint of 'reasonable' German demands over Danzig and Corridor.
	Mussolini promises to help Britain in search for peace.
	Hitler thinks of temporarily accepting Polish climb-down.

28 August	New date of German attack fixed for 1 September.
	Beck agrees in principle to direct German–Polish negotiations.
	Official British reply delivered to Hitler; Hitler demands Danzig, Corridor and parts of Silesia.
29 August	Poland persuaded by Britain and France to postpone full mobilisation.
	Mussolini urges Hitler to accept British proposals as basis for settlement.
	Hitler accepts negotiations, demanding arrival of Polish plenipotentiary on 30th.
30 August	Dahlerus brings outline of new, moderate German proposals to London.
	Polish mobilisation announced.
	Ribbentrop reads new German proposals to Henderson, but refuses to give them in writing.
31 August	Poland informs Germany that she is favourably considering British proposal of direct negotiations.
	Mussolini proposes conference to discuss Versailles grievances.
	Britain informed that Italy will not fight.
1 September	Poland invaded.
	Britain and France warn Germany.
2 September	French activity in support of Italian-sponsored conference.
	Angry scenes in House of Commons.
3 September	British and French ultimata delivered to Germany. War declared.

Bibliography

THE following list of the major sources used for this book concentrates on the years 1938–9, but a small number of works essential for understanding the background to the subject are also included.

I. DOCUMENTS AND OFFICIAL PUBLICATIONS

Documents on German Foreign Policy, 1918–1945 (H.M.S.O., 1948 on), series D, vols. i–vii, cover the period September 1937 to the outbreak of war, and some later volumes have also been consulted. They are indispensable, but when using them the remarks made about the relative insignificance of the German diplomatic machinery must be borne in mind.

This also applies to

Nazi Conspiracy and Aggression (Washington, 1946–8), 10 vols.; these are translations of documents and affidavits collected before the Nuremberg trial.

Documents and Materials Relating to the Eve of the Second World War (Moscow, 1947–48), vols. i and ii, being German records captured by the Russians. Vol. ii has been referred to as the *Dirksen Papers* in the essay.

New Documents on the History of Munich (Prague, 1958) contains mainly Czech and Soviet material on the 1938 crisis.

Soviet Documents on Foreign Policy, vol. 3, ed. J. Degras (O.U.P., 1953), comprises, of course, only official speeches and writings of the time.

Documents on British Foreign Policy, 1919–1939 (H.M.S.O., 1946 on), third series, vols. i–ix, cover the period March

H

1938 to the outbreak of war. Sometimes the letters in the appendices are more revealing than the official telegrams.

Le Livre Jaune Français (Paris, 1939) offers a few French documents for 1938 and more for 1939; since it was the official justification published after the outbreak of war, it is often interesting for what it does *not* include. The same applies to

The Polish White Book (Hutchinson, 1939).

I Documenti Diplomatici Italiani (Rome, 1952 on), 8th series, vols. xii and xiii, cover the period 23 May 1939 to the outbreak of war.

Ciano's Diplomatic Papers, ed. M. Muggeridge (Odhams, 1948), includes earlier Italian documents, but will be superseded when the official series is extended.

The Trial of German Major War Criminals (H.M.S.O., 1946 on), pts. 1–22, contains the proceedings of the International Military Tribunal at Nuremberg; documents used in evidence are collected in their original language in vols. 24–42 of the record published at Nuremberg.

Foreign Relations of the United States (Washington, 1955 and 1956): 1938, vol. i (General); and 1939, vol. i (General). Many politicians and diplomats in Europe were anxious to confide in the United States, and the result is quite often revealing.

2. DIARIES, MEMOIRS, ETC.

Ambassador Dodd's Diary, ed. W. and M. Dodd (Gollancz, 1941), contains some significant conversations between diplomats in Central Europe in the 1930's, recorded by the American Ambassador in Berlin as he counted the minutes and the marks.

J. M. BLUM, *From the Morgenthau Diaries* (Houghton Mifflin, Boston, 1959), contains a few interesting passages involving Chamberlain and Simon.

J. E. DAVIES, *Mission to Moscow* (Gollancz, 1942), contains some accurate forebodings of the American Ambassador to the Soviet Union.

Ciano's Diary, 1937-1938 (Methuen, 1952) and
Ciano's Diary, 1939-1943 (Heinemann, 1947) are vital for understanding Mussolini's behaviour in this period.

I. MAISKY, *Who Helped Hitler?* (Hutchinson, 1964) is quite useful on the Anglo-Soviet negotiations, and extraordinarily forgetful and tendentious on the Nazi–Soviet ones.

E. BENEŠ, *Memoirs* (Allen & Unwin, 1954) only fleetingly touches on the events of 1938.

K. VON SCHUSCHNIGG, *Austrian Requiem* (Putnam, New York, 1946) is a moving account of Austria's dilemma, conveying both Hitler's bestiality and the author's vacillation.

H. RIPKA, *Munich, Before and After* (Gollancz, 1939) is a Czech account of events between the summer of 1938 and March 1939.

The Confidential Papers of Admiral Horthy (Budapest, 1965) contain one or two interesting letters, memoranda, etc.

G. GAFENCU, *The Last Days of Europe* (Muller, 1947) says little that is helpful about Rumania, but is useful on Beck, more so than

J. BECK, *Dernier Rapport* (Brussels, 1951).

B. DAHLERUS, *The Last Attempt* (Hutchinson, 1947) relates the adventures of a Swedish businessman as a well-meaning and innocent tool of Nazi diplomacy during the last weeks of peace.

C. J. BURCKHARDT, *Meine Danziger Mission* (Munich, 1960) contains accounts of the High Commissioner's interviews during 1939.

The German side includes two books, at least, which can be taken as wholly sincere documents:

Mein Kampf (translated by James Murphy; Hurst & Blackett, 1939) must be read, despite the caution given in the essay, and

U. VON HASSELL, *The von Hassell Diaries* (Hamish Hamilton, 1948) provides a valuable record of events as seen by the conservative opposition to Hitler.

The memoirs of those who served the régime in various capacities need to be handled with caution. They include:

H. VON DIRKSEN, *Moscow, Tokyo, London* (London, 1951).
F. HESSE, *Hitler and the English* (Wingate, 1954).
E. KORDT, *Nicht aus den Akten* (Stuttgart, 1950).
F. VON PAPEN, *Memoirs* (André Deutsch, 1952).
P. SCHMIDT, *Hitler's Interpreter* (Heinemann, 1951).
E. VON WEIZSÄCKER, *Memoirs* (Gollancz, 1951).

The essence of Nazism is conveyed in:
H. RAUSCHNING, *Hitler Speaks* (Butterworth, 1939); and
Makers of Destruction (Eyre & Spottiswoode, 1942).

The same warning as to unreliability has to be repeated
with reference to the two French volumes which, in the
absence as yet of official publications, have to be used for
their documents:
G. BONNET, *Défense de la paix*; vol. 1, *De Washington à Quai
d'Orsay* (Geneva, 1946); vol. 2, *Fin d'une Europe* (Geneva,
1948).

The same author's *Quai d'Orsay* (Antony Gibbs & Philips,
1965) contains fewer documents and even more enormities.
Other French memoirs and diaries include:
R. COULONDRE, *De Staline à Hitler* (Paris, 1950).
A. FRANÇOIS-PONCET, *The Fateful Years* (Gollancz, 1949).
M. GAMELIN, *Servir* (3 vols., Paris, 1946-7).
L. NOËL, *L'Aggression allemande contre la Pologne* (Paris, 1946).
J. PAUL-BONCOUR, *Entre deux Guerres* (Paris, 1945-7), vol. 3.
Carnets secrets de Jean Zay (Paris, 1942).

There are several British memoirs which succeed in being
almost entirely uninformative — those of Halifax, Kirkpatrick and Simon, for instance. I include in the following
list a few books which are not strictly memoirs, but whose
value lies in the diaries, letters, and so on, which they
reproduce:
L. S. AMERY, *My Political Life* (Hutchinson, 1953 on), vol. 3:
hard-hitting and valuable.
LORD AVON, *The Eden Memoirs: Facing the Dictators* (Collins,
1962) and *The Reckoning* (1965) are somewhat reticent, but
still revealing about Chamberlain, Wilson and the author.

W. S. CHURCHILL, *The Gathering Storm* (Cassell, 1948): the highly individual record of the outstanding critic of Chamberlain's policy.

DUFF COOPER, *Old Men Forget* (Hart-Davis, 1953): valuable Cabinet revelations.

H DALTON, *The Fateful Years* (Muller, 1957): essential reading.

K. FEILING, *Neville Chamberlain* (Macmillan, 1946): contains important letters and diary extracts.

M. GILBERT, *Plough My Own Furrow* (Longmans, 1965): documents concerning Lord Allen of Hurtwood.

N. HENDERSON, *Failure of a Mission* (Hodder & Stoughton, 1940): revealing, despite its self-justifying gloss.

T. JONES, *A Diary With Letters* (O.U.P., 1954): an essential guide to the roots of appeasement.

B. H. LIDDELL HART, *Memoirs*, vols. i and ii (Cassell, 1965): invaluable insight into British military unpreparedness in thinking and *matériel*.

I. MACLEOD, *Neville Chamberlain* (Muller, 1961): a somewhat laboured apologia for its subject.

R. MACLEOD and D. KELLY (eds.), *The Ironside Diaries* (Constable, 1962): useful on the military aspects of the Anglo-French-Polish alliance.

V. MASSEY, *What's Past is Prologue* (Macmillan, Canada, 1963): emphasises the pre-war Dominion support for appeasement.

R. J. MINNEY, *The Private Papers of Hore-Belisha* (Collins, 1960): of interest on Chamberlain and the Cabinet.

A. L. ROWSE, *All Souls and Appeasement* (Macmillan, 1961): some revealing table-talk of the appeasers.

E. SPIER, *Focus* (Wolff, 1963): recollections concerning the all-party group round Churchill which tried to rally opinion against Nazism.

LORD STRANG, *Home and Abroad* (André Deutsch, 1956): more useful for its general comments on diplomacy than its record of events.

LORD TEMPLEWOOD, *Nine Troubled Years* (Collins, 1954): the sometimes inaccurate memoirs of Sir Samuel Hoare.

History of The Times, vol. iv (1952): essential letters and comments of Dawson and those around him.

LORD VANSITTART, *The Mist Procession* (Hutchinson, 1958):
the humble record of the Cassandra of the 1930's.

LORD WOOLTON, *Memoirs* (Cassell, 1959): interesting on Sir
Horace Wilson.

Two Anglo-Saxon eye-witnesses in Central Europe are
well worth consulting:

G. E. R. GEDYE, *Fallen Bastions* (Gollancz, 1939).

W. L. SHIRER, *Berlin Diary* (Hamish Hamilton, 1941).

3. SECONDARY WORKS

On the background to the period there are, among many:

Z. A. B. ZEMAN, *The Break-up of the Habsburg Empire* (O.U.P.,
1961).

D. LLOYD GEORGE, *The Truth About the Peace Treaties*, 2 vols.,
(Gollancz, 1938).

C. A. MACARTNEY, *National States and National Minorities*
(O.U.P., 1934).

E. WISKEMANN, *Czechs and Germans* (O.U.P., 1938; 2nd ed.,
1966).

G. BROOK-SHEPHERD, *Dollfuss* (Macmillan, 1961).

J. GEHL, *Austria, Germany, and the Anschluss* (O.U.P., 1963).

J. ERICKSON, *The Soviet High Command* (Macmillan, 1962).

W. LAQUEUR, *Russia and Germany* (Weidenfeld & Nicolson,
1965).

H. THOMAS, *The Spanish Civil War* (Eyre & Spottiswoode,
1961).

E. H. CARR, *International Relations Between the Two World
Wars* (Macmillan, 1947).

On Western aspects of the period there are

LORD BIRKENHEAD, *Halifax* (Hamish Hamilton, 1965),
which is excellent as a whole, but thin and out of date on
the diplomatic details.

J. R. M. BUTLER, *Lord Lothian* (Macmillan, 1960).

I. COLVIN, *Vansittart in Office* (Gollancz, 1965): a disappoint-
ing book which sets out to write fully on Vansittart and
the origins of the war, and does neither.

M. GILBERT and R. GOTT, *The Appeasers* (Weidenfeld & Nicolson, 1963).

A. J. WRENCH, *Geoffrey Dawson and Our Times* (Hutchinson, 1955).

Works on various aspects of the Axis partners include:

A. BULLOCK, *Hitler* (Odhams, 1964 edition).

H.-A. JACOBSEN and J. ROHWER (eds.), *Decisive Battles of World War II: The German View* (André Deutsch, 1965).

I. KIRKPATRICK, *Mussolini* (Odhams, 1964).

B. H. KLEIN, *Germany's Economic Preparations for War* (Harvard University Press, 1959); to be read only in the light of the *Past and Present* article mentioned below.

A. S. MILWARD *The German Economy at War* (Athlone Press, 1965) is excellent.

E. NOLTE, *Three Faces of Fascism* (Weidenfeld & Nicolson, 1965).

E. M. ROBERTSON, *Hitler's Pre-War Policy* (Longmans, 1963).

H. ROTHFELS, *The German Opposition to Hitler* (Wolff, 1961).

W. L. SHIRER, *The Rise and Fall of the Third Reich* (Pan edition, 1964).

J. W. WHEELER-BENNETT, *The Nemesis of Power* (Macmillan, 1961).

E. WISKEMANN, *The Rome–Berlin Axis* (rev. ed., Fontana, 1966) and *Undeclared War* (Constable, 1939).

Z. A. B. ZEMAN, *Nazi Propaganda* (O.U.P., 1964).

On the diplomacy of the period and various episodes within it, there are three pioneering works which have been partially superseded by subsequent documentary evidence:

L. B. NAMIER, *Diplomatic Prelude* (Macmillan, 1948)

— *Europe in Decay* (1950) and

— *In the Nazi Era* (1952).

The fresh look which has been taken at the period owes something to

A. J. P. TAYLOR, *The Origins of the Second World War* (1963 edition), however much one may disagree with some of the conclusions therein. There are useful details in

G. BROOK-SHEPHERD, *Anschluss* (Macmillan, 1963) and

E. PRESSEISEN, *Germany and Japan* (The Hague, 1958).

J. W. WHEELER-BENNETT, *Munich* (Macmillan, 1964 edition), remains well worth reading, despite the amount of documents which have appeared since it was first written.

PERTINAX, *The Gravediggers of France* (Doubleday, New York, 1944), and

H. NOGUÈRES, *Munich* (Weidenfeld and Nicolson, 1965) are useful for the details they provide on internal French politics at the time, though the latter is often unreliable and much inferior to

B. CELOVSKY, *Das Münchener Abkommen von 1938* (Stuttgart, 1958).

W. HOFER, *War Premeditated* (Thames & Hudson, 1955), sets forth the tangled last weeks of peace with admirable clarity. Two of the volumes in the R.I.I.A. *Survey of International Affairs* series contain one or two useful chapters:

A. TOYNBEE and F. ASHTON-GWATKIN (eds.), *The World in March 1939* (O.U.P., 1952).

A. and V. TOYNBEE (eds.), *The Eve of War* (1958).

As an introduction to American policy in the period there is

W. LANGER and S. GLEASON, *The Challenge to Isolation* (Harper, New York, 1952).

There are some useful essays on various individuals in

G. CRAIG and F. GILBERT (eds.), *The Diplomats* (Princeton University Press, 1953)

and on Commonwealth aspects in

D. C. WATT, *Personalities and Policies* (Longmans, 1965).

4. PERIODICALS, PRESS, ETC.

Articles on the period are scattered throughout various journals; in particular, *Foreign Affairs* should be consulted, and an article by T. W. Mason in *Past and Present*, no. 29 (December 1964). Among useful pieces in the Munich

Vierteljahrshefte für Zeitgeschichte are those on members of
the German opposition to Hitler (January 1966 and July
1962); on the Sudeten Freikorps (January 1961); and on
the Nazi planning of the border incident with Poland
which was intended to excuse aggression (October 1964).
The *Revue d'Histoire de la Deuxième Guerre Mondiale*, nos.
6, 14 and 52, contain interesting material.
I have also used the relevant volumes of *Hansard* and *Keesing's
Contemporary Archives*; N. H. Baynes, *The Speeches of Adolf
Hitler*, 2 vols. (O.U.P., 1942); and the press files of the
Wiener Library. D.N.B. has a few useful contributions,
and the reactions of the British press to Nazism are briefly
studied in R. Kieser, *Englands Appeasementpolitik und der
Aufstieg des Dritten Reiches im Spiegel der britischen Presse,
1933-1939* (Verlag P. G. Keller, Winterthur, 1964). The
Mass-Observation publications, *Britain By Mass-Observa-
tion* (Penguin, 1938) and *War Begins At Home* (Chatto &
Windus, 1940) are useful for those too young to remember
the moods of the time.

Index

Offices are those held during the period covered by this book, unless otherwise stated.

PRINTED IN GREAT BRITAIN BY ROBERT MACLEHOSE AND CO. LTD
THE UNIVERSITY PRESS, GLASGOW